# SOUTHEAST ASIA IN
# THE NEW INTERNATIONAL ERA

*Third Edition*

# SOUTHEAST ASIA IN
# THE NEW INTERNATIONAL ERA

## *Clark D. Neher*

NORTHERN ILLINOIS UNIVERSITY

Westview Press
A Member of the Perseus Books Group

Copyright © 1999 by Westview Press, A Member of the Perseus Books Group

Published in 1999 in the United States of America by Westview Press, 5500 Central Avenue, Boulder, Colorado 80301-2877, and in the United Kingdom by Westview Press, 12 Hid's Copse Road, Cumnor Hill, Oxford OX2 9JJ

Library of Congress Cataloging-in-Publication Data
Neher, Clark D.
  Southeast Asia in the new international era / Clark D. Neher.—
3rd ed.
    p.  cm.
  Includes bibliographical references (p.   ) and index.
  ISBN 0-8133-3390-3 (pbk.)
    1. Asia, Southeastern—Politics and government—1945–  2. Asia,
Southeastern—Foreign relations.  I. Title.
DS526.7.N45  1999
959.05'3—dc21                                                                98-15907
                                                                                  CIP

The paper used in this publication meets the requirements of the American National Standard for Permanence of Paper for Printed Library Materials Z39.48-1984.

10     9     8     7     6     5     4     3     2

# CONTENTS

# PREFACE AND ACKNOWLEDGMENTS

This book results from information gathered during many trips to Southeast Asia over the past thirty-five years. I am grateful to the National Science, Ford, and Fulbright Foundations, the United States Information Agency, and the United States–Indochina Reconciliation Project for their generous assistance during the more lengthy stays. I am also indebted to the faculty and staff of Chulalongkorn University, Thammasat University, Prince of Songkla University at Had Yai and Pattani, Chiang Mai University, Payap University in Thailand, and the University of San Carlos in the Philippines for their intellectual and material support of my work at their campuses.

During my career as a student of Southeast Asian politics, I have learned much from colleagues who share my interest. I am especially indebted to M. Ladd Thomas and Dwight King in the Department of Political Science at Northern Illinois University. They have provided generous intellectual and collegial counsel. Similar support has come from Ronald Provencher, Judy Ledgerwood, Susan Russell, Constance Wilson, and Mai Kyi Win, all associates of NIU's Center for Southeast Asian Studies. April Davis, Karen Schweitzer, Sandy Holloway, and Nancy Schuneman contributed outstanding administrative support, and David Oldfield, Bryan Hunsaker, Ye Myint, Ted Mayer, Robert Dayley, and Warner Winborne provided superb research assistance. Both undergraduate and graduate students at Northern Illinois University have contributed to this book as well through their enthusiastic interest in the Southeast Asian region. It is gratifying to have taught these students, many of whom are now among the new generation of scholars of Southeast Asia.

Although I accept responsibility for all errors and misinterpretations, many scholars of Southeast Asia will see their ideas reflected in *Southeast*

*Asia in the New International Era*. Among those scholars who have helped shape my views are David Wilson, Donn Hart, Michael Aung-Thwin, Ansil Ramsay, Prasert Bhandachart, Bidhya Bowornwathana, Kusuma Snitwongse, Suchit Bunbongkarn, Randy Fertel, Danny Unger, Gary Suwannarat, David Adams, Sheldon Simon, Chai-Anan Samudavanija, Tanun Anuman-Rajadhon, Sukhumbhand Paribatra, Proserpina Tapales, John McAuliff, Anek Laothamathas, Panitan Wattanayagorn, Carolina Hernandez, Ross Marlay, Nara Ganesan, and Narong Sinsawasdi.

Susan McEachern, Norman Ware, and Laura Parsons and their staff at Westview Press facilitated every stage of the project.

This book is dedicated to Arlene, Erick, Gregory, Carol, and David.

*Clark D. Neher*

# ACRONYMS

| | |
|---|---|
| AFP | Armed Forces of the Philippines |
| AFPFL | Anti-Fascist People's Freedom League |
| AFTA | ASEAN Free Trade Area |
| AIDS | acquired immune deficiency syndrome |
| APU | Angkatan Perpaduan Umnah |
| ASEAN | Association of Southeast Asian Nations |
| BSPP | Burmese Socialist Program Party |
| CGDK | Coalition Government of Democratic Kampuchea |
| CPP | Cambodian People's Party |
| CPP | Communist Party of the Philippines |
| CPV | Communist Party of Vietnam |
| DAP | Democratic Action Party |
| DPR | Indonesian Parliament |
| EOI | export-oriented industrialization |
| FUNCINPEC | United National Front for an Independent, Peaceful, and Cooperative Cambodia |
| GDP | gross domestic product |
| GNP | gross national product |
| GRC | Group Representation Constituency |
| GSP | generalized system of preferences |
| IMF | International Monetary Fund |
| IPR | intellectual property rights |
| ISI | import-substitution industrialization |
| KBL | Kilusang Bagong Lipunan |
| KPNLF | Khmer People's National Liberation Front |
| LDP | Laban ng Demokratikong Pilipino |
| LPRP | Lao People's Revolutionary Party |
| MAI | Multilateral Aid Initiative |
| MBA | Military Bases Agreement |

| | |
|---|---|
| MCA | Malayan Chinese Association |
| MCP | Malayan Communist Party |
| MIA | missing in action |
| MIB | Malay Islam Beraja |
| MIC | Malayan Indian Congress |
| MNLF | Moro National Liberation Front |
| MP | member of parliament |
| MPR | People's Consultative Assembly |
| NAFTA | North American Free Trade Agreement |
| NAP | New Aspirations Party |
| NDF | National Democratic Front |
| NEFOS | newly emerging forces |
| NEP | new economic policy |
| NGO | nongovernmental organization |
| NICs | newly industrialized countries |
| NLD | National League for Democracy |
| NLF | National Liberation Front |
| NLHS | Neo Lao Hak Sat |
| NOC | National Operations Council |
| NPA | New People's Army |
| NPKC | National Peace Keeping Council |
| NUP | National Unity Party |
| ODP | Orderly Departure Program |
| OLDEFOS | old established forces |
| PAP | People's Action Party |
| PAS | Partai Islam Se-Malaysia |
| PAVN | People's Army of Vietnam |
| PDI | Indonesian Democratic Party |
| PGNU | Provisional Government of National Unity |
| PKI | Communist Party of Indonesia |
| PPP | United Development Party |
| PRD | People's Democratic Party |
| PRK | People's Republic of Kampuchea |
| PRPK | People's Revolutionary Party of Kampuchea |
| RAM | Reform the Armed Forces Movement |
| RBAF | Royal Brunei Armed Forces |
| SEATO | Southeast Asia Treaty Organization |
| SLORC | State Law and Order Restoration Council |
| SNC | Supreme National Council |
| SPDC | State Peace and Development Council |
| UMNO | United Malay Nationalist Organization |

| | |
|---|---|
| UNESCO | United Nations Educational, Scientific, and Cultural Organization |
| UNIDO | United Nationalist Democratic Organization |
| UNTAC | United Nations Transitional Authority in Cambodia |
| WTO | World Trade Organization |
| ZOPFAN | Zone of Peace, Freedom, and Neutrality |

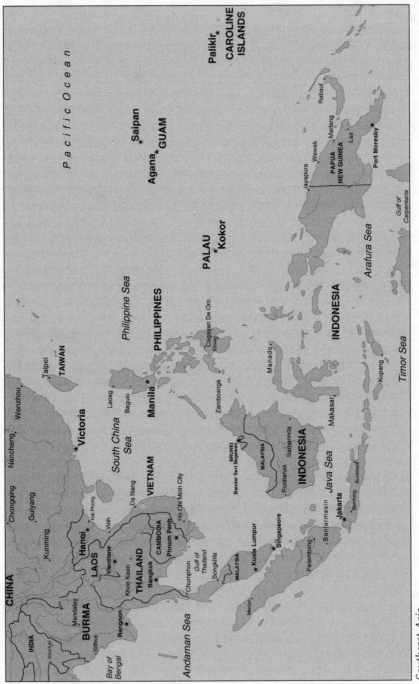

Southeast Asia

# 1

# INTRODUCTION

Writing a book about contemporary Southeast Asia can easily be seen as problematic because the region is no longer a primary focus of U.S. political attention. Weeks go by without any major media stories about this region, which, just two decades ago, dominated the discussions of government officials and ordinary citizens. Because of the many great changes in the Soviet Union, China, and Europe and the relatively stable, crisis-free environment in much of Southeast Asia, Americans have focused their interest elsewhere. Moreover, the lingering trauma, disillusionment, and cynicism of the Vietnam War period have also kept journalists, political scientists, and policymakers from focusing on Southeast Asia.

This relative indifference is all the more frustrating because significant events are occurring in the region, both politically and economically, with serious consequences for the entire world. Periodic spurts of interest in Southeast Asia have accompanied the rise and travails of Corazon Aquino in the Philippines; the remarkable three decades of economic growth of Thailand and the subsequent economic debacle in 1997; the brutal crackdown by the military on pro-democracy demonstrators in Burma; the lifting of the economic embargo against Vietnam and the establishment of diplomatic relations with that country by the United States; and the discovery, house arrest, and death of the infamous Pol Pot in Cambodia. Nevertheless, despite the region's rising economic importance, Southeast Asia has remained peripheral to U.S. foreign policy considerations.

A new era in international relations has arisen in the last several decades with important repercussions for Southeast Asia. Political, economic, and social forces of unprecedented scope have transformed the entire region. *Southeast Asia in the New International Era* analyzes contemporary politics in the context of these international and domestic political-economic realities from the perspectives of both the Southeast Asians and the international community. Each nation is evaluated in terms of its major institutions, degree of democratization, movement toward economic development, foreign policy, and the role of the state. Thailand and the Philippines are treated the most comprehensively, demonstrating two contending political and economic patterns and reflecting their intrinsic interest and importance to the region as well as the author's specific expertise.

Southeast Asia, a region of remarkable diversity, consists of ten nations with differing histories, cultural traditions, resource bases, and political-economic systems. Except for geographic proximity and a tropical ecology, few characteristics link these nations into a coherent whole. Nevertheless, most of them share certain patterns: a colonial past; a postwar struggle for independence and modernization; religious penetration by Islam, Hinduism, Buddhism, and Christianity (which are in many cases a thin veneer over animism); agricultural economies that have been overtaken by manufacturing in the past decades; reliance on patron-client bonds for achieving goals; and a strong sense of the village as the primary unit of identity.[1]

The most striking similarity among the Southeast Asian nations has been the postindependence movement from diffuse feelings of nationalism to strong nationalist loyalties. The nationalist movement has manifested itself in various ways, but the roots lie in the common colonial history experienced by all these nations (except Thailand) as well as their common subjugation by the Japanese during World War II. Many of the problems of economic and political development faced by Southeast Asian leaders today can be traced to common historical colonial patterns.

Colonial rule resulted in the formation of nation-states with viable boundaries. The imperialists guaranteed these boundaries, thus introducing a sense of stability and order to the region. Colonialism was also responsible for the growth of economic structures such as ports, railways, and roads. A money economy was introduced, and large-scale industries were established requiring skilled and unskilled laborers. Because the Southeast Asian peasants found industrial labor antithetical to traditional values, the colonialists imported Chinese and Indians to work in factories, tin mines, and rubber plantations. The Chinese and Indian communities, through their connections with Western imperialism, have thus enjoyed and continue to enjoy economic power in Southeast Asia disproportionate to their numbers.

Perhaps the most important consequence of colonialism was its direct impact on the rise of nationalism throughout Southeast Asia. The colonial nations became unified territorial states, whereas their predecessors had been nonintegrated dynastic principalities. By the late nineteenth century, the major national boundaries had been demarcated, and the entire area of Southeast Asia, except Thailand, was in European hands. This colonial heritage helps explain the strong nationalism of the Vietnamese manifested in their resistance to French, Japanese, and U.S. attempts to influence their nation. In Vietnam, Laos, Cambodia, Indonesia, and Burma, nationalism as a unifying force was exemplified by their violent struggles for independence in the post–World War II era. In the Philippines, Singapore, Brunei, and Malaysia these struggles were less violent.

Southeast Asian nations (except for Singapore and Brunei) are characterized by the agricultural base that is at the heart of their economic life. The basic economic unit is the family-operated farm, with most of the farm products being consumed by the family itself or being used to pay for the additional farm labor required. The agricultural village is the major unit of identity for the rural population, acting as its educational, religious, cultural, political, economic, and social center.

The hierarchical structure at the village level is found throughout Southeast Asian political life, with a village headman serving as the major focus of power. Essentially, these societies are organized into networks of superior-subordinate (patron-client) ties, which form the basis of the political structures of the society. These patron-client bonds act as an integrating grid of relationships that hold the society together and as linkages between the state and the citizenry. Where there are marked inequalities in wealth, status, and control and where resources are insufficient, those with limited access to the resources form alliances with individuals at a higher socioeconomic level. The relationship is one of mutual benefit in which the patron expects labor, protection, defense, or some other reward in return for dispensing benefits to the subordinate. These mutual interests provide a security that the state itself cannot provide.

Because of the great diversity in and among Southeast Asian states as well as the rapid changes they have been undergoing, categorization of these states is difficult and must be complemented by analysis of the unique attributes of each. The diversity and complexity of the region become clear when it is broken down into four political categories: semidemocracy, military authoritarianism, absolute monarchy, and communist authoritarianism. From a political perspective, the semidemocratic nations include Thailand, Malaysia, the Philippines, Singapore, and Indonesia. "Semidemocratic" refers to those nations with a semblance of citizen involvement in choosing governmental leaders, an executive leader not fully accountable to the legislative branch, a high degree of civil liberties—with some exceptions—to ensure "law and order," and autonomous groups representing the interests of the people. Burma is the best example of a military authoritarian government, featuring a dominant role for the military in all phases of political life. Brunei, however, is an absolute monarchy. Finally, communist authoritarian governments re-serve an exclusive role for the communist party in political life, establish command economies now in the process of liberalizing, and provide a low level of civil liberties. Vietnam and Laos fall into this category. Cam-bodia is in transition, constantly changing and difficult to categorize at any particular time.

Because of rapid changes experienced by most of the ten nations, as this book will show, such categories sometimes obfuscate as much as they clarify. Until the late 1970s, for example, Thailand fit into the military au-thoritarian category and could return to it at any time. In 1986 the Philip-pines ended two decades of authoritarian rule under President Ferdinand Marcos, following the extraordinary rise of "People Power" which brought constitutional government and the democrat Corazon Aquino into power. Singapore and Indonesia, both with the structural trappings of democracy, are in fact governed by an exclusive elite (civilian in Singa-pore; military in Indonesia) that periodically suppresses the rights of the citizenry.

The attempt to overthrow the military dictatorship and establish demo-cratic rule in Burma in 1988, which was reminiscent of the "People Power" revolt in the Philippines, was terminated by the military. Although continu-ity of political rule has existed in Vietnam and Laos since 1975, when com-munist governments were installed, economic liberalization programs, be-gun in the mid-1980s, have begun to change the structure of these societies. Cambodia, having undergone the horrors of the Khmer Rouge, moved to-ward a semblance of normalcy after 1979 when a Vietnamese-installed gov-ernment overthrew the genocidal regime, and then reverted to discouraged confusion under the tutelage of the United Nations Transitional Authority in Cambodia (UNTAC). In 1997, the country again devolved into chaos when Second Prime Minister Hun Sen carried out a coup d'état against the First Prime Minister, Prince Norodom Ranarridh.

Brunei, independent only since 1984 and with a population of just un-der 300,000, is an absolute monarchy; because its economy is based on oil revenues, Brunei cannot be compared to any of its neighbors. Malaysia, perhaps more than any other Southeast Asian nation, has experienced a long—albeit tenuous—period of semidemocracy and economic stability, although recent events indicate an intensification of the politics of con-frontation among the country's leading ethnic groups. The economic downturn in 1997 also jeopardizes Malaysia's stability.

This political categorization, although useful for specific times in his-tory, does not adequately portray Southeast Asian nations at all times, as none of the states fits precisely into a particular category. Thus, an alter-native listing of political categories could include, first, Leninist single-party dictatorships, based on the principle of democratic centralism, as found in Vietnam and Laos. Second, authoritarian-pluralist systems—characterized by an elitist-centered, restrictive political order with social and economic institutions that have various degrees of independence from party or state control—are found in Thailand (under the military), the Philippines (under President Marcos), Indonesia, Burma, Singapore, and Brunei. A third category is a parliamentary-democratic system, featuring free, competitive elections and limits on state power. Malaysia, the Philippines (under President Aquino and President Fidel Ramos), and Thailand (from 1977 to 1991 and 1993 to 1998) meet these criteria.[2]

Also suffering from the problem of imprecision, even this categorization does not adequately distinguish the region's political structures and behavior. The political repression in Burma, for example, is significantly greater than that in Singapore, Indonesia, and Thailand (even under the military). Although Singapore has experienced single-party rule since its independence, its style of government is qualitatively different from the absolute family rule of Brunei or the corrupt cronyism of the Philippines under President Marcos. Similarly, placing the contemporary Philippines in the same category as Thailand and Malaysia blurs these nations' strikingly different political systems. The Philippines relied on the personal charisma of President Aquino for stability and adherence to democratic procedures, whereas Thailand and Malaysia have developed these characteristics without charismatic leadership.

Another way of categorizing the Southeast Asian nations is simply geographic, with mainland Southeast Asia consisting of Thailand, Burma, Laos, Cambodia, and Vietnam and insular Southeast Asia consisting of the Philippines, Singapore, Indonesia, Brunei, and Malaysia. One advantage of this categorization is that it corresponds to religious criteria as well. All of the mainland countries practice Buddhism (with significant variations from country to country), whereas most of the peoples of the archipelagic nations practice a form of Islam. The Catholic Philippines is an exception, although important Muslim minorities are found in the southernmost islands. Singaporeans practice Confucianism, Buddhism, Islam, and Christianity.

The notion of an integrated mainland Southeast Asia was advanced in the late 1980s when Thai leaders set forth the idea of *Suwanabhum* (Golden Land), a term encompassing all the mainland nations. Thai leaders attempted to surmount the political differences among the mainland Southeast Asian nations by suggesting that these nations had a common destiny in their shared religious beliefs, geographic proximity, and desire for modernization. However, *Suwanabhum* was not accepted by the leaders of most mainland nations, as they rejected the implicit hegemonic designs of Thailand and as such conflicts were felt deeply throughout the region.

Insular Southeast Asia is a problematic category because Malaysia is as much mainland as island, sharing a long border with mainland Thailand. The Philippines, the only Christian nation, is geographically and culturally distant from the rest of the archipelago. Indonesia, with a population of over 200 million—most of which is involved with rice farming—is fundamentally different from Brunei (with its relatively minuscule population) and from the city-state of Singapore (which has no agricultural base).

The founding of the Association of Southeast Asian Nations (ASEAN) in 1967, initiated by the noncommunist Southeast Asian nations in response to a perceived communist threat, at one time led to still another means by which to categorize the Southeast Asian nations. Noncommunist ASEAN included Thailand, Malaysia, Singapore, Indonesia, the Philippines, and Brunei (which joined in 1984), while Laos, Cambodia, and Vietnam composed the communist Indo-Chinese nations. Burma, of course, remained neutral. In 1997, this categorization no longer made sense because Laos, Vietnam, and Burma all joined ASEAN. Cambodia was expected to join as soon as its government stabilized.

Thus far, ASEAN has served economic rather than military purposes. As an alliance, ASEAN was once held together largely by the members' common antipathy toward Vietnam. In the 1990s, ASEAN's fame came from the fact that separately, the member nations had emerged as among the most economically vital in the world. ASEAN became a showcase of successful economic development, at least until the member nations suffered an economic downturn in mid-1997.

Nationalism is the major reason ASEAN has not become a more meaningful alliance. The ASEAN nations are also as much economic competitors as they are collaborators. Communist ideology, rapidly losing currency among the three Indo-Chinese nations, has not erased three centuries of enmity caused by traditional Vietnamese and Cambodian expansionism. For example, Vietnam invaded Cambodia in 1979 following years of border disputes. The attempt by the communist Vietnamese to forge an Indochina Federation floundered because of the history of intense conflicts and mutual distrust among the three nations.

The difficulty in categorizing the Southeast Asian nations emphasizes the importance of viewing them as highly diverse and worthy of analysis from the vantage point of their unique attributes. Specifically, the chapter on each country will focus on the following factors: political institutions, the process of democratization, economic development (and role in the world economic system), the role of the state, and foreign policy.

Before assessing each Southeast Asian nation's contemporary political status, the impact of the new international era on politics in the region will be discussed.

# Notes

1. On June 18, 1990, the military rulers of Burma announced that the country's official name (in English) would henceforth be Myanmar and that Rangoon's name had been changed to Yangon. Because these name changes may be temporary and have not been accepted internationally, and to reduce confusion when referring to the country and its capital city prior to the name change, this book will use the names Burma and Rangoon. In 1989 the rulers in Cambodia changed their nation's name from Kampuchea to the State of Cambodia. In this text, the name Cambodia will be used throughout.

2. A detailed discussion of the similarities and differences among the ten Southeast Asian nations is included in the author's *Politics in Southeast Asia* (Rochester, Vt.: Schenkman Books, 1987). The detailed historical and cultural background discussions included in that volume are summarily repeated in the present volume.

# 2

## THE NEW INTERNATIONAL ERA

An extraordinary sweep of international change occurred in the 1980s and 1990s: the transformation of the dominant bipolar world of communists and noncommunists into a more fragmented and interdependent world of competing multipolar centers of power, with the United States participating both as an equal and as a superpower and the Soviet Union losing its vast empire. The extent of the changes, occurring in rapid fashion, stunned the world and irrevocably recast international relations.

The full dimensions of the change will not be known for decades. However, it is clear that the collapse of the communist empire, the parallel democratization of previously authoritarian political systems, and the fading of ideological distinctions will have an impact on virtually all of the world's nations, including those in Southeast Asia.

### International Changes

Since World War II, nearly all the conflicts in Southeast Asia have been related to cold war politics, but in 1998 the cold war is no longer the driving force. Today, no communist power threatens the sovereignty of Southeast Asian nations. The demise of the communist empire, led by the former Soviet Union, has generated different security concerns and needs. That empire's Russian component is no longer a major player in Southeast Asian politics, as shown by Russia's disengagement from Vietnam and Cambodia. China is more concerned with trade ties with the ASEAN nations than with support for insurgent forces in the Philippines or Thailand. Even conflict among the communist nations has decreased since former Soviet President Mikhail Gorbachev's retreat from Vietnam. Beijing and Hanoi have moved to normalize ties, and a Cambodian settlement has further reduced Vietnamese-Chinese hostilities and bad feelings.

The end of communist threats to Southeast Asia corresponds to a subordinate role for the United States in the region. U.S. foreign policy priorities are now focused on the European Union, the Commonwealth of Independent States, Japan, China, the Middle East, and Latin America. Southeast Asia has become a secondary priority, largely because U.S. interests in that area have been met and there are no crises that threaten those interests. Southeast Asia has become what the United States wanted for the region during the Vietnam War: The ASEAN nations have flourished economically (the 1997 economic recession does not undo three decades of rapid economic growth) as dynamic models of development, and enemy superpowers have withdrawn from the region.

This period of noncrisis (the 1997 economic crisis and tensions over the Spratly Islands in the South China Sea are the obvious exceptions) stems from the fact that the former historical flash points in Southeast Asia are no longer volatile: independence from colonialism, the threat from communist superpowers, communist-supported insurgency, and the Vietnam War. These crises have been relegated to history; they are no longer central considerations for Southeast Asian governments. Instead, Southeast Asia's security, both externally and internally, has never been more ensured.

As international bipolarity between the United States and the Soviet Union gives way to multipolarity (and, temporarily, unipolarity, with the United States dominant), Southeast Asian regionalism is expanding as these nations begin to form new trade alliances. This regionalism has expanded to include Vietnam and Laos as they moved toward liberalized economies. Indeed, all of the long-standing ASEAN nations have already initiated rapprochement with Indochina, as exemplified by the *Suwanabhum* (Golden Land) movement, in which Thailand has taken a leading economic role in the opening of Vietnam, Laos, Cambodia, and Burma. Enhanced regionalism in Southeast Asia reflects the fact that economics is now in command and ideology is in decline. Security issues have taken a back seat to emphasis on trade and aid issues, the role of the World Trade Organization, intellectual property rights, and economic growth triangles. Economic relations are in the forefront of the new diplomacy, necessitating a new breed of foreign policy specialists who know the unique language of economics rather than military security. However, to ensure continued budgetary and policy clout, military leaders note that the new emphasis on trading, rather than on making security matters obsolete, expands the notion of security to access to needed resources.

As ideological distinctions faded in the new international era and economic relations with new, emerging centers of power became more important than security ties, the containment of communism was no longer the central goal of the United States or its allies. Instead, trade relations assumed greater importance, with Japan, the European Union, the newly industrialized countries (NICs), and China taking center stage. Even the Persian Gulf war had little to do with political ideologies and much to do with the economic security of the United States and its allies.

A major catalyst for these changes was former Soviet President Gorbachev, who acted on the assumption that the Soviet Union would flourish only by a comprehensive reorganization (*perestroika*) and opening (*glasnost*) of Soviet society. *Perestroika* resulted in the demise of the Soviet Communist Party apparatus, the disintegration of the Soviet Union as an entity, the establishment of sovereign and autonomous republics, and the introduction of a market economy. So fundamental are these changes that all of Eastern Europe faces a long period of destabilizing transition.

For Asia, the ramifications of the demise of the Soviet Union include the Soviet withdrawal of troops from Afghanistan; the cessation of aid to insurgencies in Southeast Asia; Russian acceptance of a significant U.S. role in Southeast Asia; the demilitarization of the Sino-Russian border; and the end of Russian use of basing facilities in Vietnam. The new Russian Federation has been unable to participate in the growing economic and technological development in Asia.

Symbolic of the decline of Russia's interest in militarily influencing Southeast Asia are the abandonment of its Cam Ranh and Da Nang bases in Vietnam. Although the bases were never used to influence the course of events in Southeast Asia, they enabled potential Soviet domination over the vital waterways of the Pacific Ocean, the South China Sea, and the Indian Ocean, which are deemed indispensable for U.S. trade, access to oil by Japan, and the security of ASEAN. Russian withdrawal is a clear sign that these threats are not imminent and that Southeast Asia is not a target of expansionism, either from Russia itself or from its former client state, Vietnam. The decision to withdraw support from Vietnam reflects the new Russian view that its alliance with Hanoi had isolated Moscow from Southeast Asia's economically dynamic countries. This alliance had been a major cause of the continued ASEAN alliance with the United States and the improvement of ties between ASEAN and China.

Equally as dramatic as the transformation of Soviet domestic and foreign policy are the changes in China since the rise of the more pragmatic post-Mao leadership. During Mao Zedong's tenure, China was the Southeast Asian nations' most feared adversary. By the mid-1970s, China had emerged as the major guarantor of Thai security against possible Vietnamese aggression and as an increasingly important trade partner with ASEAN. Aid to communist insurgencies ceased. Despite the Tiananmen Square massacre in June 1989, which set back political liberalization in China, Chinese leaders regarded their goals in Southeast Asia as coincident with those of the United States. They sought to contain Soviet expansionism, develop closer economic ties with ASEAN, ensure an independent Cambodia that was free from Vietnamese occupation, and keep Southeast Asia from being dominated by any one superpower. The buildup of the Chinese navy in the South China Sea has raised the concerns of Southeast Asian governments despite Chinese assurances that the force is entirely defensive.

Since 1970, the economic dynamism of Japan has not only dramatically changed international relations but has refashioned the economies of Southeast Asia as well. Japan has become the most important U.S. ally in Asia, and Asia's economic importance to the United States increases each year. U.S. trans-Pacific commerce exceeds America's trade with Europe by over 50 percent. Although the Pacific Rim is now the largest overseas market for U.S. agricultural exports, 60 percent of the total U.S. trade deficit is with Asia (and 35 percent with Japan alone).

Despite the fact that Japan attacked and occupied all the Southeast Asian nations in World War II and was demilitarized after its defeat, it still plays a vital role in contemporary Southeast Asia. Ironically, the unrealized goal of Japan's World War II scheme for a "co-prosperity sphere" has been achieved economically in contemporary Southeast Asia. Japan has overtaken the United States as the principal economic partner of the Southeast Asian nations. Indeed, all of Southeast Asia is economically dependent upon Japan as the major source of imports, market for exports, aid provider, and foreign investor.

Japan's economic might has not been paralleled by political or military influence in Southeast Asia, mainly because Japan is sensitive to that region's concerns about allowing one superpower to assume too dominant a role, although these sensitivities decrease as each year passes and the bitter memories of World War II and Japanese occupation are forgotten. For most Southeast Asians today, Japan represents first-rate consumer goods, such as cars, televisions, videocassette recorders, and other electronic gadgets. Moreover, as U.S. influence wanes and the danger of Russian and Chinese military aggression diminishes, Japan will play an even more prominent role in all aspects of the region.

The economic interests of Japan, South Korea, and Taiwan in Southeast Asia stem from the presence of disciplined and cheap labor easily exploited by foreign corporations. The emergence of a new international division of labor, with Southeast Asians taking the role of the traditional proletariat, has led to an increase in assembly plants and other industrial facilities producing goods for export. The East Asian NICs and Japan have generated significant flows of foreign investment into Southeast Asia in response to their own rising labor costs and exchange-rate fluctuations. This dramatic change has been the engine of development as the ASEAN nations move toward export-oriented economies and away from import substitution.

Rapid industrialization has come mainly from external pressures rather than indigenous technology. A self-generating technological or research-oriented culture has failed to grow in ASEAN. Thus far, much of Southeast Asia's prosperity depends on external forces well beyond its control: outsiders' capital, technology, management, and markets.[1]

For Southeast Asian nations, this globalization of their economies made them vulnerable to economic domination by external forces, especially Japan and the East Asian NICs. Downward trends in world capital markets, a slowdown in global economic growth, the questionable viability of multilateral institutions such as the World Bank, and the rising cry for protectionism in Western nations (including the European Union) increasingly have had a direct negative impact on Southeast Asia. The crisis in the Middle East following the August 1990 Iraqi invasion of Kuwait is an example of how world events beyond the control of any of the Southeast Asian nations can directly affect these nations' economic stability and growth.

This dependence on the global economy was a principal cause of the financial disaster that hit much of Southeast Asia in mid-1997. With their currencies pegged to the American dollar, most Southeast Asian countries' exports and labor became too expensive, especially compared to that in China and Vietnam. The result was a flood of foreign capital and easy credit into Southeast Asia, massive debts, rising investments in luxury projects such as five-star hotels and condominiums, pervasive corruption, mismanagement of financial institutions, and poor decisions about investing the new capital. Global currency traders, recognizing the shakiness of these economies, bet against the Southeast Asian currencies, undermining their worth even more. The result was currency devaluation, inflation, high interest rates, unemployment, and governmental instability as Thailand, Malaysia, Indonesia, and the Philippines, as well as South Korea (the nations most affected by the downturn), struggled to resolve the crisis.

Leaders in Southeast Asia responded ineffectively to the economic crisis, allowing the downturn to spread throughout all of Asia, eventually hurting markets even in the United States. Southeast Asia's leaders seemed incapable of making the difficult decisions necessary to resolve the crisis. Instead, they hunkered down, blamed Westerners, and continued to protect cronies and undermine public-spirited technocrats. In Thailand, the devaluation of the baht necessitated a bailout from the International Monetary Fund. The $17 billion salvage plan came with tight strings attached, forcing the Thai government to raise taxes and cut government spending.

For U.S. foreign policy, at least until the 1997 economic crisis, Southeast Asia has been perceived as peripheral to its central interests in Japan, China, the Middle East, Latin America, the European Union, and the former Soviet Union. The primary reason for this low priority stems, paradoxically, from the U.S. perception that the region is politically stable, undergoing democratization, relatively supportive of American interests, and free from major international crises. In contrast to 1975, when U.S. foreign policy in Southeast Asia was paralyzed and in shambles, the present U.S. position is stronger than at any time since the end of World War II. Today it is Burma that is isolated, with its economy in chaos and its international and regional influence depleted. Insurgencies have failed throughout ASEAN, and both China and Russia are playing relatively constructive roles in the region.

Except for the interminable Cambodian imbroglio and the potential for conflict over the Spratly Islands in the South China Sea, U.S. security interests in Southeast Asia are minimal. In accordance with the principle that interests determine commitments, U.S. commitments in Southeast Asia are secondary to those in other areas of the world.

There is no clear conceptual framework for a U.S. security role in Southeast Asia, no clear Clinton Doctrine. America does have interests in the area: regional political and economic stability, economic development through capitalism, and preservation of access. The United States has determined that a home military base is no longer vital to American interests in the region. After its military bases were ousted from the Philippines, the United States found a way to replace the bases with a floating depot stationed in the South China Sea and to supply, repair, and refuel ships in new facilities ("places not bases") in the Philippines, Thailand, Malaysia, and Singapore.

This secondary interest is a complete turnaround from the period 1950–1970, when Southeast Asia was the focus of the U.S. containment policy against a perceived monolithic international communist threat.[2] During this period, the United States established security treaties with the Philippines, Thailand, and South Vietnam; participated in the Southeast Asia Treaty Organization (SEATO); acquired military base facilities throughout Southeast Asia; and eventually sent 4.2 million soldiers, spent $120 billion, and sustained approximately 58,000 deaths in the attempt to keep South Vietnam from communist rule.[3]

Although these changes are breathtaking and for the most part supportive of U.S. interests, Southeast Asia continues to be a crucial area of security concerns. Despite the end of the cold war, Asia is rearming faster than any other region in the world. In all of Asia, weapons purchases constitute 40 percent of the world total. In part, this rearmament stems from the perceived pullback by the United States from Asia as a result of the closing of military bases in the Philippines and the desire of U.S. leaders to have Japan and South Korea play a larger defense role in the region. The rearmament also stems from the perceived threat of China's moves against the Spratly Islands in the South China Sea, where Vietnam, the Philippines, Malaysia, and Taiwan also assert claims.

As Singapore, Malaysia, Thailand, and Indonesia have prospered through economic development, they have increased their weapons purchases. No longer concerned about internal insurgency or communist aggression, these nations look to their shared oceans and waterways as potential trouble areas. The Strait of Malacca, connecting the South China Sea and the Indian Ocean, is crucial, as are the fishing waters off each country's coasts. The nations of Southeast Asia are building up their air forces and navies, in particular, as part of a forward defense strategy to resist aggression at the outer limits before it reaches their own boundaries.

Fluid capital and weaponry at cheap prices, the decline of American influence in the area, the growing military strength of China and Japan, the example of the Gulf War, and a desire to ensure security are the obvious reasons for the arms race in Southeast Asia. For the Philippines, the issue is also the outdatedness of its armed forces, especially the navy, which is the oldest in the region. Because Southeast Asia's weaponry has been traditionally used to ensure domestic security, new expenditures are also required to combat those potential external problems that are at the forefront of the governments' security agendas.

Since World War II, the United States has served as a check on the development of rivalries among competitive nations in East Asia and Southeast Asia. For example, North Korean, Russian, and Chinese aggressive intentions have been restrained. Moreover, the U.S. presence has allowed the region to minimize defense budgets and focus on economic development. The absence of a strong U.S. role has already exacerbated historical animosities and regional ambitions among China, Russia, Japan, North and South Korea, and the nations of the South China Sea. The Japanese, Chinese, Taiwanese, Southeast Asians, and Koreans have all increased defense budgets and weapons purchases in the early 1990s as the U.S. defense shield has been lowered.

The collapse of the Soviet Union and the reluctance of the United States to be *the* military force in Southeast Asia could lead to more important security roles for Asia's major powers: India, China, and Japan. This potential change in Southeast Asia's international relations is an important reason that the ASEAN nations are strengthening their military capabilities and considering regional defense structures. Nevertheless, at present, because the governments of Southeast Asia cannot agree on who their probable adversaries are (or might be), the chance for a regional defense alliance is small.

Regional security concerns also focus on Japan, the area's economic superpower. Although, as previously stated, memories of Japan's depredations in Southeast Asia during World War II are waning, an increased military capability by the Japanese frightens the region's citizens. Clearly, Japan is compelled to protect its oil and trade routes in the South China Sea because its survival depends on Middle East oil. At present, Japan's government has stated unequivocally that Japan will play no military role in Southeast Asia.

## Domestic Changes in the New International Era

Coinciding with the remarkable changes in the international sphere have been indigenous developments throughout the region that make today's Southeast Asian nations fundamentally different from those of the 1970s. The clearest illustration of these changes has occurred in the three Indo-Chinese nations of Vietnam, Laos, and Cambodia, where socialist economics has been judged a failure and been replaced by market-oriented economies more similar to those in ASEAN. Ten years of economic decline following the 1975 communist consolidation or takeover of all three nations led to similar policies of renovation that ended collectivization, promoted decentralized planning, downgraded agricultural cooperatives, and terminated price controls and subsidies to inefficient industries. Foreign capital was solicited by means of liberalized foreign investment laws, and trade relations with ASEAN and Western capitalist nations were promoted.

These significant changes in Indochina, initiated in 1986, bore fruit in the late 1980s and early 1990s. In Vietnam, for example, farm production rose so that food self-sufficiency was achieved in the early 1990s. Indeed, Vietnam became the world's third largest exporter of rice, a major achievement because in the preceding decade Vietnam had been forced to import food. Laos experienced similar economic growth after promulgating the "new thinking" *(chin tanakan may)* reforms in 1986.

Cambodia's economy was also opened and decentralized by allowing entrepreneurs to run enterprises jointly with the state. Food deficits, the result of low productivity, continued in the 1980s because the populace was still traumatized by the heinous policies of the Khmer Rouge. The entire bureaucracy had been decimated during the period 1975–1979; the nation's infrastructure was almost nonexistent, and a continuing civil war was bleeding the country of its meager resources. A trade embargo, initiated by the United States, kept investment capital scarce. U.N. development programs were not allowed into Cambodia because the Cambodian U.N. seat was held by the Coalition Government of Democratic Kampuchea (CGDK), a tripartite alliance of rebel forces arrayed against the sitting government in the capital, Phnom Penh. The CGDK included the anticommunist Khmer People's National Liberation Front (KPNLF); the Sihanoukists, led by Cambodia's former ruler, Norodom Sihanouk; and the communist Khmer Rouge—the architects of the "killing fields."

Despite dismal economic conditions in Cambodia, there has been some normalization of life since 1979, when the Khmer Rouge was overthrown by the Vietnamese-sponsored Hun Sen government. The omnipresent fear and oppression that led to the deaths of some 2 million Cambodians from 1975 to 1979 have ended. The cities, once emptied, have repopulated. Nuclear families are living in accordance with Cambodian customs, practicing Buddhism, and educating the youth once again. In 1990 a dubious cease-fire was signed by the warring factions, designed to lead eventually to a freely chosen government. The eleven-year-old Cambodian war, which pitted the Hun Sen government in Phnom Penh against the three rebel forces, defied myriad attempts at resolution, at least partially because outside powers—such as the United States, China, Thailand, and Vietnam—complicated matters by using Cambodia for their own purposes. In 1993, the United Nations Transitional Authority in Cambodia (UNTAC) supervised elections designed to bring stability to the country. For the next several years, a degree of stability was achieved when the government was led by co–Prime Ministers Ranarridh and Hun Sen. Hun Sen's overthrow of his senior colleague in 1997 once again brought instability to this already suffering nation.

Changes in non-Indo-Chinese Southeast Asia have been very different, but no less important. The most obvious change concerns the process of modernization by the ASEAN nations. Since the 1970s, these states have moved from somnolent, primarily agricultural economies to vibrant, manufacturing-oriented economies with higher economic growth rates than states in any other region of the world

The rush to wealth among the ASEAN nations has led to both the best and worst aspects of westernization. Improved educational, infrastructural, and health facilities and greater opportunities in every aspect of life have been paralleled by problems such as crass materialism, pollution, intolerable traffic conditions, rising crime, corruption, alienation, and an increasing gap between the rich and the poor. Capital has poured into the region in unprecedented rates as the nations have been assimilated into the global capitalist economy. Only Burma, Laos, and Cambodia have remained isolated from incorporation into the world political economy.

The phenomenal economic growth rates, as high as 10 percent per year in the late 1980s and early 1990s, have fundamentally changed the Southeast Asian landscape. The most obvious change is the rapid increase in per capita gross national product (GNP). Per capita GNP in Thailand in 1977, for example, was $300; in 1997 the figure was $2,970. Similar leaps in the per capita GNP growth rate between the same years occurred in the other ASEAN nations: Malaysia, $660 to $4,460; Indonesia, $150 to $1,086; Singapore, $2,120 to $30,500; and the Philippines, $310 to $1,265. (The smaller growth rate for the Philippines was due to economic mismanagement during the Marcos presidency.)

Corresponding figures for Burma, Vietnam, Cambodia, and Laos show minuscule growth in per capita GNP during the same period, around $150 in each country in 1977 to $765, $270, $270, and $370 respectively in 1997. Brunei, because of its oil base, had an anomalous per capita GNP of $20,400 in 1997. For comparative purposes, 1997 per capita GNP in the United States was $28,480, in China $655, and in India $360.[4]

Quality of life indicators have also markedly improved in ASEAN. Since 1970, life expectancy in all of the Southeast Asian countries has increased by ten years to the high sixties, except for Burmese, Cambodian, and Laotian life expectancies, which are about fifty years. In Vietnam, life expectancy is sixty-eight, up from forty-three in 1980. The literacy rate throughout the region is about 90 percent, except in Laos and Cambodia, where the rate is considerably lower. Annual population growth rates have decreased since 1980 as a result of family planning policies, the rising standard of living, and the availability of birth control devices. Fertility declined more than 20 percent between 1960 and 1997. The average number of children per woman in 1960 and 1997 in each country was: Singapore, 6.3 and 1.6; Thailand, 6.6 and 3.0; Malaysia, 6.9 and 3.2; Indonesia, 5.6 and 3.1; and the Philippines, 6.6 and 4.2.[5]

These changes have paralleled the rapid urbanization of the Southeast Asian nations and the growth of an aware and involved middle class. This group is urban, educated, politically astute, materialistic, and technologically proficient. Although still a minority of the total population, the rise of the middle class is the most important socioeconomic change from the recent past. As recently as 1960 these countries' populations were 90 to 95 percent peasantry and 5 to 10 percent elite.

Similarly, a skilled blue-collar class has arisen to work in the new industries. This class, which represents the backbone of the export-oriented economies, has been at the heart of the rapid economic growth rates. Much credit for these spectacular growth rates can be attributed to the influx of industrial factories, mainly from Japan, South Korea, and Taiwan, all of which hire indigenous workers to produce products that are then exported throughout the world.

These socioeconomic changes have had both positive and negative ramifications. Life in Southeast Asia is increasingly characterized by higher standards of living, broadened horizons from a wider information flow, better health, higher levels of education, more active and meaningful participation in political affairs, and increased opportunities in virtually every sector of life. At the same time, these societies are now confronted with higher rates of crime, alienation, and corruption—social ills that are characteristic of urban centers. Air pollution, deforestation, traffic congestion, and land scarcity are a few of the environmental problems in Southeast Asia. The high levels of economic development are threatened by the assault on the region's natural resources and the governments' inability to build infrastructures sufficient to cope with the economic growth. Gaps between the few rich and the many poor are widening, despite the higher standard of living of all groups.

Although more difficult to specify, internal political changes in Southeast Asia are as important as domestic economic changes. Throughout the region there has been a tenuous, sometimes faltering trend toward pluralistic polities with stronger political institutions and less reliance on personalism. In Vietnam and Laos, for example, there is more openness in conversations and in the media regarding political issues. In Vietnam's local-level elections in November 1989, candidates were allowed to campaign with platforms that differed from the Communist Party line. Although the Communist Party retains its preeminent position in Vietnam as well as in Laos, real debates have taken place in the national assemblies of both nations. Factional struggles between conservatives and reformers have led to changes in party doctrine and government policies. Prior to 1986, such conflict and open discussion were not allowed.

In Burma, the move toward pluralistic politics climaxed in the summer of 1988 with massive demonstrations against the military government controlled by former General Ne Win. In an extraordinary outpouring of popular discontent against the government that had led Burma since 1962, thousands of citizens demanded a freely elected, democratic government. The euphoria ended abruptly on September 18, 1988, when Burma's military defense force (the Tatmadaw) quelled the movement and instituted a period of even greater repression under General Saw Maung, a protégé of former dictator Ne Win.

Despite the crackdown against those demanding democracy, the movement led to elections of members of a national assembly on May 27, 1990. In a stunning rebuke of the military rulers, and despite the fact that the most famous dissident leaders were not allowed to contest the election, opposition parties won an overwhelming majority of the seats. In the first multiparty elections in thirty years, the opposition National League for Democracy won two-thirds of the votes whereas the military-backed National Unity Party won only a small percent. However, in 1997 the military was still refusing to relinquish power, as Burma remained generally isolated from the world.

The movement toward democratization has not reached Brunei, which since its independence in 1984 has remained under the rule of its absolute monarch, Sultan Haji Hassanal Bolkiah Mu'izzaddin Waddaulah. No opposition parties have been sanctioned, and all government leaders must swear allegiance to the sultan. The immense wealth of Brunei, which comes from oil revenues, has allowed the government to set forth a comprehensive welfare and education program that, in turn, has kept antigovernment sentiment to a minimum.

The other nations have continued their slow evolution toward pluralism, stronger institutions, and civil liberties. The clearest example of the trend is the Philippines, where in February 1986 "People Power" succeeded in ousting the authoritarian government of Ferdinand Marcos and installing the democratic Corazon Aquino as president of the republic. The inability of Aquino to restructure the feudalistic socioeconomic system in the Philippines detracts from her success in revitalizing constitutional rule, free elections, freedom of the press, and autonomous institutions accountable to the public. Although personalism remained an integral part of Filipino politics under Aquino, corruption and cronyism declined compared to the Marcos era. A smooth transition from Aquino to President Fidel Ramos occurred in 1993, and he, in turn, succeeded in leading the country to higher rates of economic growth.

The Thai political system has been dominated by the military for fifty of the sixty-five years since 1932, when the absolute monarchy was replaced by a constitutional monarchy. Thailand's government was transformed into a bureaucratic military polity in which succession was determined by coups d'état rather than by heredity. Since 1970, and especially since the 1973 student-led revolt that led to the introduction of democratic procedures, two important changes have occurred: the widening of the political base with the growth of new interest groups that play important political roles outside the bureaucracy, and the strengthening and legitimizing of such formerly weak institutions as political parties and the Parliament. These changes have resulted in the gradual democratization of Thai politics, a shift from personalized, clientelist politics, and the temporary weakening of the military's role in government affairs. The 1991 military coup d'état only temporarily reversed the process of democratization.

The clearest sign of change in contemporary Thai politics was the rise to power of Chatichai Choonhavan, the first elected member of Parliament to become prime minister since 1976. Chatichai became prime minister after the July 24, 1988, parliamentary elections when he was elected a member of Parliament. As leader of the Chat Thai party, which had the largest plurality in Parliament, Chatichai formed a coalition government of five leading political parties. By 1990 the military had lost its monopoly of power in the Thai political system, although an army-led resurgence occurred in 1991 when the military deemed that the government was carrying out policies antithetical to the military's best interests. After a series of interim governments, mass demonstrations against the military, and nationwide elections in March and September 1992, democratic rule returned when the leader of the Democrat Party, Chuan Leekpai, was chosen prime minister by a majority coalition in the Parliament. Following Chuan, two more prime ministers were elected by the Parliament, although both faced criticism for leading corrupt and personalized administrations. However, in 1997 Chuan once again returned to power as prime minister.

Since Malaysia's independence in 1957, pluralist politics have been integral to the way authoritative decisions have been made. Through a system of quasi-separation of powers, competitive elections, and circumscribed civil liberties, the Malaysian government has been relatively accountable to the citizenry. Because of the ethnic communal tensions that pervade Malaysian society, the populace has accepted certain controls on its freedom, designed to ensure continued stability and consensus. Malaysia's leaders, including Prime Minister Datuk Seri Mahathir bin Mohamad, have been chosen by regularized elections, all won by the ruling Barisan Nasional (National Front) coalition.

Since achieving independence from the Netherlands in 1949, Indonesia has relied on the leadership of President Sukarno, who dominated Indonesian politics for nearly two decades until 1965, and President Suharto, who has led the country in the subsequent years. General Suharto, who was elected to his seventh five-year term in 1998, brought the military into a commanding position in Indonesian politics. At the same time, he established a constitutional order that features regular elections, which he and his Golkar political movement have controlled through skillful political management, mobilization of local-level bureaucrats, selected repression of oppositionists, workable economic programs, and unlimited access to revenue for campaign purposes. The economic crisis of 1997 brought about massive antiadministration demonstrations but did not keep Suharto from receiving unanimous support from his controlled People's Consultative Assembly (MPR) for a term to end in 2003.

President Suharto has attempted to balance the rising demands for more political openness with policies that ensure order, stability, and the continued primacy of the military. The balance is delicate because of the government's grip over mass social organizations and key areas of the economy. Suharto has followed Sukarno's dictum that Western-style democracy is inappropriate for Indonesians, who thrive in a system of consultation *(musjawarah)* and consensus *(mufakat)* in which the leaders make the key decisions for the people. Western-style democracy is viewed by Indonesian leaders as a formula for anarchy, factionalism, and revolt. Just as important, democratization is seen as a sure means for the present leaders to lose their coveted positions.

Singapore, Southeast Asia's most efficiently governed country, is a wealthy city-state and entrepôt that lacks the complexity of its larger, more populated, and more diverse neighbors. It does have the brilliant Lee Kuan Yew, who led the country since its independence from the British until November 1990, when he resigned as prime minister. Within a formal structure of democratic institutions that features free elections and a parliamentary system, Singapore has been run as a one-party system centering around Lee. By circumscribing the freedoms of the opposition and by achieving remarkable economic growth, Lee Kuan Yew obtained the support of the overwhelming majority of the people. Lee became senior minister after installing his protégé Goh Chok Tong in the position of prime minister.

The involvement of large numbers of people in the political affairs of Southeast Asian nations is a fundamental innovation, replacing traditional hierarchical patterns of rule. The leaders of virtually every nation in the region must consider the views of the populace as articulated through votes, demonstrations, interest groups, the media, dissident leaders, disaffected political factions, mobilized ethnic groups, and student associations. Moreover, national leaders must have the foresight to meet the needs of the people before these needs become impossible demands. This requirement for effective leadership in the new Southeast Asia is not only unprecedented, it is an indigenously inspired change from the centralized polities that pervaded the region for centuries. The ideas of majority rule, freedom to oppose leadership, and institutionalized rather than personalistic government are not a traditional part of Southeast Asian political culture. When these changes are viewed in conjunction with the equally momentous movement toward modernization and the international drive toward more open political and economic systems, the transformation of Southeast Asia in the new international era becomes increasingly intelligible.

The themes touched upon above are treated in more depth in the following chapters, each focusing on a particular country. Each Southeast Asian nation will be analyzed in terms of its political institutions, its processes of development and democratization, its policy issues, and the role of the state.

## Notes

1. James Clad, *Behind the Myth: Business, Money and Power in Southeast Asia* (London: Unwin and Hyman, 1989), p. ix.

2. For a detailed discussion of phases of U.S.–Southeast Asian relations, see Muthiah Alagappa, "U.S.-ASEAN Security Relations: Challenges and Prospects," *Contemporary Southeast Asia,* vol. 11, no. 1 (June 1989), pp. 1–39.

3. The figures are from Stanley Karnow, *Vietnam: A History* (New York: Viking Press, 1983).

4. All figures are from *Asiaweek* , April 7, 1997.

5. Ibid.

# 3

# THAILAND

Thailand has become an exemplary case study of how Third World countries can develop successfully. The Thai people's capacity to shape their nation into an increasingly developed society, both politically and economically, stems from a history of astute adaptation of those aspects of modernization and development that were appropriate to traditional Thai ways. Throughout their history, as citizens of the only Southeast Asian nation never to have been colonized, the Thais never had a foreign culture thrust upon them. Instead, they were able to choose and mold a political system that fits Thai culture.

Thailand's success in developing politically is all the more striking given the fact that for centuries the government was autocratic in form and spirit. Power was the privilege of a small elite as well as of absolute monarchs who were not accountable to the people and whose authority was enhanced by an aura of divinity attached to the highest levels of office. Those who ruled were believed to possess superior ability and moral excellence. Common citizens exhibited little interest in affairs beyond their own villages.

The Sukhothai Kingdom (c. 1238–1350) was the first Thai-controlled kingdom in history. In this formerly Khmer-ruled area, the Thais absorbed the cultures of the Khmers, Mons, Hindus, and Chinese and began the assimilation process that is important even today for understanding modern Thai society. Buddhism and Brahmanism were introduced to the Thais during the Sukhothai era. The Sukhothai Kingdom expanded and retracted, depending on the fortunes of military campaigns, until the Ayuthaya period (1350–1767) began.

The Thais adapted much from the Hindu-influenced Khmers, who dominated the region during the Ayuthaya period. In particular, the kings were transformed from paternalistic guardians into autocratic god-kings with the attributes of a Brahmanic deity. The perception of the kings as god-kings remains even today as an important element of the veneration shown the king by his subjects. Notwithstanding this aura of godliness, the kings did not enjoy absolute power but were limited by court factionalism and competition for power and by an assumption of kingly virtue.

During the Ayuthayan reign, important institutions were established that still influence Thai society. A *sakdi na* (power over fields) system was introduced that provided structure and hierarchy to the social and political relationships of the Thais. Virtually all persons in the kingdom were given *sakdi na* rankings according to the amount of land (or number of persons) they controlled. The ranking determined the salary of officials, the deference due them, and their labor obligations to the state. Although the quantifiable character of the *sakdi na* system had ended by 1932, the informal hierarchical nature of the system is still a significant element of Thai society.

The destruction of Ayuthaya by invading Burmese in 1767 was a traumatic event in Thai history. The political-social system was torn asunder. Despite the near-total destruction of the kingdom, the Thais displayed remarkable recuperative powers and in a short time resumed life under a new centralized government in Bangkok led by the Chakri Dynasty. Many of the Chakri kings were reform-oriented—systematizing administrative structures, freeing the slaves, bringing in highly educated technocrats, and ensuring the continued independence of the nation from Western colonialists. The present King Phumiphol Adunyadej is the ninth king of this dynasty.

Even after the 1932 revolt, which overthrew the absolute monarchy and established a constitutional monarchy, politics remained in the hands of a small elite group, now mostly civilian bureaucrats and military generals. The military, which emerged as the country's dominant institution, has controlled political power in Thailand for about fifty of the past sixty-five years, since the revolt against absolutism. Until recently, politics in Thailand was monopolized by military leaders and a small number of government officials, with no competition or balance from forces outside the bureaucratic arena. The basis of political power was highly personalized and subject to informal political manipulations and loyalties.

Thailand entered the modern period at the end of World War II in considerably better shape than most of its Southeast Asian neighbors. Having acquiesced to Japanese occupation (and thereby having suffered little war damage), and not having fought a debilitating struggle for independence, Thailand was secure and stable. Initially after the war, Thailand seemed headed toward a constitutional system of parliamentary democracy, but the army soon took power.

The most influential of the postwar leaders was Marshal Sarit Thanarat, army commander in chief, who became prime minister in 1957, declared martial law, and ruled dictatorially for six years. He was the first prime minister to make economic development the cornerstone of his rule. His successor, Marshal Thanom Kittikachorn, followed in Sarit's footsteps by keeping the military in firm control of every aspect of government and by pursuing economic development. During both administrations, the legislature was impotent, political parties were for the most part forbidden to form, and corruption was rampant.

In response to the low level of political accountability and the high level of corruption, the "great tragedy" of October 14, 1973 *(Wan Maha Wipayok)*, occurred when the citizenry rose against the Thanom government and forced the leadership into exile. King Phumiphol Adunyadej, Thailand's revered monarch, appointed the first civilian government since the immediate postwar period. The major causes of discontent included the political and economic mismanagement of the military regime, the perception that the military was increasingly ruling in its own self-interest, factionalism within the military, and the rise of an organized and aroused student population supported by the citizenry and the king.

Democratic civilian rule lasted only until October 1976, when the military again overthrew the government, proclaimed martial law, and abrogated the constitution. The 1973 revolt had raised the expectations of many Thais that fundamental economic reforms would be carried out. The succeeding three-year period, however, coincided with a worldwide recession and with inflation that temporarily ended the nation's rapid economic growth. Hence, the hopes of many Thais that democracy would improve their lives were dashed by an economic situation over which the new government had no control.

The civilian government was also faced with an international and regional situation over which it had little control. The change to communist governments in Vietnam, Laos, and Cambodia and the rise of insurgency throughout the Thai countryside shocked many Thais, who felt that only an authoritarian, military-dominated government could deal effectively with these threats. Because Thailand's traditional security ally, the United States, was withdrawing from Southeast Asia, the civilian government renewed ties with the communist nations. This destabilizing state of flux added to the uncertainty felt by many Thais.

The military remained the dominant government institution until 1988. Under General Prem Tinsulanond's prime ministership, the country began its transformation into a more democratic society. Prem included civilian technocrats in his cabinet and relied on the freely elected legislature for support of his programs. Despite two coup attempts against him, he remained in power from 1980 until 1988, when he voluntarily stepped down.

The clearest sign of democratization in contemporary Thai politics was the rise to power of Chatichai Choonhavan, the first elected member of Parliament to become prime minister since 1976. Chatichai assumed his new position following the 1988 elections, when the political party he led received the largest plurality of votes and when Prem refused to accept another term as prime minister. Prem, who had led Thailand through a period of stability and economic growth, had been deemed acceptable to both civilian and military forces and had been expected to continue in office. His refusal opened the way for civilian leadership under Chatichai.

The smooth transition from Prem to Chatichai reflected the new optimism about Thailand's evolution toward democracy. Chatichai had assumed power without relying on the support of the army. The constitutional provisions for elections worked well in the transfer of political power. Thus, the military coup d'état in February 1991 was a shocking assault on the notion that Thailand had successfully institutionalized democratic-civilian processes.

Chatichai had served as minister of foreign affairs, minister of industry, and deputy minister under previous administrations. Because his reputation was that of a big-business playboy, most analysts believed his tenure as prime minister would be short. However, Chatichai initiated a number of highly popular policies, thereby enhancing his *baramee* (charisma) in the minds of the populace.

Chatichai raised the salaries of government officials as well as the minimum wage for laborers, banned the indiscriminate cutting of trees, and stood up to the United States on trade and other economic issues. The decision to ban logging was particularly dramatic because conventional wisdom suggested that neither the cabinet nor the Parliament would ever agree to ban an industry in which many of the political and military elites had major economic interests. Although the government has yet to show that it can control illegal encroachment in the remaining forests, the ban was a first step in repairing ecological damage.

In a series of innovative proposals, Chatichai enhanced his rising reputation as a master politician among the populace. His idea to turn the Indo-Chinese battleground into a trading market was especially popular with the business community, which sought to open economic ties with the Vietnamese. His call for increased trade with Vietnam and his invitation to Cambodian Premier Hun Sen to visit Bangkok reversed Thai foreign policy, which had long opposed normalization with either Cambodia or Vietnam. Chatichai also moved to improve ties with Laos after decades of intermittent border skirmishes and diplomatic conflicts.

Chatichai's policies were supported by his coalition majority. However, oppositionists spoke against many of his initiatives, and the country's free press presented all sides of the controversies. Military leaders initially expressed support for Chatichai's administration and rejected intervention. In a move to mitigate potential military opposition, Chatichai invited General Chavalit Yongchaiyut to enter the cabinet as defense minister and deputy prime minister. Chavalit quickly tired of the criticism directed toward him and resigned his position to form the New Aspirations Party (NAP). He then campaigned throughout the country in preparation for a bid to become the new prime minister.

Despite Chatichai's widespread support, several issues raised concern about the government's stability and effectiveness. Democratization had not completely ended the personalism and factionalism that have long been a part of Thai politics. Even among the coalition partners, factional infighting remained the norm as party leaders vied for the most influential cabinet positions. The fact that much of the popularity of the administration had been focused on Chatichai personally became a source of discontent among leaders of coalition parties. Although votes of no confidence did not succeed, a minority of coalition members on occasion defected, raising the possibility that Chatichai would dissolve the government. Indeed, in December 1990 Chatichai did dissolve his cabinet as a maneuver to offset criticism of his administration. The king immediately reinstated Chatichai as prime minister, thus providing him with an opportunity to bring in new faces and to mitigate military disapproval of certain members of his cabinet. Because he turned seventy in 1990, Chatichai stated on several occasions that he was "too old" to remain in his position of leadership for much longer. The uncertainty of his tenure exacerbated factional maneuvering and set the scene for the February coup.

Related to this problem of personalism, corruption continued to be an important part of the political process. The phenomenal economic growth rates of the 1980s brought large amounts of capital into the Thai economy, and these new resources were the financial targets of public officials for private gain. Thai citizens were skeptical about the administration's professed concern for the majority, which had not gained from the economy's high growth rates. Many Thais viewed the administration as primarily concerned with big-business interests. Indeed, the military claimed that the primary motivation for carrying out the coup in 1991 was the pervasive corruption of the kingdom's politicians. Thai newspapers, unencumbered by censorship, reported daily on the rampant corruption among top-level cabinet members. Huge telecommunications projects, massive road and elevated commuter railway ventures, cable television contracts, and new oil refineries are examples of multibillion dollar deals arranged and managed (or mismanaged) by politicians whose primary aim was to perpetuate their own power base and personal wealth.

Coup leaders also cited the rise of a "parliamentary dictatorship" as another reason for the takeover, complaining in particular about rampant vote buying. The rise in the number of wealthy capitalists elected to Parliament and chosen for the cabinet had been steady in past decades but was especially conspicuous in the Chatichai administration. Although the substantial corruption was an important legitimizing rationale for the coup, the more direct cause was a pattern of slights carried out by Chatichai and perceived by military leaders as threats to their traditional prerogatives.

On February 23, 1991, Supreme Commander Sundhara Kongsompong and Army Commander in Chief Suchinda Kraprayoon abrogated the constitution, dismissed the elected government, and set up the temporary National Peace Keeping Council (NPKC) with powers of martial law and themselves as ultimate arbiters of public policy. This momentous decision was made just two hours before Chatichai was arrested on an airplane waiting to take off for Chiang Mai, where he was to have an audience with the king.

Initially, the people greeted the coup with acquiescence, though not enthusiasm, and there were no public protests or demonstrations. Realizing that times had indeed changed, the NPKC moved quickly to establish an interim constitution and to name Anand Panyarachun, a distinguished civilian, as prime minister. His appointment was a sign that the military believed the populace would not tolerate direct military rule for long. Anand's appointment, announced on March 2, was universally praised, reflecting his impeccable status and reputation as a diplomat, administrator, and businessman. Prime Minister Anand, in turn, appointed an interim cabinet consisting of outstanding technocrats, notable scholars, and senior military officials in the defense and interior ministries.

The coup leaders emphasized their commitment to policy continuity in economic matters, calling in leading Thai bankers and business executives to assure them that Thailand's market- and export-oriented economy would remain intact. Political parties were retained, and a national legislative assembly was established to approve a constitution and arrange for an election. For the overwhelming majority of Thais, the coup changed nothing except the names of the kingdom's top government leaders.

The appointment of Anand ensured that an independent-minded diplomat would lead Thailand during the interim period before elections, which were scheduled for March 22, 1992. The junta gave Anand wide leeway in running the government but also asserted its views forcefully regarding the new constitution promulgated by the interim national legislative assembly appointed by the NPKC. The final document returned Thailand's legislative body to its former system, in which the appointed upper house of Parliament was given equal power with the elected lower house in matters of policymaking. Moreover, the chairman of the NPKC was given provisional power to nominate the new prime minister, thereby providing effective power over the government for the duration of the next government's term.

Anand's independence from the military was unprecedented for a civilian who had been placed in power by a military coup. Indeed, Anand's "aberrant" confidence led him to block the military's request to buy additional weaponry, and his administration turned out to be one of the most effective in modern Thai politics. From March 1 to December 6, 1991, the government passed 127 new laws, compared to 105 for the thirty months of the preceding Chatichai government. From December 1991 to the end of his term, Anand's legislative record was just as impressive. His administration set forth measures supporting privatization, trade liberalization, deregulation of onerous restrictions on the economy, tax reform focusing on a value-added tax of 7 percent, labor constraints including the abolition of state enterprise unions, and infrastructure projects.

Anand's success was all the more surprising given the major behind-the-scenes role played by Class 5 military officers, who formed an elite group that had managed to win control of key positions in the NPKC and the army. Army commander Suchinda was the strongman of Class 5; his colleagues in the same class were made ministers of communications and the interior, and other colleagues controlled the top five posts in the armed forces. Their influence over the new administration continued following the 1992 elections.

Once the new constitution was approved and an election law passed, campaigning began in earnest. The major theme of newspaper articles was vote and candidate buying by parties looking for candidates to run under their banner. Despite the establishment by Anand of a "watchdog committee" to monitor campaigning, many parties distributed money aimed at enlisting electable candidates to position themselves as the core of the next coalition government. For months before the election, an unseemly move among candidates toward wealthy parties occurred, with no concern whatsoever for the stance of the party on issues or ideological direction. For the majority of candidates, the only principle concerned which party offered the most money.

Political parties sold their names and vote-mobilizing organizations to candidates. In return, candidates each received up to several hundred thousand dollars for campaign purposes, but these funds were often

given in cash and could not be accounted for. The practice of party jump-
ing became common because parties rarely set forth coherent policy statements and were used largely to support particular candidates.

The elections were carried out with bureaucratic efficiency, although
the campaign included election-law violations. Poll-watch volunteers
monitored the campaign expenses of individual candidates, which were
limited to $40,000. Vote buying entailed the following tactics: giving cash
to voters in return for promises of support, offering food and alcoholic
drinks free of charge, serving free food at village festivals, and promising
cash to voters if the candidate they were told to vote for won. To discourage vote buying in the 1992 election, radio, television, newspapers, and
banners featured slogans designed to discourage people from "selling
their freedom."

There is conflicting evidence as to whether vote buying is an effective
means to garner votes. Most researchers have found that money is a primary incentive for determining a citizen's vote. Candidates must have an
effective network of support, run by canvassers (*hua khanaen*) who have
close ties with village leaders such as headmen, teachers, and respected
elders. Because candidates need to ensure that the money they hand out
will not be wasted, they distribute it through a network of canvassers.
Voters tend to vote for those candidates close to village or town leaders
who have helped the voters out in the past. If these leaders have funds
from candidates to divvy up, villagers are all the more likely to support
the leaders' choice.

Nevertheless, the government's anti-vote-buying campaign suggested
to voters that they should not accept money from a candidate but that if
they did, they should then vote for that candidate's opponent. This more
cynical response resulted in voters sometimes accepting favors from
many candidates. Although vote buying occurred throughout the kingdom, poll watchers found few cases of outright fraud such as ballot box
stuffing.

To ensure that the military continued its dominance, military-backed
parties, which were close to General Suchinda, formed a joint campaign
scheme to minimize competition and to elect candidates supporting the
NPKC. The parties included the Samakkhi Tham, under the leadership of
Narong Wongwan; the Chat Thai (Thai Nation) party led by retired Air
Chief Marshal Somboon Rahong; and the conservative Social Action
Party, with Montri Pongpanit as leader. All three party leaders agreed
that they would consider a nonelected prime minister and might well integrate into leadership positions even those politicians who had been
charged with being "unusually wealthy," a euphemism for corrupt, by
the anticorruption investigative group appointed by the NPKC. It is
ironic that the Chat Thai party was included in the group since that was

Prime Minister Chatichai's party when he was overthrown by the very coup leaders his party later supported. Those who staged the coup joined with those whom they accused of being unworthy of holding public office to form a new government. Most commentators suggested that the Samakkhi Tham leaders cajoled the Chat Thai leaders into the fold by promising that they would be cleared of corruption charges once the new government was formed.

Opposition parties were viewed as those that opposed the continuation of military dominance and pledged to support amendments to make the constitution more democratic. In another irony, the leading opposition New Aspirations Party was led by former army General Chavalit, the mentor of coup leader General Suchinda. Thailand's most popular politician, Bangkok Governor Chamlong Srimuang, gave up his position to lead the Palang Dharma party. Buoyed by Chamlong's reputation as an incorruptible ascetic, Palang Dharma swept all but 3 of Bangkok's 35 seats. The third major opposition group was the Democrat Party, Thailand's longest-lived political party, whose candidates campaigned against the NPKC leadership and in favor of a return to democratic rule.

The March 22 elections resulted in a narrow victory for parties aligned with the NPKC. The pro-military Samakkhi Tham won 79 of 360 seats, Chat Thai 74, New Aspirations Party 72, Democrat Party 44, Palang Dharma 43, Social Action Party 31, Prachakorn Thai (Thai Citizen) 7, Solidarity 6, and Rasadorn 4. The Samakkhi Tham, Chat Thai, Social Action Party, and two minor parties forged a coalition of 195 seats, or 55 percent of the total. The other major parties (New Aspirations, Democrat, Palang Dharma, and Solidarity) formed the opposition.

The pro-military coalition initially nominated Narong Wongwan as the next prime minister. His credentials as a civilian four-term elected member of Parliament (MP), a former cabinet member, and a leader of the political party winning the largest plurality made him an attractive choice for the NPKC leaders. As a billionaire businessman, his considerable fortune helped build up the Samakkhi Tham party in less than a year. His leadership would mean that the military could dominate political policy-making. However, on the day he was nominated, the U.S. State Department confirmed that Narong had been denied a visa in July 1991 because he was alleged to be involved in drug trafficking from his business base in the Golden Triangle area of northern Thailand. Narong had made a fortune in a wide variety of businesses: tobacco, transportation, mining, timber, and holiday resorts. He had also been investigated for possessing "unusual wealth" when a member of the Chatichai cabinet, but those charges were later dropped.

With Narong's reputation besmirched, military leaders began to distance themselves from him, while political party leaders spent the following week attempting to forge a coalition agreement to name a prime minister. Newspaper stories speculated that the military, having long known about Narong's involvement in drug trafficking, had deliberately recommended him for prime minister as a ploy to create a crisis of leadership, which the military would resolve through the nomination of General Suchinda, the 1991 coup leader. Indeed, Narong backed down from the nomination, and the coalition named Suchinda despite his prior unequivocal declaration that he would not accept the prime ministership. His nomination was approved by the king and the Parliament with the concurrence of the speaker of the Parliament as well as General Sundhara, the chief of the NPKC. In what Thais referred to as "the second coup" or "the silent coup," General Suchinda, by engineering military control over the position of prime minister, reversed the steps Thailand had taken toward democratic government. To express dismay, some 50,000 protesters demonstrated against the new government following the announcement of Suchinda's appointment.

Prime Minister Suchinda announced a controversial cabinet, including eleven members who had been investigated by an antigraft panel (established by Suchinda after the coup) to see if they had enriched themselves while in office. Three of the eleven were declared "unusually wealthy" but were nevertheless selected for the new cabinet. Critics of Suchinda pointed out that these appointments gave lie to the original claim of the coup leaders that their purpose in overthrowing the Chatichai administration was to curtail corruption.

To reduce concerns about the economic direction of the administration, Suchinda reappointed a conservative economist as finance minister. Nevertheless, the rest of the cabinet was made up principally of wealthy business executives and military leaders who had no national or international reputation for administrative competence. For example, the communications minister was a major financier of the Chat Thai party noted for corruption.

Suchinda's tenure as prime minister had parallels with that of General Prem, who ruled Thailand from 1980 to 1988. Both leaders were generals who refused to be parliamentary candidates and who followed a difficult era of hectic civilian rule. However, Prem had solid support from a majority coalition in the Parliament, the army, and the citizenry, whereas Suchinda led a divided coalition and was viewed as the person who ended democratic rule, however inept such rule had been. In Bangkok, the Palang Dharma sweep and the strong showing of the Democrats in the southern provinces in the March 1992 elections demonstrated the high degree of opposition to a return to military rule. The fact that many members of the majority coalition were precisely those politicians deemed corrupt by Suchinda and ousted in the 1991 coup augured poorly for the stability of his administration.

In his favor, Suchinda could count on the overwhelming support of the appointed Senate, which was dominated by leading military officers, top bankers, wealthy industrialists, and business executives. The 270 senators had the power to participate in nonconfidence votes and to take part in general debates on governmental policy. The economic elite in the Senate consisted of the presidents of Thailand's largest corporations and banks. Military or police officers held 60 percent of the seats.

The conflict between Thailand's reverence for tradition and its headlong plunge into modernity was the key factor in the events that drove Prime Minister Suchinda from office after only a forty-eight-day reign. He bet that the forces of tradition as exemplified by the military would prevail, and he underestimated the power of the ideal of democracy among the country's increasingly educated and sophisticated citizens. The massive anti-Suchinda demonstrations by hundreds of thousands of Thais in May 1992, and the deaths of hundreds of persons when the military tried to stop them, were the tragic consequences of Suchinda's hubris and miscalculations.

First, Suchinda did not understand that the days were long gone when the military could dominate every aspect of Thai politics without much public demur. The 1991 coup did not undo almost two decades of new participatory values during which Thai urbanites as well as rural peasants learned how to promote their own interests through political activities.

Second, Thais were much more attuned to international events, both through the media and through their burgeoning economic contacts. Suchinda did not understand the importance Thais placed on their international reputation. Thais were profoundly embarrassed that their country had suffered another coup just as much of the rest of the world was moving inexorably toward more open and liberal regimes. When Suchinda maneuvered himself into the position of unelected prime minister, breaking a solemn promise not to do so, and then used draconian military force to stay in power, he underestimated the depth of Thais' sense of humiliation and their desire for his removal.

Third, Suchinda misunderstood the reaction he would generate by approving a violent response to the antigovernment demonstrations. The declaration of an emergency effectively took away civil liberties, while censorship of the media and the sight of police officers and troops bludgeoning demonstrators ended any semblance of legitimacy Suchinda might have had. His claim that the demonstrators and their leaders were pawns of "communist" elements that desired the end of the monarchy was vintage rhetoric from the 1960s, irrelevant to contemporary realities.

Suchinda's military backing was shaky because he relied solely on his military academy Class 5 army colleagues, many of whom he had helped to top positions. Officers from other classes, especially at the level of colonel, disapproved both of his seizure of power and his decision to send in the troops. Chamlong Srimuang, for example, the unofficial leader of the opposition, whose hunger strike galvanized the demonstrators, was a former leader of the Class 7 army faction.

In essence, Suchinda believed that he could run the country in the same way he ran the military. He often spoke of the importance of honor and pride among military men and the need to fight to keep that honor when insulted by politicians; obedience, he noted, was the essence of military life. Obedience was not, however, the priority of interest groups that increasingly contested the military's dominance. These groups, including the new middle class, provincial leaders, those active in nongovernmental organizations (NGOs), and the business elite, were imbued with values contrary to those revered by the military. When Suchinda sent in the army against the antigovernment demonstrators, he showed his contempt for the crucial difference between civilian and military life.

When the crisis of May 1992 reached a stage of potential civil war, King Phumiphol stepped in, and his extraordinary intervention on May 20 forced the resignation of Suchinda and placed the immense prestige of the monarch on the side of democratic rule. On television screens throughout the world, the sight of Suchinda and Chamlong kneeling at the feet of the monarch illuminated the unique position of the king in Thailand. By agreeing to amnesty for all persons involved in the demonstrations, by supporting constitutional amendments designed to reduce the military's dominance, and by directing Suchinda and Chamlong to peacefully resolve the crisis forthwith, the king succeeded in ending the violence.

The establishment of a civilian administration was more difficult than the removal of Suchinda, who went into hiding protected by troops loyal to him. The majority coalition of parties in the Parliament agreed to support Somboon Rahong, the head of the Chat Thai party and close confidant of the disgraced military leaders. Although he was an elected member of the Parliament and enjoyed the support of a majority in the Parliament, Somboon was anathema to the opposition parties and to the demonstrators who believed that he was a lackey of the generals.

In a second extraordinary intervention, the king rejected Somboon and instead approved the return of Anand Panyarachun as prime minister. The king's decision occurred just before the Parliament overwhelmingly passed constitutional amendments requiring prime ministers to be elected members of Parliament and reducing the role of the military-dominated Senate. The first amendment was designed to apply to prime ministers named before the amendments were promulgated so that Anand could rule.

Anand's appointment was met enthusiastically by most Thais, who recalled that he had won international praise for running an honest and efficient government during the interim period following the 1991 coup.

His appointment was seen as a brilliant stroke to end the stalemate following the catastrophic events of May. After appointing a distinguished group of technocrats and diplomats to his cabinet, Anand pledged to serve only for four months to prepare the country for parliamentary elections, to repair the damage done to the nation's reputation, and to revitalize the economy.

Anand succeeded in demoting the kingdom's top military leaders, who were deemed responsible for the violence. He removed important state enterprises from military control and planned for the second national election in one year. These decisions were considered courageous because they directly challenged the traditional prerogatives of the army.

The September 13, 1992, election featured 2,417 contenders from sixteen parties contesting 360 parliamentary seats. Few of the candidates were newcomers, although many candidates jumped parties. Parties changed names and distanced themselves from the tainted, "satanic" affiliations they formerly had with the military. The wealthier parties paid potential candidates to join. For example, the Chat Thai party paid $120,000 to any former MP, $200,000 to anyone who had won a seat in the last election, and $280,000 to a former minister who could deliver a team of MPs. The mass exodus from parties affiliated with the military and the embarrassing game of musical chairs were indications that candidates were primarily self-interested and that they had little concern for party policy positions. In the September election, personalism remained the chief characteristic of political parties in Thailand.

The pro-democracy "angel" parties—Democrat, Palang Dharma, New Aspirations, and Solidarity—plus one party that had supported the military in the previous administration formed a government under the leadership of a civilian politician as leader of the country. Chuan Leekpai, the soft-spoken, moderate leader of the Democrat Party from Trang Province in the south, assumed the position of prime minister. He led a 207-seat coalition in the 360-member House of Representatives.

Chuan's immediate challenge was to find a balance between democratic rule and sensitivity to the traditional prerogatives of the military. He also faced the challenge of keeping together his fragile administration, which included leaders of the coalition parties who themselves coveted the prime ministership. Opposition leaders pointed to Chuan's lack of charisma and leadership and his lack of policy initiatives and new programs.

Part of the difficulty for Chuan was that many of the problems his administration needed to solve were intractable. Even with a cabinet considered to be one of the brightest in Thai history, the first six months of Chuan's tenure generated few proposals for solving the problems of traffic congestion, pollution, environmental degradation, child labor, acquired immune deficiency syndrome (AIDS), centralized decisionmaking, water shortages, and ubiquitous corruption.

Despite these difficulties, Chuan attempted to democratize a corrupt, military-dominated political system. He led the country from September 1992 to May 1995, becoming the longest-serving elected civilian prime minister in Thai history. His coalition fell apart as a result of differences and conflicting demands among the ruling political parties, and elections were called for July 2, 1995. Chuan's majority in the elected lower body, the House, was tenuous, and the coalition eventually collapsed over controversies about decentralization, a contentious issue in the highly centralized arena of Thai politics.

In the July 1995 election, some twelve political parties and 2,300 candidates vied for the 391 House seats. About 40 million people voted. Campaign issues were vague because political parties in Thailand generally do not offer platforms or represent particular ideologies. Thai politics has long been characterized by candidates moving from one party to another depending on how much competing parties offered them for their services. Parties offered up to 5 million baht ($200,000 in 1995) to any competing candidate with a good chance of success who would switch parties. Voters were offered 100 to 300 baht ($4 to $12) if they promised to vote for a particular candidate.

Other campaign issues included rural poverty, environmental degradation, Bangkok's notorious traffic congestion, land reform, and bureaucratic inefficiencies. Chuan ran as "Mr. Clean" and emphasized his stewardship over the vibrant economy. His reputation as an unexciting leader without charisma was detrimental. The other major personality in the campaign was Banharn Silapa-archa, leader of the Chat Thai party. Party members noted Banharn's vast experience: He was a billionaire business executive with six terms in Parliament and former minister of agriculture, industry, interior, finance, and transportation. Because he represented a rural constituency, he was viewed as someone who understood the average Thai. Banharn's campaign opponents charged that he was corrupt. He was disdainfully described as "Mr. ATM" to remind Thais that he had bought himself into power. Banharn was scorned by Bangkok voters (Chat Thai did not win any seats from Bangkok constituencies) and by the intellectual elites who viewed him as a country bumpkin.

The elections resulted in a triumph for the Chat Thai, which captured 92 seats. Banharn moved to mobilize a coalition of parties, while Chuan, whose Democrat Party won 86 seats, became the leader of the opposition. The "satanic" party victory showed that money politics had returned. Banharn's victory was an apt reflection of politics as usual.

Ministerial portfolios were allocated as rewards for loyal service by MPs rather than on the basis of expertise. The new cabinet was highly factionalized and received negative assessments from Thailand's outspoken press, mainly because old-style politicians dominated the cabinet rather than new-style technocrats.

Banharn's administration turned out to be a disaster characterized by corruption, a lack of direction, personal dishonesty (Banharn allegedly lied about his plagiarized law thesis and his birth date), and economic malaise. He was forced to call new elections in November 1996, reportedly the most expensive in Thai history. The New Aspirations Party gained defections from Chat Thai, winning the most seats (125) in the Parliament. NAP party leader Chavalit Yongchaiyut became prime minister, leading a group of conservative parties. Like Banharn, Chavalit was unpopular among Bangkok's elites and the leading newspapers, although he had achieved popularity in the rural areas for his support of developmental projects, especially in northeastern and southern Thailand.

Chavalit was immediately faced with two tremendous challenges: drafting a new constitution and solving the economic crisis. A major political crisis was averted when the Parliament overwhelmingly passed a new constitution on September 27, 1997. This approval returned some legitimacy to Chavalit. His support for passage, however reluctant, allowed him to survive a potentially disastrous censure vote but only because his supporters feared that he would dissolve Parliament rather than resign, which would have forced the country into precipitous elections. Chavalit's administration was increasingly tenuous, with large demonstrations opposing his leadership on a daily basis. Elections were called for early spring 1998.

Much of the protest centered around Chavalit's inability to resolve the economic crisis. Indeed, his imprudent supervision, his lack of direction, his administration's refusal to provide anything more than a Band-Aid for the ailing economy, and his ambivalent enforcement of laws designed to prevent corruption were all reasons for the Thais losing confidence in his leadership. Hence, it was no surprise when Chavalit announced in November that he would step down as prime minister, an office he had held for just 11 months.

Chavalit's resignation culminated six months of economic chaos and the seeming inability of the government to bring order to the situation. Most Thais blamed the political system for the economic crisis, believing that politicians are more concerned about perpetuating their own power and profits than they are about the public good. Chavalit's coalition was made up of competing political and financial ambitions that rendered it impossible to make the difficult decisions necessary to impose discipline on the nation's economy. When Chavalit stepped down, the baht had lost half its value against the dollar, the stock market had fallen precipitously, and the International Monetary Fund had been forced to bail out the country with a loan of some $17 billion.

Because Chavalit's resignation came at precisely the time that the Thai Parliament was acting on provisions to launch the new constitution, the country faced the prospect of an interim prime minister until elections could be called in 1998. Thai newspapers speculated that one of several former prime ministers would be called to take over temporarily: General Prem Tinsulanond, who served for three terms from 1980 to 1988; Anand Panyarachun, who was twice placed in the prime ministership by the military in 1991 and 1992; and Chuan Leekpai, head of the opposition Democrat Party and prime minister from 1992 to 1995. In November, Chuan managed to forge a coalition majority and took over the top position.

Thailand has not been able to establish a systematic process for transferring power in its sixty-five years as a constitutional monarchy. Nevertheless, with few exceptions, successions have proceeded with a minimum of the violence and dramatic upheavals characteristic of the kingdom's neighbors and other Third World societies. Policy continuity has been a feature of the process of succession, with new leadership generally meeting with acceptance and legitimacy among the political aware. This legitimacy stems from the fact that elections and coups have rarely obstructed government processes or undermined the principal underpinnings of the state: nation, king, and religion.

The May 1992 crisis serves as an exception to these generalizations. This succession crisis included excessive violence perpetrated by a military bent on perpetuating its power. That violence changed the Thai citizenry's views on the acceptability of military rule and significantly undermined Suchinda's legitimacy. The king's interventions were indicative of a system that had not yet established succession processes independent of assistance from the ceremonial head of government.

The struggle between, on the one hand, state officials led by the military, and on the other, politicians and business elites, continues to be a centerpiece of Thai political activity. The other central focus is the struggle between urbanized Bangkok and the more traditional countryside. The 1991 military coup d'état and the subsequent debate on how to fashion a new government were examples of both the attempt and failure to resolve these struggles. The public explanations for the coup—corruption and parliamentary dictatorship—were rationalizations presented by a segment of the military to secure prerogatives thought threatened by civilian leadership. Once elections took place, that same military segment decided it would be intolerable for a leading politician and that politician's supporters among the financial elite to become prime minister.

The rise of a middle class, far more educated and aware than any previous generation, suggests that the battles for political power in Thailand in the near future will be between this new Bangkok-centered civilian force and the formerly entrenched military. The long history of military participation in politics implies that the changes many Thais hope for will not occur easily. Nevertheless, the Thais' traditional capacity to cope with change by balancing tradition and modernity suggests that the new international era in Thailand will be increasingly in the direction of democracy.

The reasons for optimism about continued, stable, democratic rule and moves away from military-dominated, highly authoritarian, self-serving centralized government are many. First, Thailand has successfully ended internal insurgency. Second, the kingdom is free from serious outside threats to its security. Third, the nation enjoyed three decades of remarkable economic growth, and could return to rapid development once the 1997 crisis is resolved. Fourth, the armed forces are being professionalized, and army generals are embarrassed about the 1991 coup. In 1997 the army commander in chief stopped Prime Minister Chavalit from initiating emergency rule when he was beset by daily demonstrations against his rule. The international movement toward democratization has penetrated most of the major groups in Thai society, including the military.

The rise of an educated, more cosmopolitan middle class is often viewed as the sine qua non for stable government. In Thailand, that class has become more and more a focal point of economic and political decisionmaking. Supporting the middle class are new interest groups, including NGOs, that are demanding rights and resources formerly thought available only to the elites. Along with political parties and the Parliament, these new institutions are taking on the functions formerly carried out by patron-client networks.

## Institutions and Social Groups

### Patron-Client Ties

Historically, the key to understanding Thai society has been the patron-client relationship. Patron-client ties are hierarchical, face-to-face relationships of reciprocity. However, the relationship is not one of balance, as the superior has power over the subordinate. When individuals have few resources at their command but have various needs, persons who can supply the resources and meet the needs attain power over them.

At every level, from the village to the central government in Bangkok, patron-client groups have disseminated information, allocated resources, and organized people. These groups have formed a network of personal relations that extends throughout Thai society and that traditionally has formed the heart of Thai politics. Although both personalism and patron-client relationships remain important, in the past several decades Thai politics has evolved in the direction of decreased personalism and more formalized participation in political structures.

## Constitutions

The Thai propensity for changing constitutions has been referred to as *faction constitutionalism*, whereby each successive draft reflects, legitimates, and strengthens major shifts in factional dominance. Thai constitutions have not been considered the fundamental laws of the land; rather, they have functioned to facilitate the rule of the regime in power.

Since 1932, Thailand has been governed under fifteen constitutions, five of which were democratic and based on the parliamentary model with the executive accountable to the Parliament. Military leaders were not allowed a dominant role in this model. In the six constitutions that were semidemocratic, the prime minister did not have to be an elected member of Parliament, and the upper house was controlled mostly by military and civilian bureaucrats, who were appointed. Four constitutions were undemocratic, providing for neither an elected Parliament nor political parties.[1]

The 1978 constitution (abrogated by the 1991 coup) struck a balance between democracy and military dominance. It called for a bicameral Parliament with an appointed upper body, the Senate, and an elected lower body, known as the Assembly. This constitution enjoyed greater longevity and stability than previous documents and was the underpinning for the semidemocracy that emerged. Semidemocracy refers to the balance between Western-style democracy and continuing authoritarian values that favor and buttress military involvement in governmental affairs. The balance is uniquely Thai: a blend that was legitimated in the minds of the rulers and ruled until the February 1991 coup.

Thailand's next constitution was promulgated in 1991 by the interim national legislative assembly appointed by the NPKC. The final document returned the kingdom to its former parliamentary system, whereby the appointed upper house was given equal power with the elected lower house in matters of policymaking. Moreover, the chair of the NPKC was given provisional power to nominate the new prime minister, thereby providing effective power over the government for the duration of the next government's term.

Massive citizen demonstrations throughout the country in December 1991 forced the Assembly to back down on controversial provisions under which the electorate would vote for party slates rather than for individual candidates. The slate system had been promoted by the newly formed Samakkhi Tham party, which had close links with NPKC members. The demonstrators also forced the Assembly to drop the proposed number of appointed senators from 360 (the same number as the elected representatives) to 270. The final change came when the Assembly scrapped a clause that would have allowed civil servants and military officers to join the cabinet without resigning from their current positions. The provision that the prime minister did not have to be an elected member of Parliament went unchanged until 1992, when the Parliament passed constitutional amendments requiring prime ministers to be elected members. The Parliament also passed amendments designed to reduce the role of the military-dominated Senate.

Led by former Prime Minister Anand Panyarachun in 1996–1997, a "People's Committee" drafted a new constitution designed to reduce corruption, enhance human rights, decentralize the political system, make the Senate accountable (through direct elections), separate the executive from the legislative branch (by requiring ministers to resign from the Parliament), provide the judiciary with more authority, and strengthen political parties. One hundred of the five hundred members of Parliament are to be elected by a national vote from a list of party-nominated candidates, whereas the other four hundred are to be elected by single-member constituencies. The new constitution emerged as Thailand's most democratic ever.

## Military

Since the overthrow of the absolute monarchy, the Thai military has played the dominant role in Thai politics. Of the fifty cabinets during the 1932–1997 period, twenty-four must be classified as military governments, eight as military dominated, and eighteen as civilian. The civilian governments, which were the most unstable, were often replaced by military regimes following army coups.

The reasons for military dominance include the weakness of civilian governments and the fact that the military is the most highly organized institution in the kingdom. Because of perceived external and internal threats to Thai security, the military has proclaimed itself the only institution capable of protecting Thai sovereignty. Moreover, the hierarchical nature of the military is congruent with the nation's highly centralized political culture. Because Bangkok, as Thailand's primary city, dominates every aspect of the country's political and economic life, the military has needed to control only this one city in order to control the entire kingdom. Military, police, communications, and government agencies all emanate from Bangkok. Bangkok is to Thailand what Washington, D.C., New York, Los Angeles, Chicago, Philadelphia, and Dallas together are to the United States. Army divisions that have jurisdiction over Bangkok can control those ministries that are necessary for dominating society: defense, interior, and communications.

Reacting to the view that neither internal nor external threats are menacing Thailand or its institutions, and that the regional situation has changed from one of confrontation to one of peaceful coexistence, the army initiated a comprehensive modernization program. Following the Indonesian model of dual function (*dwi fungsi*), with the army playing a national developmental as well as security role, the military launched civil development projects manned by army units in all four regions of the country. The most prominent project, Green Northeast (*Isaan Khiaw*), was designed to improve irrigation and reforest denuded hillsides in Thailand's most impoverished region. Likewise, the army's New Hope (*Harapan Baru*) project in the southern provinces was also planned to legitimize the military's new role as chief developer of the kingdom. Neither program achieved its stated goals.

The military's role in development stems from a government order in 1980 placing responsibility for defeating communist insurgency on the army. Order 66/2523 suggested that stable government and higher levels of economic development were necessary before the Communist Party of Thailand could be destroyed. The military was believed to be the most effective instrument for bringing about these conditions.

The fact that there was no successful coup d'état from 1977 to February 1991 is testimony to the increased professionalization of the army compared to the first four decades of constitutional monarchy beginning in 1932. The fact that communist insurgency, which plagued Thailand in the 1960s and 1970s, had been quelled and that there was no external threat to Thai security also undermined the major rationales for military intervention into governmental affairs.

The strengthened role of political parties and the Parliament as well as a general attitudinal change more favorable to democratic civilian rule, especially among the politically aware, also reduced the military's influence. The fact that Prime Minister Chatichai gave the armed forces a free hand in personnel matters, provided generous budgets to all branches of the military, and supported the army's development projects mollified the military. Perhaps most important, the Thai king's determination to oppose a military coup greatly reduced the chance that such a coup would succeed. Nevertheless, two unsuccessful coup attempts in 1981 and 1985, and the successful coup of 1991, are reminders that military factionalism and personalism are still a part of Thai politics.

Conventional wisdom suggested that as Thailand moved toward the status of a newly industrialized country (NIC), military coups became anachronistic, no longer a suitable means to change administrations. The kingdom's remarkable annual economic growth rates of 11 percent (the highest in the world for three years), its more politically aware and highly educated middle class, and its strengthened political institutions (political parties, interest groups, and the Parliament) were factors thought to provide a buffer against intervention by the military. Moreover, the lack of foreign or domestic threats to Thai security and the disapproval of venerated King Phumiphol toward the failed 1981 and 1985 coup attempts seemed to insulate contemporary administrations from a military takeover.

The traumatic events of May 1992, when military authorities violently quashed pro-democracy demonstrators, was a turning point in the way Thais viewed the role of the military. The military went on notice that future coup attempts would lead to an outpouring of hundreds of thousands of citizens. Nevertheless, a downturn in the economy, as in 1997, or a collapse of the civilian democratic regime could once again open the way for the military to step in for the sake of stability and security. When Prime Minister Chavalit was inundated with antiadministration protests and the Thai economy was in crisis, the army commander in chief announced publicly that the military would not intervene. Nevertheless, scholars of Thai politics, most of whom had argued that the 1991 coup would not and could not occur, have been more circumspect about predicting the future of the military's role in Thailand.

## Bureaucracy

For most of the contemporary era, Thailand has pursued a bureaucratic polity with the arena of politics within the bureaucracy itself. The bureaucracy has been the bedrock of stability in a political system in which top leadership positions have changed unpredictably. Although coups may bring new factions into power, the bureaucracy continues its conservative policy role with little change in direction.

The formerly exclusive role of the bureaucracy has been widened in recent years by the new role of technocrats, who have attained important positions and brought a more rational mode to policymaking. These highly trained and educated officials have public-regarding values rather than the traditional values of hierarchy, personalism, and security. The technocrats lost much of their luster in 1997 when the Thai economy collapsed, at least partly because they did not adequately interpret the warning signs of the coming disaster.

The bureaucracy is no longer the only arena of politics. Extrabureaucratic groups, such as Parliament, political parties, and pressure groups, and, of course, the military, now play a significant role in determining public policy. Still, the bureaucracy is powerful in determining the direction and implementation of policies.

## Parliament

At one time, elections in Thailand were held only when the ruling group became convinced that it could control the process so that elections would merely enhance its power. Today, elections provide more meaningful choices among candidates who represent alternative ideas. The bicameral Parliament, no longer just a rubber stamp for the prime minister, engages in public debate about important issues.

In the recent form of semidemocracy, the upper house—that is, the appointed Senate—was still dominated by the military. However, the Senate has lost much of its influence, especially after the passage of the 1997 constitution, which made the House the primary body for making policy, while the formerly appointed Senate became an elected body. Another sign of the Parliament's higher standing has been the diminished criticism of members of Parliament by military leaders.

The Parliament includes an unprecedented number of Sino-Thai business executives. In the past, Thailand's Chinese minority had stayed mostly in the economic sphere, and this community's greater involvement in political affairs has raised concerns that an emerging "bourgeois polity" will be dominated by Chinese Thai.

The new politics of contemporary Thailand is characterized by the strengthening of the Parliament and the political parties. The elites who dominate policymaking have come increasingly from both institutions. For example, Chuan's, Banharn's, and Chavalit's cabinets consisted of party leaders who were elected members of Parliament. The Parliament is no longer peripheral to authoritative decisions, thanks originally to a greater role granted it by Prime Minister Prem, under whose leadership the Parliament began to act independently, particularly on economic matters.

## Political Parties

In the past, political parties centered around individual personalities. The parties had only rudimentary organization and were almost devoid of disinterested programs or issues. Elections often involved more than twenty parties, most of which were established for a particular candidate in a specific election.

Since the short-lived democratic period of 1973–1976, there has been a movement toward party institutionalization and longevity. The organizational apparatus for the major parties remains intact after an election and plays an important role in the strategies of both the ruling coalition and the opposition. The parties are beginning to build long-term links with the citizenry along with party discipline, so that they can exert greater influence on policymaking and assure themselves of an important role in coalition governments.

Thai political parties can be visualized as falling along a spectrum that runs from liberal to conservative, but most parties fall into the moderate and nonideological category. Ideological positions are not paramount in campaigns because only a minority of voters make choices based on issues. In the last several elections, parties have been fewer in number, more coherent in structure, and better able to represent citizens' demands.

In the September 1992 elections, the tarnished "satanic" parties attempted to change their image by changing their names and, in some instances, their leadership. Former Prime Minister Chatichai returned from exile to set up a new party (Chat Pattana, or National Development). Although the election was considered the fairest in recent history, successful candidates still had to spend up to $1 million. Candidates switched parties in accordance with whichever group provided them with the most financial support. Party platforms played almost no role in determining candidate or voter affiliation, except for the broad notion of pro-military or pro-democracy.

The pro-democratic "angelic" parties included the Democrat (79 seats), New Aspirations (51 seats), and Palang Dharma (47 seats). When the Social Action Party (22 seats) agreed to join the coalition, these parties controlled the appointment of the prime minister. The pro-military "satanic" opposition parties were led by Chat Thai (77 seats) and Chat Pattana (60 seats). Altogether, eleven parties won seats after a voter turnout of 61 percent. The pro-military parties came close to forging a majority coalition, which would have meant that little had changed from the Suchinda period. Despite urban disdain for the pro-military groups, rural voters supported those candidates who could best help their provinces with new roads, schools, irrigation canals, and temples. Candidates also achieved votes by offering rural Thais a sum of money.

The 1995 elections resulted in a coalition with seven parties: Chat Thai (92 seats), Palang Dharma (23), New Aspirations (57), Social Action (22), Nam Thai (Thai Leadership) (18), Prachakorn Thai (18), and Muanchon (Mass Party) (3). The coalition controlled 233 of the Parliament's 391 seats.

Chat Thai did not win any seats in Bangkok or the south, but did well in rural areas where the party dominated patronage networks. With unlimited funds, Chat Thai overcame its reputation as a "satanic" party and spread its wealth among regional voters. With its 86 seats, the Democrat Party formed the centerpiece of the opposition, followed by Chat Pattana (53 seats), Seritham (Freedom) (11), and Solidarity (8). Party voting was clearest in the south (where the Democrats maintained their hold on power by winning 46 of 51 contested seats) and in Bangkok, but in most other areas voters split their votes among more than one party.

The November 17, 1996, election was the most expensive ever, with the NAP leader Chavalit appointing a coalition with basically the same parties as in the previous administration: Chat Thai, Social Action, Prachakorn Thai, and Muanchon. One major difference was that the Chat Thai party (which was highly unpopular because of Banharn's leadership) was replaced by the Chat Pattana Party led by former Prime Minister Chatichai.

Campaign spending continues to be an important part of the electoral process. Candidates with solid financial support and with patron-client arrangements with wealthy Thais have a significant advantage, which helps to explain why an increasing number of elected MPs are in business.

## Monarchy

Theoretically and legally above politics, the Thai monarch is the national symbol, the supreme patron who reigns over all, and the leader of the Buddhist religion. The prestige and veneration of the monarchy have grown since the coronation of King Phumiphol Adunyadej, who recently became the kingdom's longest reigning monarch. In 1996 King Phumiphol celebrated fifty years on the throne.

In the 1980s the king became more involved in Thai politics. He supported the government of Prime Minister Prem Tinsulanond in both 1981 and 1985 when military coups attempted to overthrow Prem's administration, but he chose not to intervene in the 1991 coup. The king's strong resistance to the earlier coups helped to defuse the crises and to heighten his prestige and influence.

The king's most important intervention occurred during the May 1992 crisis when pro-democracy demonstrators called on General Suchinda to step down as prime minister. The military's violent response brought the country to the brink of civil war. King Phumiphol admonished the nation's leaders to settle the conflict peacefully, and he demanded the resignation of Suchinda. The king subsequently vetoed the choice of a new prime minister suggested by the majority coalition in the Parliament and brought back Anand Panyarachun to be interim leader until elections could take place.

The Thais' universal veneration for their monarch has raised concerns about a potential succession crisis. The king promoted his daughter, Princess Sirindhorn, to the rank of *Maha Chakri* (crown princess), thereby placing her in the line of succession along with her brother, Crown Prince Vachiralongkorn. The crown prince has often been criticized for his lack of commitment and discipline, whereas the princess has been universally admired for her dedication. At present, however, the crown prince has become involved in ceremonial duties and is being trained to succeed his father. Because the king is the symbol of all that is great in Thailand, a contentious succession could undo the present high level of stability by unleashing forces now held in check by the knowledge that the king would object to them.

## Peasantry

About 65 percent of the Thai people live in rural areas as farmers. However, they are not the passive peasantry once depicted in textbooks. As modernization arrived, Thai farmers became sophisticated economic actors, moving from subsistence to surplus agriculture. Increasing numbers of rural Thais engage in political activity, contact officials, join special interest groups, participate in village projects, and have knowledge of governmental processes.

Changes in the countryside over the past several decades have significantly affected the lives of the vast majority of Thais. Roads now penetrate into formerly isolated areas. Electricity is almost universally available. Transistor radios, motorcycles, televisions, and daily newspapers are integral parts of village life. Agricultural diversification has introduced cash crops into the Thai economy. Whereas rice constituted more than 90 percent of agricultural output twenty years ago, today the percentage is less than 50.

## Sino-Thai Business Community

Traditionally, the Chinese minority (about 10 percent of the population) has dominated the Thai economy while the Thai majority has prevailed in politics. Since 1980, however, a fundamental change has occurred in Thai politics, with the Sino-Thai becoming more involved. Because of the high degree of Sino-Thai assimilation (compared to all other Southeast Asian nations), the expansion of the middle class, the new importance of technocrats in the running of ministries, and the realization that government policies affect the economy, business interests have become increasingly involved in politics.

The importance of the middle class (in a nation that had no such class until recently) suggests that Thailand has become a bourgeois rather than a bureaucratic polity. This new class of entrepreneurs, technocrats, and government officials views military rule as an anachronism, unsuited to the nation's well-being. It supports the move away from the personalistic politics of the past to the more stable, pluralistic, and institutionalized politics of the period of semidemocracy.

## Intellectuals

Thai students and intellectuals were leaders of the 1973 revolt against the military that ousted the ruling generals and placed civilians in power. Although the period of civilian democratic rule lasted only three years before the army returned to regain its dominant role, Thai politics has never been the same. The interim democratic period brought new groups and attitudes to Thai politics and showed that the military is not an invincible force.

During the regimes of Chatichai and Anand, leading Thai academicians played an important role in fashioning domestic and foreign policies. Chatichai's "new nationalism" and opening of relations with Indochina were examples of policies formulated by his academic advisory council, consisting of a group of prominent university scholars. The advisers were criticized by officials of the Ministry of Foreign Affairs as well as by the military for allegedly overstepping their legitimate sphere of influence.

## Women

Women have never been serious contenders for positions of power in Thai politics. The percentage of women in the Parliament is minuscule, only one woman has been appointed as a provincial governor, and except for the "appropriate" positions in health or human services, women have not served in cabinets. There are no women generals in the military.

Nevertheless, women play an important role in Thai society, especially in the professions. The percentage of women doctors, lawyers, accountants, and professors is higher than that in the United States. The same number of women as men vote in elections for the Parliament. A more important point, however, is that a societal double standard exists whereby men are allowed far more leeway of behavior and participation than are women. The social patterns in Thailand continue to reflect the traditional view that women should defer to men in the public sector.

## Democratization

The history of politics in Thailand is a history of authoritarian rule. Thailand's political culture, with its emphasis on deference to authority and hierarchical social relations, is not conducive to democratic rule. Democracy entails citizen involvement and a tolerance for different points of view. For involvement to occur, an individual must feel competent to exert influence and to cooperate with fellow citizens in common cause. Thus, weak perceptions of self-competence, unwillingness to work in concert, and low tolerance for different points of view make the prospect for democracy in Thailand problematic.

The strength of Thailand's semidemocracy was partially a function of the economic boom and the government's resulting capacity to meet the needs of the citizenry. When basic needs are met, other nondemocratic values become secondary. However, when a government is perceived as unable to meet citizens' needs, the values of security and stability, for example, take precedence. Hence, a severe downturn in the economy or an unexpected external threat to Thai sovereignty could undermine the evolution toward democracy. Thais expressed concern and fear about democracy's continued prospects when their country's economy collapsed in 1997.

Another potentially serious threat to Thai democratization relates to monarchical succession. The Thais' veneration for their king is also directed to his daughter, the crown princess, rather than to the crown prince. Although it appears that the crown prince is being groomed to succeed his father (there has never been a reigning queen in Thai history), the role of the monarchy as the symbol of all that is great in Thailand could change fundamentally with his succession. At worst, Thai citizens will denounce the inheritance and insist that the crown princess become the monarch. More likely, the Thais will acquiesce to the prince's ascension and simply ignore the monarchy, or tone down their attitude of veneration. In either case, the Thai monarchy will no longer be the kingdom's bedrock of stability and legitimacy. The Thai king has consistently moderated governmental policies and on recent occasions has acted to prevent the military from undermining democratic rule.

Democracy requires a political culture supportive of democratic values. Modernization has brought high levels of education, literacy, access to the media, and travel—all of which has heightened Thais' awareness of democratic values and expanded their horizons. Democracy also requires a model of a time when democratic government was successful; however, the 1973–1976 period of democracy is viewed by most Thais as a time of chaos, disorder, and economic travail. In the Chatichai period, semidemocracy was sanctioned by the people because of the high level of societal order and economic growth. The Chuan, Banharn, and Chavalit administrations suffered from a perception of weakness and inability to solve the myriad problems facing the kingdom.

In the past, the Thais' democratic orientations have been formalistic in the sense that these orientations have had little depth. Other values—such as security, development, deference, personalism, and economic stability—have taken precedence over values more directly related to citizen participation in governmental affairs. Thus, the status of democratization in Thailand has been tenuous.

## Economic Development

During the 1970s, 1980s, and early 1990s, Thailand sustained a 7 percent
rate of annual economic growth, a pace equaled by only a few other developing nations. More remarkably, the kingdom's economic growth in
1987, 1988, and 1989 averaged over 10 percent, higher than in any other
country. During these boom years, inflation was under 4 percent.

Coincident with these high growth rates was an increase in the export
sector, which in the late 1980s grew by about 24 percent each year. Foreign
investment has also grown at a rapid rate, with Japan, Taiwan, the United
States, Hong Kong, and South Korea the leading investors. Manufacturing is now responsible for a larger share of the gross domestic product
than is agriculture.

Although 65 percent of the Thai people are involved in the agricultural
sphere of the economy, the number of those in rice farming is decreasing.
Thai farmers have diversified into crops such as vegetables, fruits, maize,
tapioca, coffee, flowers, sugar, rubber, and livestock. Although farming
areas have not developed as rapidly as urban areas, the standard of living
in the countryside has improved noticeably since the 1970s. Nevertheless,
the urban bias of Thai economic development is clear from both the emphasis on manufacturing and the higher percentage of budget allocations
centered on Bangkok.

The factors responsible for the kingdom's economic successes have included a commitment to free-market, export-driven policies carried out
by highly trained and generally conservative technocrats. These new officials were not as steeped in personalistic, clientelist politics as were their
predecessors or their peers in neighboring countries. Those in charge of
economic policy carefully screened pending development projects to ensure that they would contribute to overall economic growth.

An important component of sustained economic development is political stability. Although coups have been the standard mechanism for
changing governments, they have rarely undermined the continuity of
the policy process. Even following the 1991 coup, Thai politics adhered to
a consistent set of policies, with incremental (rather than fundamental)
changes to the norm.

The vital involvement of Thailand's Chinese minority cannot be over-
estimated as a factor explaining the vibrancy of the economy. This dynamic minority has provided leadership in banking, export-import manufacturing, industrialization, monetary policy, foreign investment, and
diversification. The autonomy granted the Chinese has resulted in an entrepreneurial minority's reinvesting its profits into the kingdom, with
comparatively little capital leaving the country.

Liberal regulations on foreign investment made possible a capital influx
from industrial nations. Thailand, now further integrated into the world

capitalist system, has had access to foreign credit and technical assistance in addition to enjoying flourishing trade relations throughout the world. Thailand has been a favorite site for production plants owned by Japanese, South Korean, and Taiwanese firms. The Thai government's decision to move toward an export-oriented industrialization strategy emerged from high-level technocrats in the development agencies, most of whom were insulated from political pressures by other bureaucratic and societal forces.

In just one generation, Thailand has managed to lower its population growth rate from 3.0 percent to 1.4 percent. The decrease resulted from a massive government-sponsored education program that has changed attitudes about the optimum family size and made birth control devices available throughout the kingdom. This has resulted in a higher standard of living for families, higher educational attainment and literacy, and lower poverty rates.

The nearly three decades of sustained economic development came to an abrupt halt in mid-1997 after the Chavalit administration stopped propping up the baht. Having futilely spent billions of baht from foreign reserves on a lost cause, on July 2 the administration unpegged the baht from the U.S. dollar and allowed it to float. Within weeks, the currency had lost 40 percent of its value. Simultaneously, the stock market continued its precipitous decline, losing 70 percent of its value. To strengthen the economy, the Thai government accepted a $17 billion bailout from the International Monetary Fund and from other Asian nations.

There are many reasons for the debacle including poor political leadership, the refusal of recent governments to make hard decisions about fiscal responsibility, pervasive corruption that blocked important infrastructure projects and educational reform, and the undisciplined opening of the economy to foreign capital, with dollars flowing into Thailand at interest rates below those offered by domestic banks. Offshore debt grew steadily as Thais borrowed dollars at cheaper rates than they could borrow baht. The money was spent primarily on real estate and a wide range of investments that offered meager returns such as convention centers, hotels, condominiums, and private hospitals. Bad loans flourished. The baht became overvalued when the dollar gained value against the yen, making Thai labor and exports more expensive and therefore less competitive. Speculators then bet on the devaluation of the baht, borrowing baht at one price and selling the currency back at a devalued rate, thereby making tremendous profits.

The Thai government's hope is that the devaluation will boost exports, curb imports, and cut the current-account deficit. To keep the budget balanced, the Chavalit government raised the value-added tax from 7 to 10 percent. Interest rates were raised to guard against a surge in inflation.

One obstacle to solving the crisis is the poor state of Thailand's infrastructural facilities. Automobile traffic in Bangkok is gridlocked (although there have been reports of fewer cars and less traffic as a result of the economic downturn), and port facilities cannot handle the growing ship traffic. Electricity and telecommunications are unreliable.

A second problem is the depletion of Thailand's natural resources, especially its forests. Despite recent legislation banning logging, floods, soil erosion, and droughts have resulted from the government's almost total lack of control over the implementation of the legislation. In recent years Thailand has suffered catastrophic natural disasters. Flooding and landslides, directly attributable to deforestation, have killed hundreds of people and devastated villages and towns.

The AIDS crisis also has the potential to undermine economic growth. Depending on prevention practices and behavioral changes, some 2 to 4 million Thais will be diagnosed as positive for the AIDS virus by the year 2000. Billions of dollars will be spent to care for these victims. Between 1991 and 2000, the direct and indirect costs of projected AIDS cases will total between $7.3 and $8.7 billion. AIDS deaths during the decade could reach a half-million. AIDS is likely to have an even broader impact on the Thai economy, particularly on tourism, direct foreign investment, and remittances from abroad.[2]

The number of college graduates in the "hard" sciences and technology is not sufficient to meet developmental needs. Thai universities graduate only one-third of those needed in engineering. Many graduates move into the private rather than the public sphere because of the former's higher salaries. The total number of youths matriculating from Thai high schools is lower than in most of the other Southeast Asian countries, also leading to a dearth of trained persons for Thailand's new industries. Compared to Asian NICs, Thailand's trained engineers and scientists are too few to move the economy into industrialization.

Foreign investment and trade have made the economy vulnerable to the vagaries of the world's capitalist system. Thailand is integrated into the global economy with all the advantages and disadvantages that entails. Until recently, the country's economic policymakers diversified imports and exports sufficiently to ensure that a downturn in one sector would not cripple the overall economy. The new crisis has undermined that shibboleth.

## The Thai State

Thailand is an interesting case study of the role of the state because the kingdom's economy has grown rapidly, and there is considerable controversy over the role the state has played in economic as well as political development. The state refers to public officials, elective and appointive, who decide public policy that is binding upon all members of society. The state represents the totality of authoritative, decisionmaking administrators and institutions as they promote the public good, independent of societal forces.

Until the 1980s, scholars referred to Thai politics as a "bureaucratic polity" in which politics took place within the bureaucracy and extrabureaucratic institutions were negligible. External institutions, such as the Parliament and political parties, were deemed to have little influence over the state's policy decisions. The bureaucratic polity included the military, as many of the generals held important government posts (including the position of prime minister). The state, then, was considered strong and autonomous, independent of such societal organizations as political parties, business associations, farmers' groups, and labor unions. When these groups began to emerge, they were co-opted, manipulated, or oppressed by the bureaucracy, which used the military as its controlling force. By integrating the military into the political process, the government established a broad-based regime. Utilizing both collaborative and coercive forces, the state increased its stability and capacity.

Since the student-led revolt against the military in 1973, however, Thai political institutions have increased in number and have broadened their bases considerably, strengthening the role of the legislature, political parties, and business associations while reducing direct military domination. As societal groups have come to play a more important role in Thai politics, the state has lost some of its autonomy and consequently become weaker. On the other hand, Thai authorities enjoy autonomy from societal actors, especially rural citizens who are politically passive. Because rural citizens constitute about 65 percent of the population and make few demands on the central authorities, this notion of passivity is central to the argument that the Thai state can act autonomously.

Similarly, state autonomy has derived from the fact that Thai authorities have successfully co-opted nonbureaucratic but nevertheless elite groups. The state has managed the political-economic affairs of the kingdom effectively and, with exceptions, in the best interests of potential countervailing groups, such as business elites; thus there has been little need for these groups to challenge the authorities.

This view of state autonomy stems at least partially from the success of Thai authorities in preserving the state's independence and sovereignty. The government is legitimate precisely because of this success, and with the related outcome of political continuity and stability as well. Having averted colonial rule, established a stable political system, and met the basic needs of the majority of the citizenry, the Thai state has proved its effectiveness.

In the past two decades, Thailand achieved one of the highest economic growth rates in the world. That record of success can be partly attributed to the state authorities' knowing when to get out of the way of society's entrepreneurs, including the ethnic Chinese, who have been the engine of the Thai economy for generations. Moreover, Thai state authorities promoted the kingdom's economic strength through generally conservative policies (such as supporting technocrats, forming economic development agencies, devising five-year plans, and the necessary but unpopular devaluing of the currency in the face of intense opposition from business and military leaders).

The strength of the state has also been shown by the progression from authoritarian to semidemocratic rule between 1970 and 1997. From the 1973 student-led revolt against the military dictatorship to the 1991 coup, Thai politics had steadily become (albeit with fits and starts) a more open and responsive system. Ironically, as the Thai state has shown the capacity for effective adaptability, formerly nonstate institutions such as the Parliament and political parties have become focal points for public policy discussions. Indeed, these significant changes in Thai politics attest to a system that has effectively coped with changing internal and external demands. However, these changes also reflect a political system in which the number of authoritative decisionmakers has expanded.

In terms of criteria characterizing a strong state—citizen compliance with state demands, citizen participation in state-run institutions, and legitimation (acceptance) of the state authority—the Thai state's progress toward democratization has been strong. From the standpoint of state strength, defined in terms of autonomy from societal actors and institutions, democratization has moved the kingdom's state toward weakness.

The Thai state has gained citizen conformance to its demands through a highly centralized administrative system with control over the police and other essential institutions. The fact that these policies have not been considered intolerable has made the state's efforts easier to carry out compared to states in which the authorities have thrust unwanted burdens on the populace.

Legitimation is a potent factor accounting for the strength of the state. Here again, the Thai state has managed to receive acceptance, even approbation, of its rules of the game. The primary reason for this is that contemporary Thai authorities have basked in the aura of the king, the symbol of unity of the Thai state. Thais have accepted the state's symbolic configuration within an ideology of king, state, and religion. Through socialization and the deliberate exploitation of the king's popularity by whichever regime is in power, the Thai state has become identified with the king and Buddhism, resulting in an extraordinarily high level of acceptance.[3]

Even scholars who view the state as weak agree that Thailand has had remarkable achievements. However, they do not believe that the state is responsible for these achievements. Instead, they argue, various organizations—such as the National Economic and Social Development Board, the Bureau of the Budget, and the Bank of Thailand—have, as individual agencies, produced the economic growth that has in turn provided political stability.[4] When the economy declined, these scholars had to revise their analysis about the competency of these extrabureaucratic organizations.

Despite these achievements, the Thai state has failed to carry out public policies in many areas. Its failure to collect personal and corporate taxes in a fair and efficient manner, for example, has resulted in meager state resources and the inability to build an infrastructure or establish adequate health, environmental, and educational services. As a proportion of gross domestic product, Thailand's public investment is one of the lowest among the developing world economies.[5]

Public policies approved by institutions with newly expanded authoritative powers, such as the national Parliament, are often ignored due to the inability of the government to implement and monitor these policies. For example, the law to ban logging operations, promulgated in 1988, has done little to end the practice. Nor has the government realized its goals of adopting the value-added tax, privatizing state enterprises, or improving revenue collection. In these cases, the state has not been able to enforce its policies effectively.

The Thai state does not always implement its policies consistently, effectively, and reliably. Thai policymaking has at times been characterized by a lack of coordination among governmental ministries, a muddling-through approach to economic policy—in contrast to South Korea and Taiwan, where policy is more coherently and strategically dictated by the state.

The Thai state, for example, has not played an active developmental role in the country's economy. Instead, the state has refrained from intervention in the economy in terms of regulation and investment, allowing the private sector to take the lead. The low level of state activity in industrial development as well as the initiatives of the private sector in what amounts to a laissez-faire economy suggests that Thailand's growth has been achieved in spite of the state, not because of it.

If autonomy is a key variable for assessing strength, the Thai state is weak, for the officials who make authoritative decisions are not insulated from patronage networks. In fact, Thai officials are integrated into a network of patron-client exchange relationships that are the very heart of the political process. These relationships act as links between state officials and societal groups in business, agriculture, labor, the aristocracy, and the intelligentsia.

Prior to the 1973 revolt, the bureaucratic polity insulated state officials from these societal forces. As a result, virtually all political decisions were made within the bureaucracy where intrabureaucratic patron-client ties prevailed. In the post-1973 period, the patron-client network widened as new groups formed alliances with state officials. Whereas the centralized state had formerly precluded the development of societal interest groups and political parties, the recent Thai polity has nurtured, co-opted, manipulated, and controlled new groups. The present government is seeking a balance between centralization of authority and an open polity with a strong legislature and political parties. Such a balance is difficult to attain because both civilian and military authorities feel threatened by societal groups while simultaneously the new technocrats and westernized officials are committed to a more democratic polity. At present, these societal groups have shown only a limited capacity to perform their functions.

Political parties remain largely self-interested patronage groups, revolving around particular personalities. The Parliament as well has had difficulty developing public-regarding policies and forwarding alternative sets of policies for state officials to implement. The state, led by the military and the bureaucracy, has dominated policymaking, at least in the areas deemed important to these institutions.[6] However, as democratization has taken hold, societal groups enjoy more autonomy and clout in policymaking as long as they do not unduly press upon the prerogatives of the more dominant bureaucratic and military interests.

Thailand's remarkable economic growth up to mid-1997 can be explained in many ways. Certainly, the generally prudent state policies since 1977 have been crucial in providing the necessary stability and environment. In some respects, the Thai state has been "strong" enough to get out of the way of the dynamic Sino-Thai entrepreneurial class, while in other respects the government has supported the demands of these entrepreneurs for an open, market-oriented economy. Conversely, since the 1970s, business organizations have initiated, transformed, or even blocked important economic policies and legislation they have deemed antithetical to their interests.[7]

Thai success in economic development does not require a strong-state explanation. Examples abound of strong states that have produced disastrous economic policies because they were insulated from societal groupings. Nor does Thai success require a weak-state explanation, which could lead as well to economic stagnation stemming from the state's attempts to meet demands made by a variety of forces. A weak state may not be able to maintain order in an environment of conflicting, multiple demands.

A better explanation is that the Thai state has achieved a proper balance between the state and civil society.[8] In a period of rapid development, this state is coping with the changing demands of its citizenry as well as those of the international arena. The adaptive ability of the state partially explains why societal forces have not taken over the traditional roles of the bureaucracy and the military. At the same time, the Thai state has opened its policymaking process to new institutions such as political parties, business associations, and the Parliament. The result has been that new ideas have been assimilated and occasionally acted on for the best interests of the public. All of this is happening while traditional, informal personalism, mostly in the form of patron-client relations, remains central to modern Thai politics. In some respects, therefore, the Thai state has been flexible and responsive to changing political-economic circumstances.

Thus, the Thai state can be viewed as either strong or weak, depending on the issues and state components one chooses to emphasize. These characterizations can also change over time.

A factor encouraging state strength is massive societal dislocation, which severely weakens the capacity of a society to inhibit the growth of a strong state.[9] The most common forms of dislocation are wars, revolutions, mass migrations, and economic depressions. The "strong states" of China, Korea, Vietnam, Taiwan, Cuba, Japan, and Israel have undergone such dislocation to varying degrees.

Inasmuch as Thailand is the only Southeast Asian nation that did not experience formal colonialism by Western imperialists (Thailand also did not suffer grievously from the Japanese invasion in World War II), its experience is in sharp contrast with the ordeal of Indonesia, which suffered severe dislocation from the Japanese occupation and the independence war against the Dutch at the end of World War II. Moreover, Thailand has not lost large areas of land or experienced mass migrations, wars, or revolutions comparable to those of states deemed strong. Even the overthrow of the absolute monarchy in 1932 did not appreciably change conditions in the kingdom. Thailand did not face the horrors of mass executions, as did the Indonesians in the mid-1960s following the rise of the military government.

Indeed, relative to its neighbors, Thai society has been characterized more by continuity and stability than by dislocation. And whereas Indonesia was faced with the very real prospect of communist rule (the Communist Party of Indonesia included some 19 million persons in the early 1960s), the communist threat to Thailand was negligible. At its height, the Communist Party of Thailand had only 60,000 members. From these perspectives, then, Thailand does not meet the necessary conditions for the emergence of a strong state.

Dislocation is more likely to lead to a strong state if it occurs at a historical moment in which external political forces favor concentrated social control. When a threat of foreign invasion exists, the impetus toward a strong state is even greater. For Thailand, U.S. economic and security dominance in the postwar period provided the best bulwark against the perceived communist threat. As both the internal and external communist threats were minor compared to those against China, Taiwan, Korea, and Vietnam, the impact on the Thai state was correspondingly small. Most important for strengthening the state was the Thai military's claim that the communist threat necessitated its primary role in state control over the society. Indeed, in the postwar period, Prime Ministers Phibun Songkran, Sarit Thanarat, and Thanom Kittikachorn were able to parlay the threat into temporary strongman rule. Since 1975, the internal insurgency threat has receded. Moreover, no serious analyst of Southeast Asia believes there is an external threat to the security of Thailand. In contrast, Cuba, Israel, North and South Korea, and Vietnam have all been invaded at least once since World War II. Both China and Taiwan have had reason to expect such an invasion. Thus, on this condition as well, Thailand does not fit the conditions necessary for a strong state.

The next condition important for creating a strong state is the "existence of a social grouping with people sufficiently independent of existing bases of social control and skillful enough to execute the grand designs of state leaders."[10] The issue is whether there are bureaucrats, technocrats, and socioeconomic leaders who identify their ultimate interests with those of the state. Although the military-dominated bureaucratic polity in Thailand brought technocrats into leading policymaking positions, these technocrats had no autonomous political base or constituency. Although aristocrats and intellectuals have had strong constituencies outside of the bureaucracy, they have not constituted a separate power base opposing the interests of the authorities in power.

The economically powerful Chinese minority was similarly co-opted by Thai authorities through the system of "pariah entrepreneurship," wherein Chinese business executives and the Thai political authorities agreed to respect and support each other's spheres of influence. The Chinese provided much of the financing for political leaders, who used the funds to concentrate their political power. Until the 1980s, the Chinese only rarely participated in political affairs. With increased intermarriage and assimilation of the Chinese into Thai society, it became increasingly difficult to keep these spheres of influence separate. The important point is that the business class has rarely acted as an autonomous force, separate from the interests of the ruling authorities.

Thailand does not have strong autonomous societal groups whose primary loyalties are with religious, regional, economic, or ethnic sects. The principal extrabureaucratic groups have interests that coincide with those of the state. In this respect, Thailand meets the condition of a strong state, requiring independent groups skillful enough to execute the grand designs of state leaders.

The last condition concerns skillful leadership, which must be present to take advantage of the conditions to build a strong state. Among Thailand's dozen prime ministers in the past twenty-five years, quality and strength have varied, but few have been so incompetent as to jeopardize the fabric of the kingdom. Most have been carefully selected bureaucrats who have set forth generally conservative policies, adapting those aspects of modernization and development that were appropriate to traditional Thai ways. The exceptions to this generalization include Prime Ministers Banharn and Chavalit, both of whom were partially responsible for bringing down the Thai economy. In addition, the fact that there has been only one successful coup d'état since 1977 is testimony to the growing professionalization of the army. Thai leaders have both enhanced and undermined the conditions necessary for a strong state.

## Foreign Policy

Thailand's foreign relations must be seen in the context of the new international era brought on by the end of the cold war. The most obvious manifestations of this "new world order" include the perception that there are no regional or great-power threats to Thai security and that the U.S. security role in Southeast Asia has declined.

Internal considerations have also brought changes in Thai foreign policy–making. Thailand's sustained economic development and the rise of business and other nonbureaucratic interests in the political sphere are partially responsible for the new directions. Prime Minister Chatichai surrounded himself with his Council of Academic Advisers, which viewed these international and domestic changes as an opportunity for Thailand to reassess its foreign policy and to initiate new policies more appropriate to the new international order. The thrust of these initiatives was in the direction of a "new nationalism," toward normalization of relations with the Indo-Chinese nations and toward economic rather than security relations. Chatichai emerged as the leader in implementing these new priorities, and the Ministry of Foreign Affairs had to subordinate its views to those of the academic advisers.

The new nationalism took the form of relating to the United States as an equal rather than as a client. Under Chatichai, Thai foreign policy lessened security dependence on the United States, asserted a policy of equidistance in its relations with allies and adversaries, and launched a dramatically new Indochina policy without seeking U.S. support.

The clearest example of the new era of Thai-U.S. relations concerned the intellectual property rights (IPR) controversy. From the perspective of the United States, the issue involved the lack of effort on the part of Thai authorities to prevent the copying of U.S. products, such as computer software and pharmaceuticals, as well as fairness in trade relations. From the Thai perspective, the issue was defined in terms of U.S. protectionism, U.S. bullying of a long-term ally, nationalism, and economic development.

The IPR issue symbolized the new importance of economic concerns and the decline of security considerations in relations between the two nations. Moreover, the issue demonstrated the realignment of various forces in determining Thai foreign policy. Until the period of semidemocracy, the military had dominated foreign policy in Thailand, with leading bureaucrats in the Ministry of Foreign Affairs, cabinet ministers, and political party leaders playing secondary roles. However, during the time of the IPR negotiations, a new political scenario had developed in Bangkok. The United States had to consider the reactions of the military, the Ministry of Foreign Affairs, advisory councils of the prime minister, the prime minister himself, the Parliament, the mass media, and activist students, all of which played a role in resolving the dispute. The IPR negotiations were far more complex than negotiations of the past, when U.S. officials could deal directly and exclusively with military leaders.

Economic relations have replaced security ties as the kingdom's major foreign policy concern. The Thai economy is now integrated into the world capitalist system; therefore, the nation's stability is increasingly vulnerable to external pressures and fluctuations, which explains why the perceived protectionism of U.S. trade policy has been regarded with alarm. Although Thailand has enjoyed an annual billion-dollar surplus in trade with the United States, the importance of the trade relations is asymmetrical. With Thai exports to the United States accounting for only 1.2 percent of U.S. imports, and U.S. exports constituting almost 20 percent of Thai imports, the U.S. market is more vital to the Thai economy than the Thai market is to the United States. The United States is Thailand's second-largest trading partner after Japan.

As cold war considerations continued to ebb, the importance of the United States to Thai security concerns correspondingly decreased. Cuts in U.S. security assistance to Thailand, the reluctance of the United States to play a major role in resolving crises in Vietnam and Cambodia, and Thailand's new nationalism have diminished the importance of U.S. security and contributed to the intensification of Thai efforts to forge closer ties with China, Indochina, Japan, Russia, and the country's ASEAN neighbors. Nevertheless, Thai leaders continue to prefer an American presence as a "balance wheel" in the area, especially to offset the influence of China and Japan.

The new tone of Thai-U.S. relations reflects Thailand's growing importance in the world economy. Major aspects of Thai-U.S. relations continue to include financial aid, joint military exercises, collaboration on Thai-

Cambodian relations, common efforts to care for Indo-Chinese refugees, cooperation to wage war on narcotics activities, and support for the Peace Corps. The larger point, however, is that the relationship has irrevocably changed as both nations find their way in the new era of international relations and domestic political and economic forces.

A centerpiece of Chatichai's new foreign policy initiatives was the movement toward normalization of relations with Vietnam, Laos, and Cambodia. This abrupt change in policy resulted from, first, the view of the prime minister's advisers that Vietnam no longer constitutes a direct threat to Thai security; second, the fact that Vietnam itself desired normalization; third, the feeling that closer economic ties would do more to lessen tensions between the two nations than would confrontation; and finally, the fact that Thailand could be master of its own destiny. The last point refers to the Thai government's willingness unilaterally to forge new relations with its neighbors without consultation with the United States or ASEAN allies.

In 1989 Thailand and Laos began cooperating in securing their common border. High-level meetings reduced the tensions between the two countries that began after the 1975 communist takeover in Vientiane. The resolution of border fighting over disputed territory in 1987–1988 facilitated the warming of relations. The major element of the new ties is flourishing trade, symbolized by an Australian-built bridge across the Mekong River, which forms much of the border between the two countries, that has facilitated the transport of trade items.

During the Anand and Chuan administrations, Thailand was criticized for undermining U.N. attempts to resolve the crisis in Cambodia. As the only frontline state involved in the Cambodian imbroglio, Thailand was faced with the problem of keeping negotiations open with all involved Cambodian factions. The Khmer Rouge, which controlled an area bordering Thailand, was participating in lucrative cross-border trade. For Thailand, the trade was worth tens of millions of dollars. Gems (mostly rubies), arms, and logging were controlled by well-connected Thai business executives, military leaders, and rebel forces that have operated in the area for generations. Thai officials claimed that it was impossible to control the long border.

Thailand's economy-driven foreign policy has also been manifested in the country's leading role in the negotiation of an agreement by ASEAN members to create a free trade area to enhance security. The January 1992 agreement to create this area (the ASEAN Free Trade Area, or AFTA) was a cooperative action aiming to compete with the European Union and the North American Free Trade Association (NAFTA), and to respond to concerns about economic dependence on Asian superpowers, namely, Japan. AFTA, which would comprise a market of 320 million people in a rapidly growing region, was based on the principle of "open trade," with participating nations lowering trade tariffs on one another's goods.

Altogether, Thailand has responded effectively to issues appropriate to the new international era. These initiatives have been toward a "new nationalism," toward normalization of relations with the Indo-Chinese nations, and toward economic, rather than security, relations. Thailand has been an active participant in ASEAN and other regional forums. The country supported Burma's application to ASEAN as part of its "constructive engagement" with the Burmese regime. The purpose of this approach, which counters the policies of most of the world's nations (which want to isolate Burma because of its human rights violations), is to gain access to Burmese resources and reduce tensions between the two countries. In the 1990s Thai foreign policy lessened security dependence on the United States, asserted a policy of equidistance in relations with allies and adversaries, and launched a new Indochina policy without seeking U.S. concurrence.

## Conclusion

Thailand has evolved into a semidemocracy, with new institutions available for more effective political participation. These new institutions have been assimilated into existing patterns in ways that fit traditional methods of political activity. The Thai leadership has been able to cope with the tensions that have arisen from the process of democratization. The political system, with its modified, open form, meshes with the personalism and hierarchy that have traditionally been important parts of Thai culture.

At a formal level, until the 1991 coup, open participation in the political process, a free press, and free elections prevailed. At an informal level, Thai society is still dominated by the small proportion of the society that controls the military, economic, and political spheres. During the 1990s the Thai people deemed that their government is legitimate because of both democratization and steady economic growth. The prospects for sustaining parliamentary democracy depended on the capacity of the government to meet the needs of the people, the continued vibrancy of the economy, the restraint of military leaders, and a smooth monarchical succession. The prospects also depended on the continued strengthening of such institutions as the Parliament and political parties and a concomitant decrease in personalism and self-interested, corrupt policymaking. The 1997 economic debacle is now the single greatest threat to democratization because it has undermined the government's legitimacy and the people's view that the authoritarian aspects of the government were worth tolerating for the sake of economic growth.

Thailand today is fundamentally different from Thailand of just twenty years ago, when the military-dominated bureaucracy controlled society. As democratization and economic development flourished simultaneously and new groups emerged to challenge the traditional power elites, Thai society evolved into one that was more independent, confident, stable, and thriving. Thai history is replete with examples of successful management of problems to ensure the independence and stability of the kingdom.

Semidemocracy involves the participation of most groups within the society; thus the political system has been accepted as legitimate by the rulers and the ruled. Until the 1991 coup, Thais did not feel oppressed by their government leaders, and (with rare exceptions) civil liberties have been protected. Thailand's continuing capacity to cope with changing demands and to assert its own destiny has been sustained despite the interlude of martial law in 1991 and the economic crisis in 1997.

## Notes

1. A portion of the following section consists of updated material from the author's previous writings on Thailand. See "Change in Thailand," *Current History*, vol. 89, no. 545 (March 1990), pp. 101–104, 127–130; and "Changing Perceptions of U.S.-Thai Relations: American Perspective," in *U.S.-Thailand Relations in a New International Era*, ed. Clark D. Neher and Wiwat Mungkandi (Berkeley: Institute of East Asian Studies, University of California, 1990). Material has also been excerpted from Clark D. Neher, "Political Succession in Thailand," *Asian Survey*, vol. 32, no. 7 (July 1992), pp. 585–605.

2. See Mechai Viravaidya, Stasia A. Obremskey, and Charles Myers, "The Economic Impact of AIDS on Thailand," working paper no. 4 (Cambridge: Harvard School of Public Health, Department of Population and International Health, March 1992).

3. Joel S. Migdal, *Strong Societies and Weak States: State-Society Relations and State Capabilities in the Third World* (Princeton: Princeton University Press, 1988).

4. Daniel Unger has written persuasively on Thailand as a weak state. Many of his insights are incorporated into the next section of this chapter.

5. For a detailed discussion of the state's role in the economy, see Anek Laothamatas, *From Bureaucratic Polity to Liberal Corporatism: Business Associations and the New Political Economy of Thailand* (Boulder: Westview Press, 1991).

6. One of the best analyses of the Thai state can be found in Chai-Anan Samudavanija, "Thailand: A Stable Semi-Democracy," in *Democracy in Developing Countries: Asia*, ed. Larry Diamond, Juan J. Linz, and Seymour Martin Lipset (Boulder: Lynne Rienner Publishers, 1989).

7. See Laothamatas, *From Bureaucratic Polity*, for a lengthy discussion of the greater role of businesspeople and business associations countrywide in determining Thai economic policy.

8. This point is made in Diamond, Linz, and Lipset, *Democracy in Developing Countries*, p. 22.

9. Migdal, *Strong Societies and Weak States*, p. 269. The following section is based on the framework developed by Joel S. Migdal. Donald Emmerson, in his unpublished essay "Beyond Zanzibar: Area Studies, Comparative Politics, and the 'Strength' of the State in Indonesia" (paper presented to the Association for Asian Studies, Chicago, April 1990), has adapted Migdal's framework in his evaluation of the Indonesian state. The following section of this chapter follows Emmerson's adaptation.

10. Migdal, *Strong Societies and Weak States*, p. 274.

# 4

# THE PHILIPPINES

In the quest for political and economic development, the experience of the Philippines has been different from that of Thailand. Whereas the Thais have shown an ability to meld traditional cultural values with selected modern values in order to achieve development, the Filipinos have had considerably less success finding the appropriate blend. In contrast to the Thais, who have never had a foreign culture thrust upon them through colonialism, the Filipinos, colonized for four hundred years by the Spanish and then for forty-eight years by the Americans, were not as free to choose those aspects of westernization most conducive to development. Instead, the nation is beset even today by the same difficulties that arose during colonialism: oligarchic politics, personalism, economic inequality, and institutional decay. Political development in Thailand was viewed from the perspective of the Thai political system's large capacity to cope with the changing needs and demands of the people through strengthened and expanded political institutions and through the reduced importance of personalism in determining public policy. In the Philippines, this process toward development and democratization has been stymied and in some cases reversed, diminishing the system's capacity to cope with the people's demands. The result is more often institutional decay rather than development and authoritarianism rather than accountability.[1]

The long Spanish and shorter (but profound) U.S. domination of the Philippines left a mixed legacy. From the Spanish, the Filipinos inherited a highly inequitable system of land tenure dominated by a powerful landowning class. The landed families and the hierarchical society, still powerful in Filipino politics, were rooted in clan warfare and Spanish feudalism. The U.S. presence from 1898 to 1946 integrated the Philippine economy into the U.S. economy, nudged the country's political structures toward competitive democracy, introduced a system of public education that vastly improved literacy rates (along with incorporating English as the national language), and fostered the rise of highly trained technocrats, bureaucrats, and entrepreneurs. The economic relationship between the Philippines and the United States was built on the primary products produced by Filipinos for the U.S. market. Sugar, under the control of a few landholding "barons," was the forerunner of crops grown for the foreign market.

Philippine independence, proclaimed on July 4, 1946, followed World War II and the Japanese occupation and began a period of semidemocratic rule within the context of a continuing oligarchy. A series of democratically elected presidents ruled over a society still pervaded by personalism in the form of patron-client ties. Civil liberties flourished, as did violence perpetrated by the private armies that surrounded the nation's elite families.

When Ferdinand Marcos was first elected president in 1965, the Philippines was experiencing economic growth and political stability. The vital Liberal and Nacionalista Parties, despite their fluid, nonideological nature, ensured the nation a lively competition for public office. At the same time, Philippine society suffered from problems that originated during the colonial era, the most salient of which were social and economic inequality, corruption, food shortages, and widespread violence.

In 1969 President Marcos became the first president in the postindependence Philippines to be reelected. His reelection was "bought" in the sense that he gave government funds to local officials who manipulated the vote in his favor. A constitutional provision precluded a third term, so Marcos planned to stay in power by abrogating the constitution and asserting that national crises demanded extraordinary measures. His proclamation of martial law in September 1972 ended formal democratic rule and began a fourteen-year period of authoritarian rule.

A majority of Filipino citizens supported Marcos's initial steps to end the breakdown of law and order, his promise of land reform, and his strengthening of the army against insurrections by communists throughout the archipelago and by Muslim dissidents in the southern islands. This support dissipated as it became clear that Marcos's achievements did not match his rhetoric and that the "temporary" period of martial law was merely a pretext to perpetuate his personal power.

Acting with the wholehearted support of the United States and using his martial law powers, Marcos was both executive and legislator. To give legitimacy to his regime, he instituted referenda, all of which turned out a 90 percent vote in favor of his continued tenure, and elections, all of which were fraudulent. Press censorship of antigovernment criticism, jailing of dissidents, lack of basic civil liberties, absence of a secret ballot, and control of ballot counting were the methods Marcos used to win approval for his rule.

By the mid-1970s, Marcos's "New Society" began to disintegrate with the rise of lawlessness in the countryside, the realization that the "constitutional authoritarian" government was more authoritarian than constitutional, the imprisonment of respected political leaders such as Marcos's rival, Senator Benigno Aquino Jr., and the growing awareness of a mismanaged economy. This last problem was perhaps the most crucial in generating citizen antagonism toward martial law. Unemployment rose to over 20 percent and underemployment to 40 percent, real income shrank as inflation increased, and corruption reached an intolerable state under "crony capitalism" whereby Marcos's friends were placed in charge of business conglomerates despite their lack of business acumen.

The "lifting" of martial law in 1981 temporarily improved the image of the New Society but did not significantly change the authoritarian political order. The government continued to be based on personalism with no legitimacy granted to governmental institutions. Compared to the period before martial law and to conditions in neighboring countries, Philippine politics during the Marcos era was increasingly characterized by decay rather than by development. As the regime lost its legitimacy, the Armed Forces of the Philippines (AFP) became less professional, the economy worsened, and the Communist Party of the Philippines (CPP) and its military arm, the New People's Army (NPA), strengthened, thereby undermining the original rationale for martial law.

By 1983, after the hierarchy of the Philippine Catholic Church and business leaders had turned against Marcos and when Marcos's health was known to be precarious, Senator Aquino returned to the Philippines after several years of exile in the United States. Aquino, the single greatest challenger to President Marcos, was assassinated in August 1983 the moment he stepped out of the airplane that had flown him back to his country. The almost universal belief of Filipinos in the government's complicity in this assassination released long-suppressed grievances.

The Marcos regime would no doubt have fallen even without Aquino's martyrdom, for Filipinos already knew that Marcos and his associates were responsible for the country's low vitality, whereas other noncommunist Southeast Asian nations were flourishing.[2]

After Aquino was assassinated, the Philippines suffered disastrous declines in industrial and agricultural production and in wages and employment as well as capital flight, high inflation, severe undernourishment for children in rural areas, a rich-poor gap wider than in any other nation in the region, and negative economic growth, while the other noncommunist Southeast Asian nations were boasting of the world's highest growth rates.

A momentous event in contemporary Philippine politics took place during three remarkable months, from December 1985 through February 1986. Bowing to intense pressure from the United States, wishing to take advantage of his improved health during a remission of his illness, desiring to end opposition attacks on him, sensing the disarray of potential opposition candidates, and confident about his capacity to engineer a mandate, Marcos called for snap elections to be held on February 7, 1986.

From the moment Marcos announced the elections, the key question was whether the opposition could unite around a single candidate, and the answer was unclear until the final filing day. Previously, the opposition had been able to unite only in its disdain for Marcos. Because of the highly personal nature of Philippine politics, the competing ambitions of potential leaders, and Marcos's ability to manipulate and co-opt rival forces, the opposition had a difficult time presenting a serious alternative.

Structurally, the opposition suffered from the disintegration of the two-party system during martial law. Instead, there were now many parties and organizations, each with an ambitious leader who wanted to be the candidate to run against Marcos. Corazon "Cory" Aquino, the widow of the martyred Senator Benigno Aquino Jr., emerged as the person around whom all the oppositionists could coalesce. Her genuine reluctance to lead added to her attraction as a sincere, honest, and incorruptible candidate, precisely the antithesis of the president. A grassroots groundswell of support culminated in a petition with over a million signatures from Filipinos urging her to run for the presidency. Mrs. Aquino met with Senator Salvador Laurel, himself a major contender for the presidency, and fashioned an eleventh-hour agreement whereby she and Laurel would be the presidential and vice presidential candidates, respectively, under the banner of Laurel's United Nationalist Democratic Organization (UNIDO). For the first time since 1972 when martial law was declared, the opposition had achieved unity.

Candidate Aquino, realizing that she could not match the president in financial or organizational strength, proclaimed a "people's campaign." Marcos, her opponent, had easy access to government money during the campaign, which allowed him to raise officials' salaries, decrease taxes, and lower fuel and utility rates. By the end of the campaign, some $500 million from the government treasury had been spent to reelect the president. In contrast, the opposition spent $10 million, all of it raised from donations.

Whereas Aquino's first campaign speeches stressed her sincerity and honesty and her empathetic qualities as a sufferer under Marcos, her later speeches focused on issues and her program to reform the government. She vilified the president for his corruption and immorality as she cited evidence that the president had lied both about his role as a hero in World

War II and about his fortune of several billion dollars in real estate around the world. The former issue arose after investigations of U.S. Army documents disclosed that Marcos's claim that he had headed a guerrilla resistance unit during the Japanese occupation of the Philippines was "fraudulent" and "absurd." U.S. congressional investigations also documented the president's wealth overseas. Aquino's major theme was that Marcos had brought economic ruin and political dictatorship to the nation and that she would restore integrity.

Marcos's campaign focused on his experience, including his wartime record, in contrast to his opponent's "naïveté." He stressed the need for "strong" male leadership rather than "weak" female leadership, suggesting that a woman's place was in the bedroom rather than in the political arena. Marcos claimed that communists had taken over Aquino's campaign and that only he could handle the communist insurgency. He accused Aquino of planning to cancel the Military Bases Agreement with the United States and to dismember the republic by giving away the southern island of Mindanao.

The voting was marred by fraud committed by Marcos supporters. When the "official" count gave Marcos 54 percent of the vote, the National Assembly—the final arbiter for voting controversies—proclaimed Marcos the winner, but the opposition launched a peaceful crusade of civil disobedience to bring down Marcos and allow the real winner, Aquino, to assume office. The U.S. government, official observers, journalists from dozens of nations, the Catholic Church, and most Filipinos agreed that Aquino had actually won the election by a large margin.

As Aquino's civil disobedience campaign took hold, Defense Minister Juan Ponce Enrile and Lieutenant General Fidel Ramos, vice chief of the armed forces, defected from the Marcos camp and called for his resignation and for Aquino's ascension to the presidency. This rebellion by former Marcos supporters began a series of defections from the president, leaving him with only a small, hard-core group of backers.

When Marcos threatened to retaliate by bombing the headquarters of Enrile and Ramos, thousands of Filipinos—urged on by the archbishop of Manila, Cardinal Sin—surrounded the building, some even lying in the streets to keep the tanks from approaching. This display by students, farmers, nuns, and shop owners became known as "People Power." The tank commanders eventually retreated and many defected to the opposition. The United States signaled its support of the rebellion, thereby undermining Marcos's claim that only he enjoyed the confidence of the superpowers. On February 25, 1986, Aquino and Laurel proclaimed the people's victory and were sworn in as president and vice president. The next day, Marcos fled the country with his family to live in exile in Hawaii, where he died on September 28, 1989, at the age of 72.

With little bloodshed, "People Power" had triumphed over a regime that had dominated the political, social, and economic life of the Philippines for twenty-one years. The republic was awash with optimism that a new era in Philippine politics had arrived. Indeed, in the first months of the Aquino regime the executive, legislative, and judicial institutions were revitalized, the military curtailed, political parties refurbished, electoral processes made honest and effective, the media freed, the Marcos cronies undercut, and the citizens given back their rights. However, the monumental problems faced by Filipinos remained: oligarchic politics, personalism, economic and social inequalities, and weak institutions incapable of meeting the needs of the people.

In both the political and economic realms, President Aquino's administration achieved notable gains. Filipinos again could express pride in their country's government after years of corrupt and demeaning leadership. Governmental institutions were rejuvenated under a president whose commitment to democratic values and procedures was irrevocable. Even during Aquino's first year as president when she had virtually unlimited powers, she focused on restoring the democratic process. Civil liberties were reinstated, including the writ of habeas corpus, the release of political prisoners, and the holding of free and regularized elections. These gains came about through the promulgation of a new democratic constitution approved by over 75 percent of the Filipino people in a February 1987 referendum.

Contending with a desperately sick economy resulting from mismanagement by the previous regime, the Aquino administration achieved slow growth. The Philippine economic growth rate had been negative during the last years under Marcos, but the rate under Aquino was positive 6.7 percent in 1988 and 5.5 percent in 1989 while inflation decreased. Growth was highest in the industrial sector, as confidence in the economy grew and construction projects flourished. But the growth rate plummeted to just over 1 percent in 1992–1993. Philippine exports increased 25 percent in 1987, 1988, 1989, and 1990, and capital flight ended by 1989.

These achievements were even more remarkable in light of the fact that Aquino had inherited a legacy of cronyism and corruption, persecution and privilege. The fact that the Aquino administration was able to survive at all was in itself an achievement. The fall of Marcos meant that the cronies were at risk as well. Within a four-year period after assuming the presidency, Aquino survived six coup attempts.

Aquino had raised the expectations of the people with promises of reform in all areas of life. She promised the end of the politics of personalism and the beginning of the politics of principle. Compared to the recent past in the Philippines, the Aquino administration earned high marks, but judged against higher standards such as those of its Asian neighbors, its record was weak. Although the level of corruption and privilege decreased significantly under her administration, Aquino failed to change the system in a fundamental way. As with all Philippine presidencies during the country's postindependence period, the Aquino administration was characterized by oligarchic rule, economic and social inequality, desperate poverty, and the politics of personalism.

Even the higher economic growth rates during Aquino's presidency were not clear achievements. The benefits of the recovery were reaped almost entirely by the economic elites, with the rural population seeing little if any benefit. The rural poor were in fact set back by 16 percent inflation in 1989 alone for such basic commodities as food and energy.

Aquino's initial and unsuccessful attempts to end communist insurgency were based on reconciliation, a policy the armed forces vigorously fought against, claiming that the NPA insurgents were taking advantage of the military's soft line by strengthening their positions. To keep the military from rebelling, Aquino's counterinsurgency policy eventually moved toward a more conservative, harder line, including support for community vigilante groups established to repulse the rebels. These localized anticommunist self-defense organizations proliferated with the failure of peace negotiations between the Aquino government and the NPA. Aquino's endorsement of vigilantism was a sign that the communist movement was still extremely active, despite her administration's reforms.

In January 1988, the Asian Human Rights Commission criticized the Philippine government for "serious and unjustifiable" violations of human rights, citing abuses committed by government-supported vigilante groups. These groups were viewed as having "turned the whole of the Philippines into a battlefield pitting civilian against civilian."[3]

Most Filipinos believed that stability would not return to their country without a resolution of the tragedy of Senator Aquino's assassination. In September 1990, a special court found a former air force general and fifteen other servicemen guilty of the assassination, sentencing them to life imprisonment. But even this verdict did not still the widespread belief that the assassination would not have occurred without the approval of persons high in government, namely the Marcoses.

Aquino, in short, failed to institutionalize the overwhelming personal support she received from the populace. She did not develop a political party that could carry on her reform policies when she was no longer in office. Her followers expected that she would solve the nation's problems single-handedly. The proliferation of political parties during her administration weakened administrative discipline, as the leaders of various organizations vied for power rather than cooperating for the common good. Personalism once again triumphed over institutional legitimacy.

Personalism also became an issue when Aquino ineffectively dealt with allegations of corruption among her own family members. As a member of one of the wealthiest families in the Philippines, Corazon Cojuangco Aquino was raised in the tradition of family loyalty, and these ties precluded her from halting the improprieties of some of her Cojuangco relatives, several of whom had been Marcos cronies.

The Cojuangco family has been split both politically and financially. Supporting the president was her brother, José "Peping" Cojuangco, the leader of a major political party, the Laban ng Demokratikong Pilipino (LDP). On the other side was her first cousin, Eduardo "Danding" Cojuangco, a close friend of former President Marcos, whom he joined in exile. Eduardo amassed one of the country's largest fortunes as a result of favoritism shown him by Marcos in numerous business ventures. He was the ultimate patron in his home region of Tarlac Province, where he was known as a one-man social security system. He is said to have awarded 25 million pesos in loans and scholarships to more than 25,000 people in the province.[4]

This familial problem was exacerbated by Aquino's reluctance to move more forcefully toward meaningful land reform. Because Aquino's family owned a 6,000-hectare hacienda, Luisita, in Tarlac Province on the island of Luzon, her detractors viewed this reluctance as self-interest. Aquino had the opportunity and power to put forth a comprehensive land reform program when she had revolutionary powers during her first year in office before the National Assembly was constituted. However, she waited to promulgate her Comprehensive Agrarian Reform Program until after assembly members had had a chance to gut those parts of the reform that were damaging to their own interests. Because 130 of the 200 elected members of congress were leaders of established landowning families and another 39 were relatives of these families, the final land reform program was characterized by compromise and loopholes that guaranteed the continuation of the status quo. Even Luisita was not broken up and divided among its tenant farmers.

The Aquino administration was also reluctant to act forcefully on the equally important problem of population growth. At the present rate, the Philippines' population of 65 million will increase to 100 million by the year 2020. There is no longer a frontier to which a "surplus" population can move and be productive, and over 750,000 new jobs are needed each year just to maintain the status quo. Despite studies showing that the economy and environment could not sustain the country's population growth, the Aquino administration was reluctant to offend the Catholic hierarchy by advocating contraception.

The reasons for the country's high (2.3 percent) annual population growth are many. First, high levels of poverty generally correlate with high population growth rates. Moreover, the leaders of the Catholic Church, in a country in which over 90 percent of the population practices Catholicism, have opposed governmental involvement in family planning. Parish priests, on the other hand, have long been sympathetic to their parishioners' use of contraception. The country's machismo culture has also kept birth rates high because male prowess is defined in part by the number of children fathered.

An exception to Aquino's overall weak record on reform measures was the successful passage of the 1991 Local Government Code, which was designed to decentralize decisionmaking away from Manila. It is not yet clear if the devolution of powers has simply increased local bossism and corruption or placed governmental responsibilities in the hands of the officials most responsive to the people.

Public opinion surveys showed that President Aquino's initial, almost universal support decreased steadily as her tenure in office lengthened. Various nuisances frustrated Filipinos every day, especially those living in Manila. Electrical brownouts, for example, lasted for at least three to four hours each day without any hope for a solution. (Ironically, the brownouts were caused by a higher-than-projected growth in demand as a result of the improved economy.) Traffic jams were endless, and crimes of all sorts were on the upswing. Water shortages caused comfort and health problems, and drainage systems were clogged by sewage that might be left uncleared for weeks. The same streets in Manila were repeatedly under repair, an example of inadequate coordination among ministries. The Metropolitan Waterworks and Sewerage Company would dig up the streets to lay water pipes; the telephone company would dig up the same streets again to install telephone lines; then the Ministry of Public Works and Highways would dig up the streets a third time for flood control.[5]

Beginning in December 1989 with a military coup attempt that temporarily destabilized the government, a series of dreadful events occurred that many Filipinos saw as ominous indications that the government's mandate was tenuous. A horrendous earthquake in July 1990, which devastated much of northern Luzon, was followed by the Iraqi invasion of Kuwait, which raised the price of oil in the Philippines, undermining the fragile economy. This was followed by a typhoon that swept over half of the archipelago in November, claiming nearly four hundred lives. Half a million persons were left homeless by the typhoon, and crops were ruined in a dozen provinces.

Even more devastating was the eruption in June 1991 of Mount Pinatubo in central Luzon, a volcano that had been dormant for five hundred years. Considered the worst in modern history, the eruption killed over five hundred persons, caused hundreds of thousands to lose their homes and livelihoods, and affected weather patterns throughout the world. The eruption also caused economic devastation in an already impoverished area and hastened the withdrawal of American troops from Clark Air Force Base, which was situated only about twenty miles from Mount Pinatubo and was buried beneath several feet of ash.

Unbearably, five months later the Philippines suffered through tropical storm Uring in the Visayas. The storm and consequent flooding caused some eight thousand deaths and the devastation of tens of thousands of farms. Much of the flooding could be attributed to the fact that many of the islands' mountains had been denuded from deforestation.

In the midst of these natural tragedies, the Philippine Senate rejected the Military Bases Agreement with the United States, ending America's military presence in the country. Although the rejection could well be in the best long-term interests of the Philippines, the immediate effect was the loss of 70,000 jobs and $500 million in U.S. foreign aid.

After intense debate and speculation, Aquino decided not to seek a second term. (The constitutionality of a second term was part of the debate.) Seven candidates declared their intention to become president, all but one of whom (Miriam Defensor Santiago) represented traditional interests. Aquino endorsed her minister of defense, Fidel V. Ramos, who was subsequently elected in May 1992 with only 23.4 percent of the popular vote. (No runoff is required among those candidates with the highest votes.)

The most prominent candidates included Ramos, Santiago, Salvador Laurel (vice president under Aquino), House Speaker Ramon Mitra, former first lady Imelda Marcos, rural boss and Aquino cousin Danding Cojuangco, and liberal Senator Jovito Salonga. These candidates split the votes evenly, allowing Ramos to win the largest plurality.

Ramos was known for his heroism in turning against his former boss, Ferdinand Marcos, in 1986 and for his competent leadership in defending Aquino against army-initiated coups. Nevertheless, he was laconic and careful to a fault.

Ramos was faced with many of the same crises Aquino had been unable to solve: chronic crime exacerbated by a string of kidnappings of Chinese children; continuing insurgencies by communists, rightist soldiers, and Muslim separatists; a debilitated economy with the lowest growth rate among the ASEAN countries; and daily brownouts, sometimes lasting most of the day. Ramos appointed commissions and directed his vice president to head up committees to solve these extraordinary problems. He also engaged in intensive travels around ASEAN to discover which of each nation's policies the Philippines could most effectively emulate.

During his six-year term (1992–1998), Ramos became known as the nation's most effective president of the postindependence period. Under his administration, the Philippines joined the rest of Southeast Asia as an economic tiger. Ramos took on the major oligarchic families and firms that he believed restrained the nation's progress. He promoted a more open market system and strengthened the nation's sagging infrastructure. He gave foreign investors the right to 100 percent ownership in Philippine companies; transformed Subic Bay, the former U.S. naval base, into an enterprise zone with investment from American and other foreign companies; privatized state enterprises including Philippine Airlines; and pushed through a fast-track mechanism for privatizing power companies, a decision that has helped solve the ubiquitous problem of electrical shortages.

Ramos's economic program was implemented under the slogan "Philippines 2000," indicating the target year for joining the ranks of the newly industrialized countries (NICs). Ramos's vision was to transform the Philippines into an economic power within the framework of a democratic political system. His success is shown by record growth rates approaching 7 percent, an end to the power shortages that had undermined the country's growth for decades, the privatization of huge firms that formerly had been controlled by the oligarchic families, and the growth of exports. Moreover, by continuing in his predecessor's spirit of political liberalism, Ramos proved that he was both a democrat and a developer.

Ramos's popularity was high as he approached the end of his six-year term. His major strengths have been (1) his personal reputation for honesty; (2) his willingness to open the country to foreign investment, to eliminate corruption, and to create a workable tax system; (3) his success in 1994 in forming a coalition between his party and the main opposition parties; (4) his support from the business community, important factions of the military, and the U.S. government; and (5) his ability to nurture a commitment to democratic institutions among Filipinos. His weakness have been (1) his lack of charisma and his unwillingness to make critical decisions; (2) his inability to break up the dynastic-controlled provincial economies; (3) his impotence in coping with the horrible natural disasters that continue to devastate the islands; and (4) his lack of a mandate, after receiving less than one-fourth of the presidential vote to start off his term. Because the constitution allows for only a single term in office, Ramos's friends began campaigning for a constitutional amendment that would allow him to run for a second term. This attempt was strongly opposed by numerous opposition groups and by Cardinal Sin, who viewed the effort as a throwback to the days of the Marcos dictatorship. Finally, in the face of massive protest demonstrations, Ramos was forced to announce publicly and straightforwardly that he would not seek a second term. Even many of his supporters believed that enacting a constitutional amendment to allow a second presidential term would set a bad precedent.

Ramos's achievements went beyond economic growth. He also kept the more professionalized military under wraps (not a small success, given the fact that he was defense minister under Corazon Aquino), oversaw the reduction of crime in Manila (taking over as "anticrime czar" from Vice President Joseph Estrada), and brought the Philippines into the new international era through his trips abroad and his active role in regional associations. Importantly, he was primarily responsible for a 1996 peace accord between insurgent Moro National Liberation Front (MNLF) forces and the central government.

## Institutions and Social Groups

### Patron-Client Relations

The Philippine government can be described as clientelist, a form of societal organization in which political life centers around relationships that are largely person to person, informal, hierarchical, reciprocal, and based on an obligation of indebtedness *(utang na loob)*. Because they are too weak, interest groups, political parties, the legislature, and other government institutions have been supplanted by clientelist relationships. Thus, political life in the Philippines has consisted of constantly changing coalitions of clientele groups that serve both to articulate mass interests and to ensure government control over the people.

The need for patrons to provide resources to their clients has been a major cause of corruption throughout Philippine society. Indeed, public office has been used both for private gain and for the support of clients. Clientelist systems rely neither on rational allocations of resources nor on market forces; their first priority is to perpetuate the power of those who already rule.

Under President Marcos, the clientelist nature of Philippine society was most evident in the president's grant of monopoly privileges to selected followers. Marcos put the control of numerous industries in the hands of his clients and assured them of immunity from loss; when the economy began to collapse and his authority lost legitimacy (after the assassination of Senator Aquino), Marcos lost control, first over the resources he used to reward his clients and eventually over the entire society.

With the rise of President Aquino, Marcos's clientele lost its source of favors, and new patronage groups emerged in the same fashion as has occurred throughout Philippine history. President Aquino found it impossible to ignore these relationships and eventually relied on her own clientele, albeit in a less corrupt manner than Marcos. Her reliance on clientelism further undermined the importance and legitimacy of political institutions, resulting in the continued decay rather than development of Philippine politics. Fidel Ramos was the first president to attempt to end clientelist politics and to strengthen government institutions and laws as a way to replace cronyism.

## Constitutions

The Philippine experience with constitutions is less than one hundred years old. The Malolos constitution of 1899, promulgated by Filipino nationalists under the leadership of Emilio Aguinaldo and the first democratic constitution in Asia, was based on South American and Spanish models and embodied the ideas of liberal democracy, representative government, separation of powers, and a system of checks and balances. This constitution endured only a short time before the United States ended the short-lived republic.

The U.S.-sponsored constitution of 1935 provided for a representative democracy based on the U.S. model. A bill of rights safeguarded the people's involvement in the polity through the electoral process. A bicameral legislature, an independent judiciary, and a chief executive (elected for a fixed term of four years) provided for a separation and balance of powers. This constitution remained in force until 1973. In 1972, Marcos had convened a constitutional convention to draft a new constitution based on a parliamentary rather than a presidential model. However, Marcos's declaration of martial law silenced debate on his proposed constitution; a few months later a constitutional convention approved the new document, which called for a parliamentary form of government led by a prime minister and allowed the interim president (Marcos) to decide when to convene the interim national assembly, further allowing him to make and execute all laws until he convened the assembly. The constitution was then approved by people's assemblies *(barangay)* and went into effect on January 17, 1973.

President Aquino's victory led to a "Freedom constitution," a provisional document issued by presidential proclamation. It provided for presidential appointment of a constitutional commission to draft a new, permanent constitution. Meanwhile, until the commission presented a new constitution, which resembled the one of 1935, President Aquino held executive and legislative powers. A plebiscite on February 2, 1987, supported the new document, with 75 percent of the voters approving.

Under the 1987 constitution, the powers of the president are more circumscribed than under previous Philippine constitutions. The presidential term is six years, with no reelection permitted. To curb the familial patronage of the Marcos years, the president's spouse and all close relatives are barred from appointment as public officials. Martial law powers are also circumscribed, providing both the legislative and judicial branches the power to review legal bases for the imposition of martial law.

The Aquino constitution is the most democratic in all of Southeast Asia, providing for citizens' civil liberties, a meaningful separation of powers, and rights of participation in choosing government representatives.

## The Legislature

In the postindependence period, the Philippine legislature has been both a bulwark for freedom and a tool for legitimizing presidential decrees. The Aquino constitution gives numerous prerogatives to the Congress, including the sole power to declare war, to withdraw presidential emergency powers, and to determine revenue origination and appropriation. Whereas the Marcos constitution of 1973 allowed President Marcos to exercise both legislative and executive powers, the 1987 constitution in contrast makes a clear separation between these powers.

The new constitution called for a bicameral Congress, consisting of a 24-member Senate elected at large for six years and for not more than two consecutive terms and a House of Representatives of not more than 250 members, most of whom are elected from legislative districts apportioned on the basis of population. About 20 percent of the House members are elected through a party-list system. For the first three terms of the Congress, half of the representatives are to be from labor, the peasantry, the urban poor, women, youth, and other underrepresented groups.

## Political Parties

The Philippines had a two-party system for most of its democratic period (1946 to 1972) when the Liberal and Nacionalista Parties held power in alternation, with neither party ever able to get its presidential nominee reelected.[6] The ideological differences between the two parties were negligible, and neither party appeared to represent the interests of the vast majority of Filipinos. For the most part, the two parties functioned as mobilizers of votes for specific candidates.

Under Marcos, one party dominated the political scene. Marcos's New Society movement (*Kilusang Bagong Lipunan*, or KBL) was a noncompetitive, authoritarian party devoted to keeping Marcos in power and to maintaining the support of the U.S. government. Through his magnetic personality, his dominance of the bureaucracy and the legislative and executive branches, his fraudulent plebiscites and referenda, and his manipulation of nationalist symbols, Marcos controlled every aspect of the party and its program.

When Marcos allowed other political parties to be established in 1978 in preparation for elections for an interim national assembly, some thirty parties emerged with regional constituencies. However, these parties were fragmented and unable to find financial backing. Thus, President Marcos thwarted every attempt to achieve a semblance of opposition activity.

In the post–martial law era after 1981, the KBL continued to dominate politics. However, as Marcos's support deteriorated, opposition parties began to emerge. The most important of these was UNIDO, formed in 1979 by Salvador Laurel, who had broken from the KBL. UNIDO, largely an alliance of establishment politicians who had lost out when Marcos took control, was united primarily in its opposition to his domination of the political scene. Thus, UNIDO became an umbrella organization encompassing a number of smaller parties under the leadership of prominent politicians such as Senator Benigno Aquino Jr., who established LABAN! (Fight!) while still a political prisoner of Marcos. These parties formed the core of support for Corazon Aquino when she became a candidate for the presidency.

After Marcos fell from power, KBL members scattered to different parties, including the once moribund Nacionalista Party now led by Juan Ponce Enrile, defense minister under Aquino (and later implicated in coup attempts against her). Vice President Laurel joined Enrile in the Nacionalista Party when he, too, broke with Aquino. At the other end of the ideological spectrum, former communist and labor leaders formed the Partido ng Bayan to contest elections for the National Assembly.

No one party emerged around Aquino's centrist-reform administration. Instead, a series of parties under the leadership of prominent politicians were established to enhance these politicians' political ambitions. However, in contrast to the two parties of the pre–martial law era, these new parties had ideological as well as personal causes. The centrist and left-of-center parties gave support to Aquino, although they disagreed among themselves over power sharing. The right-of-center parties, which opposed her leadership, also squabbled over a sufficient number of issues to prevent them from uniting. Thus, party politics remained largely an elite-establishment activity, based on patronage and personalism. Political parties played almost no role in the 1992 presidential election. Instead, voting was determined primarily by the general public's attitudes toward individual candidates.

The 1992 election included so many candidates that voters identified less with political parties and more with personalities. The power of old-time political machines ebbed as party organization weakened. Instead of parties, personalities prevailed. The runner-up to Ramos in the 1992 election was Miriam Defensor Santiago, who threatened to chop bribe takers into a thousand pieces and throw them to the sharks in Manila Bay. She lacked any party machinery. Even former first lady Imelda Marcos won votes with the support of one faction of her husband's old party, the KBL. Ramos himself cobbled together a last-minute party when "his and Corazon Aquino's" party, the LDP, was taken over by a faction led by House of Representatives Speaker Ramon Mitra.

## The Military

Although long involved with supporting particular candidates for office, the military has never played the dominant role in Philippine politics. In contrast to Thailand, the Philippine military has been subordinated to civilian leaders and given the orthodox task of providing external defense and security against domestic subversion. (This second task was exploited by Marcos to protect his personal interests.) Fidel Ramos is the first president to have been a military general.

The AFP had total personnel of 37,000 in the 1940s. In the 1960s the figure was 62,000; between 1975 and 1976 the number jumped from 90,000 to 142,000; and today the total is about 154,000. Marcos expanded the army to three-and-a-half times its former strength during his tenure, which increased military involvement in civilian life, including the militarization of internal security forces.[7] Under Marcos, the military was deprofessionalized through his appointments of cronies and fellow Ilocanos (from northern Luzon) to the commanding positions. The clearest such example was Marcos's appointment of his cousin, Fabian Ver, as armed forces chief of staff. Ver, who was subsequently determined by a government-appointed investigatory commission to have been a planner in the assassination of Senator Aquino, politicized the military, turning it into a security force for Marcos and the enforcer of his martial law. In return, Marcos provided military leaders with access to financial benefits.

A group of reform-minded soldiers who reacted against the politicization of the military and its diminished professionalism organized into the Reform the Armed Forces Movement (RAM) and led the army rebellion against Marcos after the elections of 1986. Juan Ponce Enrile, a RAM leader, was awarded the position of minister of defense in Corazon Aquino's government for his role in ousting Marcos and supporting Aquino. He along with other RAM officers eventually turned against Aquino and led coup attempts against her government.

In response to RAM demands, Aquino changed her policies by replacing cabinet ministers who were antimilitary, taking a harder line against communist insurgents, and increasing the defense budget. She moved to professionalize the military by dismissing "overstaying" generals who had kept their positions out of loyalty to Marcos and by regularizing the promotion system.

Despite these reforms, members of the elite Scout Rangers and the marines led the most violent and threatening of the coup attempts against Aquino on December 1, 1989. They captured air bases, the Fort Bonifacio army camp, and two television stations and attacked the presidential Malacañang Palace. To repulse the attack, Aquino asked the United States to provide air support to forces loyal to the government. U.S. F-4 Phantom jets, flying from Clark Air Force Base, immobilized the rebel forces, who had occupied hotels and office buildings in Manila; the rebels agreed to a negotiated settlement. One of the principal rebels, Gregorio Honasan, leader of previous coup attempts and a RAM founder, once again evaded capture.

This coup attempt, thus far the best funded and organized of all attempts to overthrow Aquino, came as a surprise, as the military seemed to have grudgingly acquiesced to Aquino because she had moved closer to their viewpoint on countering communist insurgency. The leadership of the coup was traced to RAM, which had also led previous mutinies. Except for a call for President Aquino's resignation, no specific demands were made by the rebel forces. An eight-member provisional junta was to have been set up, consisting of military leaders (including Honasan), former Defense Minister Enrile, and former Vice President Laurel. Following the coup attempt, however, both Enrile and Laurel were charged with involvement, but the charges were dropped when no concrete evidence was found to substantiate them.

During the coup attempt, which was devastating to the Aquino regime, seventy-nine people were killed and six hundred wounded. Moreover, the image of stability, so important for the country's continued economic growth, was shattered. Also, Aquino lost face because of her decision to request U.S. support. Finally, the role of the U.S. military in this domestic issue complicated later negotiations on the American bases and exacerbated nationalist and anti-U.S. sentiments that were already near the surface.

During the Ramos presidency, no military coups were attempted. Ramos was the first Philippine president to view security in broad terms, taking into account military, political, economic, societal, and environmental factors. The absence of an external threat to Philippine security was fortunate, since the armed forces were incapable of defending the country from external aggression. The army has demanded a larger share of the national budget to make up for the U.S. military aid lost after the Senate terminated the Military Bases Agreement, under which the armed forces had received an annual subsidy from Washington. Ramos provided the military with its basic needs and ensured professional leadership.

## The Bureaucracy

In Thailand, the bureaucracy along with the military has been the dominant institution of government. In the Philippines, on the other hand, the bureaucracy has been subordinate to the politicians, in particular to the president. The original bureaucratic unit in the pre-Spanish period was called the barangay, which was responsible for law and order and for the collection of tribute. The Spanish centralized the bureaucracy and transformed it into a patronage-oriented institution designed to keep the rulers in power.[8]

When the Americans came, they assumed the top positions in the bureaucracy for themselves and attempted to make bureaucratic institutions more accountable to the public. Nevertheless, the bureaucracy remained highly personalistic, centralized, and administratively inefficient. Under Marcos, the bureaucracy was mobilized for the president's personal benefit. Graft and corruption in the bureaucracy have accounted for annual losses of some 10 percent in the country's GNP.[9]

Despite personalism, the Philippine bureaucracy has attracted highly educated and technologically proficient civil servants. Even under Marcos, technocrats were placed in key positions, lured by other bureaucrats from the better-paying private sector. Often, however, the technocrats have had difficulty putting their policies into effect because they do not have the requisite political skill or clout. One of Ramos's strengths was to provide the bureaucratic technocrats with the power to carry out their mandate. The results, in terms of economic development, have been positive.

## Women

Traditionally, women have played only minor roles in Philippine politics. Women have never held key positions of power in the legislature, cabinet, military, or bureaucracy. The rise of Imelda Marcos and Corazon Aquino to positions of immense power is anomalous rather than a pattern, as both were the wives of famous and powerful politicians. Marcos, who was governor of Metro Manila and minister of human settlements until her husband was overthrown in 1986, owed her claim to leadership to her husband's authoritarian rule. Aquino was the saintly widow of Senator Benigno Aquino. The power of these women is more a function of their familial ties to prominent male politicians than their successful surmounting of the formidable barriers that have traditionally kept women out of political positions of power.[10]

Filipinas are socialized to play subordinate roles to men in most areas of life, although many women are prominent in the professions and in the business world. In rural areas, women are responsible for performing traditional duties as well as farming chores. Women generally work many more hours each day than do men. Wealthy Filipinas are more active in social affairs because they can afford to hire helpers to take care of their children and manage household tasks. Even among the wealthy, however, women are socialized to let the men lead and to do so demurely. Imelda Marcos's flouting of such conventions caused her to be ridiculed by Filipinos of both sexes.

Corazon Aquino's rise to power was facilitated by the perception of her male associates that she would be a pliable and temporary leader whom they could easily manipulate. However, her refusal to step aside and allow her vice president, Salvador Laurel, to control her cabinet choices and policy decisions surprised Laurel, the military, and other influential leaders. Ironically, however, her unexpected strength and popularity and her commitment to democratic procedures were major causes of six coup attempts against her by forces who continued to believe that she was only a transitional phenomenon.

## Insurgents

The revolutionary opposition in the Philippines gained strength during the 1950s and 1960s but became a meaningful threat to the nation's security during Marcos's rule. The CPP, the central organizational unit of the revolutionary opposition, is the largest communist party in ASEAN and the only such group to remain a viable threat into the late 1990s. Serving as the military arm of the CPP and consisting of some 12,000 to 20,000 armed fighters, the NPA has actively engaged in insurgency activities throughout the archipelago's 73 provinces. The NPA at one time controlled some 20 percent of the country's territory.

The NPA's strength has come from disillusioned peasants, especially tenant farmers and day laborers, whose hopes for a better life were lifted by Marcos's announcement of a New Society and then dashed by unfulfilled promises and expectations. Similarly, the rise of Corazon Aquino initially weakened the NPA until her promises of meaningful land reform and improvement in the standard of living went unmet. Students and intellectuals were persuaded to join the NPA by the movement's claim to represent the nationalist struggle against imperialism and the peasant-worker struggle against feudalism and dynastic politics. Other citizens supported the NPA as the only viable force against the corruption and abuses of rights perpetrated by local dynastic politicians and military units.

President Aquino began her administration with a conciliatory policy toward the NPA, inviting its members to join her government and to become contributing citizens. However, the military balked before such a conciliatory attitude and the NPA rejected her cease-fire proposals outright, forcing her to return to a harder line. During the first four years of Aquino's term of office, the NPA continued to perpetrate violent acts designed to undermine the legitimacy of the administration and to steer the populace toward support for the insurgents.

Thailand's success in countering insurgency stemmed from combining a policy of reconciliation and amnesty with economic development. In the Philippines, however, Aquino's reconciliation policy was not matched with a concomitant improvement in the standard of living. Although very little outside support is provided to the NPA, it was able to capitalize on the negative growth of the national economy and on the consequent extreme poverty suffered by nearly half of the population. The nation's interminable economic difficulties made it difficult to resolve the protracted guerrilla war.

During the Ramos presidency, the NPA was largely a spent force, factionalized and deprived of leadership. The nation's improved economy undermined the chief issue the NPA used to mobilize supporters.

## The Church

As citizens of the only predominantly Christian country in Asia, Filipinos have felt themselves to be different from and even superior to their Asian neighbors. With 84 percent of the population Roman Catholic, over 12,000 priests and nuns throughout the archipelago, the largest land holdings in the nation, and control over thousands of parishes, schools, and hospitals, the Catholic Church is a significant political, economic, and social institution. Factionalized among conservative, centrist, and progressive forces, the church has played a crucial role in all areas of Philippine life.

The current leader of the church in the Philippines is Jaime Cardinal Sin, archbishop of Manila and head of the centrist faction. Cardinal Sin, in conjunction with church bishops and clergy, played an important role in undermining President Marcos's administration and in fashioning the compromise that unified the opposition under Corazon Aquino.

The church's role in bringing down Marcos and Cardinal Sin's close relationship to President Aquino provided the church with an important voice in policy matters. Church leaders have been outspoken in their condemnation of corruption and other dishonest practices and in their support for programs that favor the poor and greater social justice.

Because of her devout religious beliefs, President Aquino acquiesced to the pronouncements of the church on most issues. The most contentious controversy concerned the wish of many government officials to launch a family planning program to slow the highest birthrate in Asia. The church's condemnation of family planning, specifically the use of contraceptives, has kept the government from implementing a comprehensive plan designed to improve health standards and reduce poverty. With 49 percent of the population living below the poverty level and the population growth rate at 2.3 percent a year, chances dimmed for solving the poverty crisis.

The other church-government controversy concerns the rapid rise of AIDS cases in the Philippines. By the end of 1990, government health officials expressed alarm that AIDS was possibly a far greater crisis than had previously been believed. The church's stand against homosexuality and artificial contraception made it difficult for condoms and sex education to be made available to those most in need. President Aquino chose not to disagree with the church on these issues. When Ramos, the first non-Catholic president in Philippine history, set forth an anti-AIDS program that included the distribution of condoms, Cardinal Sin denounced both the plan and the president himself. Notwithstanding these controversies, the church has emerged as the primary symbol of peaceful change, warning against political excesses by government and opposition groups alike.

Cardinal Sin was the leader of the coalition of groups opposed to amending the constitution to allow Ramos to serve a second term.

## Democratization

The Philippines was once known as Southeast Asia's "showcase of democracy," and in terms of the formal institutions of government, that description is accurate. In the postindependence period up to the time of martial law, the Philippine government carried out its functions on the basis of constitutional guidelines, through the separation of powers and by adherence to a bill of rights.

Behaviorally, however, the picture is much different. Since the Spanish colonized the Philippines almost five hundred years ago, the nation has been ruled by a small number of family dynasties that have controlled both the economic and political spheres through decidedly undemocratic means. From the great haciendas of the Spaniards to the patronage politics of the U.S. period, these dynasties have ruled in a baronial, feudal manner, each controlling a particular area of the archipelago.

Even today, following the "People Power" revolt, a group of provincial barons commands the rural areas. In Cebu Province, for example, the governor, the mayor of Cebu City, and the congressman elected to the national legislature are all named Osmeña and are from the politically powerful clan once led by a former president. This example, which is multiplied throughout the republic, is indicative of a system that has remained essentially undemocratic throughout Philippine history.

The country's archipelagic nature is partially responsible for the decentralized, dynastic system. Pervasive poverty also helps explain why the poor learn to rely on their wealthy patrons. Dynastic families sponsor the weddings of their laborers and tenants, pay for children's education, and care for the sick, thereby forming a tie of dependency that keeps the poor deferential and loyal. Without strong government institutions, patron-client relations develop to meet the needs of the majority poor.

The dynastic nature of Philippine politics is also due to cultural factors. A Filipino's loyalty is directed first to family, then to close friends, then to the local community, then to personally known political leaders, and finally to distant, impersonal governmental agencies. Although all of these concentric circles of allegiance place emphasis on the personal nature of loyalty, an individual's family and patron family demand the deepest loyalties.[11]

These feelings of loyalty and deference have been strengthened by a ritual kinship (compadrazgo) in the form of godparents (compadre). This means of formalizing a friendship is employed between persons of higher status and lower status. In the compadre system, a reciprocity is formed in which the higher-status compadre renders material benefits and prestige and the lower-status family provides loyalty, deference, and support. Thus, a candidate for office may be asked to sponsor a marriage or a newborn baby in return for a family's electoral support, and the family then has the right to seek political patronage from its new compadre.[12] Politicians are equally desirous of becoming sponsors to ensure a wide base of electoral support.

A report on Philippine values commissioned by the country's Senate in 1988 attempted to explain the reasons for the lack of democratic values. The report's major conclusion was that Filipinos suffer from a colonial mentality that suggests that everything Philippine is second-rate and everything Western is first-rate. This report suggested that Filipinos have a feeling of national inferiority; hence, support for the nation's governmental system is weak compared to support for family and patrons. The report also suggested that Filipino elites are often alienated from their roots and from the masses of the people, most of whom they scorn. The elites' first priority is to take care of themselves and not to concern themselves with the public good. Such values, of course, are not conducive to democratic rule, a form of government that requires mutual trust and respect for different points of view.

For democratization to take root in the Philippines, the formal institutions of government must become more than facades for oligarchic rule. Inasmuch as the overwhelming majority of newly elected senators and representatives are members of families who have dominated Philippine politics for centuries, the election of Corazon Aquino was in reality more a restoration of certain families (and the demise of other families who had aligned with Marcos) than a revolution. Although the persons in charge of the government have changed, and despite Fidel Ramos's efforts to reform the system, there have been too few fundamental changes in the character of the Philippine political system.

## Economic Development

If Thailand has been the favorite case study for capitalist development of agricultural societies in the last several decades, the Philippines became the model for what not to do. On a par with Thailand in the mid-1970s, when each nation had an annual per capita GNP of just over $300, the Philippines later slipped behind, achieving a $1,265 per capita GNP in 1997 in contrast to Thailand's $2,970. In the 1980s, until the time Marcos left office, growth rates in the Philippines declined, making the republic the only ASEAN state not to share in this period of economic growth. Per capita GNP in 1984 had fallen to the levels of a decade earlier.

Under the Aquino government, the Philippines achieved growth rates of 6.7 and 5.5 percent in 1988 and 1989, respectively, but these figures are still far below Thailand's 10 to 11 percent growth rate. Moreover, the August 1990 Iraqi invasion of Kuwait brought about a rise in oil prices that affected the Philippines more than the other Southeast Asian nations. The Philippines imports almost all of its oil from the Middle East; thus, the crisis there doubled the oil import bill, worsened the trade deficit, dislocated 65,000 Filipino overseas workers, ended foreign exchange remittances from these workers, and added to the nation's already staggering budget deficit.

Economic growth rates since Aquino took office, however, although more satisfactory than those under Marcos, ignore the country's 2.3 percent population growth, the highest in Southeast Asia. Real growth, then, was only 4.1 and 2.9 percent in 1988 and 1989, respectively, and in 1991 and 1992 growth rates fell to zero percent. Moreover, the figures do not indicate that the standard of living for laborers has decreased steadily for two generations due to the decline of the economy, high unemployment and underemployment, and inflation. Concentration of wealth and land has long been more pervasive in the Philippines than in any other Southeast Asian nation. The slight improvement in the economy has enriched the nation's higher-status economic classes but not the vast majority of the people.

The Philippine economy has been skewed since the days of Spanish colonialism, which thrust a feudal economic system upon the Filipinos. When Americans refined the Philippines with their neocolonialist system, the Philippine economy fell under the control of outside forces, including multinational corporations, and of a group of fabulously wealthy Filipino families (mostly of Spanish or Chinese background). Philippine minerals and primary food crops were exported to U.S. markets, thereby integrating the economy into the global capitalist system. Neocolonial relations between Americans and Filipinos were characterized by exploitation rather than cooperation for the mutual good, with the bulk of the profits gained by businesses in the Philippines going to Americans.

The Philippine economy at the end of World War II was in a shambles because of the widespread destruction in Manila and of basic infrastructure throughout the archipelago. The United States became the primary supervisor of the Philippine economy. President Marcos later supported U.S. dominance of the Philippine economy while placing his cronies into positions of power.[13] Thus, the state became the major player in the economy, opening it to greater penetration by multinational corporations, foreign banks, and international funding agencies such as the World Bank. Only a small group of Marcos-centered industrialists and financiers benefited from this new form of state capitalism, while small businesses and labor groups were weakened.

As with most Southeast Asian nations in the 1950s, the Philippines adopted an import-substitution industrialization (ISI) strategy to develop the economy. In essence, the ISI strategy restricted imports of foreign goods in order to improve the balance of payments and to generate new industries to make the nation more self-sufficient. The United States had already penetrated the domestic Philippine economy, so this policy was not opposed by the Americans. Initially, the policy worked well in terms of benefiting domestic manufacturing industries, and between 1950 and 1980 the share of manufacturing in the total economy rose from 8 to 25 percent, whereas the share of agriculture declined from 42 to 23 percent.[14] Manufacturing accounted for more than half the value of Philippine exports in the 1970s, just a decade after accounting for only 6 percent. At the same time, however, every economic indicator showed the Philippines to have the least effective economy in the region.

The lack of success of ISI-led international agencies such as the World Bank to change their advice and to recommend an export-oriented industrialization (EOI) strategy for economic development. Thailand employed an EOI strategy to achieve high economic growth rates. However, interference by Marcos cronies kept protectionist measures intact so that the new strategy never worked effectively.

During the 1970s the rise in oil prices and the price collapse of the major Philippine exports, sugar and coconuts, caused a recession and a foreign trade deficit crisis. Unemployment rose and the standard of living deteriorated. These economic conditions occurred simultaneously with the people's growing disenchantment with the New Society's authoritarian ways and gross corruption.

The Philippines is characterized by a large tenant farmer population, which is prone to join revolutionary movements; thus, the failure of the Marcos land reform scheme to improve the farmers' lot further alienated a large sector of the population. Only a minuscule percentage of potential recipients were awarded certificates of land after the 1972 land reform decree. By the early 1980s, farm prices had dropped so low that starvation was a real threat in the major sugar areas.[15] In contrast, the large majority of Thai farmers owned their own land and did not suffer the same degree of decline in their standard of living; consequently, they rarely engaged in radical political activities.

Similarly, urban laborers grew increasingly angry about the erosion of their wages and the deterioration of working conditions, while employers found themselves losing profits because of the increased costs of energy and pressure from the Marcos administration to raise wages. Both of these groups as well as the farmers could see that President Marcos's family and cronies were living in ostentatious luxury. Marcos had given his best friends monopoly control over the sugar and coconut sectors, which led to their amassing fabulous riches. These riches ended up in Swiss and U.S. bank accounts and in real estate investments throughout the world, a capital flight that subverted the economy to an incurable state.

All these factors so undermined the economy that only a spark was needed to bring Filipinos to the streets to demand change. That "spark" turned out to be the return home and assassination of Senator Aquino in August 1983. For Filipinos, the regime was not only a disaster economically but morally as well.

All of these difficulties kept foreign investment at a minimum, in contrast to Thailand where Japanese, Taiwanese, South Korean, and U.S. capital stimulated and sustained economic growth. The decline of Marcos led to increased international investment abroad, and six military coup attempts frightened away both trade and aid. The Multilateral Aid Initiative (MAI), also known as the Philippine Assistance Program, budgeted $3.5 billion for the Philippines to be funded primarily by the United States, the World Bank, and Japan; it was to be an Asian equivalent of the Marshall Plan, which had been so successful in rebuilding Europe after World War II. The money was meant to furnish infrastructure, relieve the massive debts of the Marcos administration, and provide aid to the needy. However, the continued instability in the country slowed the pace by which MAI money reached the Philippines.

Corazon Aquino and later Fidel Ramos inherited a profoundly difficult and complex situation that was not easily resolvable by even the outstanding economists they were able to bring into their administrations. The problems that beset the Philippines were the same as those of the past: economic inequality, land disputes, monopolistic industries, corrupt leadership, and an elite class more concerned with self-interest than with the public good. These are problems that can be resolved only by fundamental changes in all areas of Filipino life, including the social, economic, cultural, and political realms.

Fidel Ramos focused his presidency on improving the Philippine economy. He liberalized virtually every facet of the economy, allowing technocrats and the market system to prevail. By 1994 the economic growth rate had reached 5.1 percent, not outstanding by Southeast Asian standards but high compared to previous performance in the Philippines. By 1996, growth had reached 6.8 percent, an unprecedentedly high figure, helped by the lack of any major natural calamities during the year. Exports continued to grow, capital formation consistently increased, and the agricultural sector flourished. Inflation was under control. Many signs of growth were visible, most strikingly in Manila as new buildings were constructed, streets were repaired, tourists came in increasing numbers, and a middle class arose. The 1997 economic debacle that began in Thailand caused a devaluation of the peso, and the first signs in several years of an end to the growth period.

For most Filipinos, the standard of living remained lower than in much of Southeast Asia. This is a galling fact for a people who live in a country with rich natural resources and who form the most literate and highly educated population in Southeast Asia, with more experience with democratic rule than any of their neighbors.

## The Philippine State

The Philippines is as interesting a case study as Thailand for analyzing the role of the state, but for different reasons. Thailand was known as a bureaucratic polity, where politics was enacted within the bureaucracy (including the military) and societal institutions were of secondary importance. Only in recent years have extrabureaucratic groups become important in making authoritative decisions that have an impact on all of society. The Thai legislature, political parties, and business associations have all contributed in diminishing the direct domination of the military.

The Thai state lost some of its autonomy with the rise of competing groups and democratization. On the other hand, because of effective centralized administration, Thai authorities have shown a high degree of state strength by achieving their aims and meeting the needs of the citizenry. Thus, the Thai state has gained authority from its demonstrated high capacity to meet the needs of the people and from the legitimacy provided by the king.

If autonomy from societal institutions is a key variable in assessing strength, the Philippine state is weak because its authorities are integrated into a web of patronage networks that limits their power. The Philippine state cannot establish a coherent program because its authorities are not free from the oligarchic connections that have been a major part of Philippine politics for five hundred years. In this respect, the Aquino years are not different from the Marcos years.

The Philippines is an example of a state that intervened in the economic system with devastating results. President Marcos undermined market forces by setting up incompetent cronies in businesses, then providing them with subsidies that relieved them of the need for accountability and efficiency. However, Marcos's "crony capitalism" was different from that of his predecessors and successors only in degree. In contrast to Thailand, the Philippine state has critically hurt the economy through its corrupt intervention and its subservience to the economic dynasties. The result has been an economy of gross inequality, slow growth, and resistance to change; it has been unable to integrate with the international economy (except in an exploited manner).

As discussed in the chapters on other countries, the first condition necessary for state strength is massive social dislocation. Unlike Thailand, which had no colonial heritage, the Philippines experienced two colonial regimes, both of which had a massive impact on every aspect of the country's life. Moreover, and again in contrast to Thailand, the Japanese interregnum was a period of dreadful trauma and devastation, and as a result of the war Manila was all but destroyed. In terms of social dislocation, then, the Philippines has the necessary conditions for development as a strong state.

A strong state is more likely to emerge when at a historical moment external political forces, such as a threat of foreign invasion, favor concentrated social control. In 1972 President Marcos used the internal threats of insurgency and civil war in the Muslim provinces to buttress his arguments for martial law. This insurgency and insurrection remained viable threats under his martial law as well as during Aquino's presidency. Thus, on this condition also the experience of the Philippines is conducive to the rise of a strong state.

A social grouping that is independent of existing bases of social control and is able to execute the policies of state leaders is the third condition for a strong state. As if trying to fulfill this condition, the Philippine government has co-opted bureaucrats, technocrats, and business executives who identify their ultimate interests with those of the state. The dynastic families, on the other hand, have a separate power base (their regional clientele) that is often at odds with state authorities. The economically powerful Chinese also have not acted as an autonomous class. (Corazon Aquino is a descendant of a Chinese immigrant.)

More than Thailand, the Philippines has strong autonomous societal groups whose primary loyalties are to their religious, regional, and economic clienteles. Catholic Church leaders play an important political role in contrast to Buddhist leaders in Thailand, who are apolitical. In their home provinces, the dynastic families carry out policies almost autonomously, independent of central government dictates. Intellectuals, students, and insurgents also have interests that are opposed to the central authorities. In this respect, then, the Philippine state is weaker than Thailand, lacking legitimacy and the capacity to integrate independent groups that are skillful enough to execute the designs of state leaders.

Philippine leaders have differed in strength and accordingly have either strengthened or weakened the state. Marcos amassed tremendous powers for himself and his clientele, but he was sufficiently incompetent to jeopardize the fabric of the republic. Aquino reinstated democratic government, but she was unable (or unwilling) to form policies that undermined the oligarchic power structure.

Thus, the Philippines has experienced the necessary conditions for the development of a strong state: massive social dislocation and external support. However, the state has remained personalistic, characterized by ineffective leadership and low capacity to meet the needs of the people.

## Foreign Policy

The United States, the Philippines' closest ally, also represents the republic's biggest foreign policy problem. Since the colonial period, the United States and the Philippines have had a "special relationship," a term that aptly describes the close and complex ties shared by the two nations for almost a hundred years.

The Philippines, as Asia's most Americanized country, shares a common Christian heritage and the widespread use of the English language. In clothing, music, art, education, and politics, Filipinos have emulated Americans rather than their Asian neighbors. The result, therefore, has been a love-hate relationship. Many Filipinos look to the United States as their hope and even their future home at the same time that they demonstrate against U.S. interference in their affairs. The classic illustration of this ambivalence is the equal number of Filipinos demonstrating against American policy in front of the U.S. embassy and the number of Filipinos waiting there in line for an immigrant visa.

U.S. support of President Marcos, which was believed to have sustained and prolonged his rule, was applauded by some and denounced by others. The last-minute U.S. endorsement of President Aquino, after it became clear that Marcos was finished, together with help in persuading Marcos to leave the country only partially helped to undo the damage.

Meanwhile, the presence of U.S. bases on Philippine territory intensified the conflicting emotions Filipinos feel toward the United States. These sixteen facilities (later reduced to six) were negotiated in the 1947 Military Bases Agreement (MBA), which was to run for ninety-nine years. In 1966, however, the term of the MBA was reduced to twenty-five years (to 1991), to continue thereafter subject to one year's notice of abrogation by either party.[16] Negotiations commenced in 1990 to determine the future of U.S. bases in the Philippines.

The great importance that both nations placed on the negotiations made a settlement difficult. For the U.S. negotiators, the issue was the continuation of the military's forward defense strategy in the Pacific. Moreover, as the Pacific Rim continued its dynamic economic growth and political development, the region became increasingly important for the United States economically, politically, and strategically. The defense of Pacific sea and air lanes was an important mission for Subic Bay Naval Station and Clark Air Force Base in the Philippines; these bases provided the U.S. Seventh Fleet with maximum flexibility for operations throughout Southeast Asia, in the Indian Ocean, and in Northeast Asia (especially in the vicinity of Japan).[17]

Subic was the largest naval supply depot outside of the United States, and Clark was the center of all air operations from Hawaii to the Indian Ocean and the Persian Gulf. Troops could be airlifted from Clark to the U.S. base at Diego Garcia in the center of the Indian Ocean in case of emergencies in the strategically and economically indispensable Persian Gulf.[18] From the vantage point of U.S. negotiators, the bases were an integral part of an interdependent global network of alliance relationships and strategic facilities among the noncommunist countries of the world.[19]

Those who supported retention of the bases noted the economic benefits they provided the Philippines. Indeed, an estimated 3 percent of the Philippine GNP was generated, directly or indirectly, by the bases: by the 30,000 U.S. personnel, by the 45,000 Filipinos who worked on the bases, and by Filipino businesses established near the bases, as well as by taxes paid by all these employees. An estimated $500 million, a huge amount in a poor country, was generated by the bases each year and fed into the local economy. In addition, compensation for use of the bases was $962 million over a three-year period between 1988 and 1991.

Supporters of the bases also argued that the American presence guaranteed a U.S. defense umbrella for the Philippines, thus keeping the Philippine military budget relatively low. If the United States withdrew, Philippine tax money would have to be diverted to the military, away from other needed programs. U.S. support for the multibillion dollar multiple aid initiative would also be jeopardized. Moreover, U.S. withdrawal would make a military coup easier to carry out. U.S. air power was used to put down the December 1989 coup, which came close to overthrowing the democratic government of President Aquino. Potential coup leaders would be less willing to attempt a takeover if the U.S. military could be quickly deployed against them.

For the Filipino negotiators, the crucial points did not involve strategic advantage but rather issues of nationalism, constitutional principles, compensation, and social problems. Those who argued from a nationalist point of view stated that because the Philippines was no longer threatened by an outside adversary, the U.S. bases were no longer necessary to protect Philippine security and sovereignty. From this viewpoint, the bases were an affront to Philippine sovereignty, a continuing illustration of the dependent relationship between the Philippines and the United States.

The other disputed issue was the impact the bases had on the quality of life in surrounding areas. From one perspective, the bases perpetuated a "moral cesspool" in Olongapo (near Subic) and Angeles City (adjacent to Clark). In Olongapo alone, some 16,000 prostitutes serviced sailors on leave; AIDS and other sexually transmitted diseases were rampant. Unfortunately, the economies of these towns had become dependent on socially undesirable activities, a situation that fostered a negative image of all Filipinos.

After months of negotiations, the Philippine Senate rejected the bases agreement and requested that the Americans leave Subic. Prior to this decision, the United States, as a result of the destruction from Mount Pinatubo and differences over the amount of rent, had begun their withdrawal from Clark Air Force Base. The United States dispersed its military presence among several locations in the area. Indeed, such a dispersal is advantageous in that it has made U.S. forces less vulnerable. Singapore, for example, offered port facilities; Guam became a primary repair base; and Australia, South Korea, Japan, and Micronesia all provide air support facilities. Thailand, Malaysia, and Indonesia also provide services to the American navy and air force.

The Philippine Senate's determination was based on the desire to move from a dependency relationship with the United States to a more nationalistic posture. The decision led to tensions and challenges as the nation substituted the traditional view of reliance for security on the United States to a more broadly based view. Even though the Philippines remained under the American nuclear umbrella, there was no clear threat from abroad to Philippine security, and there was the luxury of time to carry out the transformation from reliance on American forces to reliance on Philippine forces.

In the short run, the decision to oust the Americans worsened foreign confidence in Philippine stability, thereby worsening the already desperate economy. However, the long-term gain could be important for the country's psyche: The government was taking responsibility for the nation's ills, rather than blaming "American dominance" for every difficulty that cropped up, and at the same time was undermining NPA propaganda about American "neo-imperialism." Shouldering responsibility should oblige Filipinos to look more creatively and determinedly for appropriate solutions to their problems. One reason for such hope is the fact that the United States was not an issue in the 1992 presidential campaign.

In an attempt to find a compromise between the short-run disadvantages and the long-run advantages of the American withdrawal from Subic and Clark, President Ramos announced in November 1992 that American ships, aircraft, and troops could continue to have access to military installations in the Philippines. The policy of giving Americans a lease on part of Subic was designed to reduce Philippine defense expenditures, undercut the military's insistence on a bigger budget, ensure American involvement in case of an attack on the Philippines, recoup rental payments, and improve ties with the United States. The disadvantages of the policy were the potential for revived furor over a continuing U.S. presence and the delays such a presence could cause in plans to convert Subic into a privatized economic development zone.

Shortly after Ramos's announcement, some Filipino senators questioned the effectiveness of the Mutual Defense Treaty between the United States and the Philippines, which commits the two countries to mutual support in the event of external aggression. U.S. diplomats responded with frustration that the Philippines could end up as the only ASEAN country that does not allow U.S. ships refueling and visitation rights.

For the Philippines, the Spratly Islands imbroglio became the next major flash point. China is viewed as the greatest threat to Philippine security because of its immense size and military capability. Philippine officials believe that there are vast untapped resources, including oil and natural gas, in the South China Sea, where the Spratlys are located. The

South China Sea is also a strategic waterway for the vital trade routes linking the Persian Gulf with Japan, Taiwan, and South Korea, all of which rely on free passage for their oil imports.

Philippine interest in the South China Sea involves its claims to eight of the Spratly Islands and to maritime jurisdiction over a wide expanse of the sea's resources. Philippine officials have defined the problem in terms of respect for Philippine territorial rights and sovereignty. The military, in particular, has made the dispute over the Spratlys a matter of national prestige and overall security, thereby precluding compromise with the other claimants: Malaysia, China, Taiwan, and Vietnam. Still, President Ramos's administration prefers to rely on diplomatic negotiation for a favorable settlement.

The ambiguous status of the Mutual Defense Treaty has raised questions about American assistance to the Philippines. Caught in the contradiction between the desire for autonomy from the United States and the desire for American support for Philippine claims, Filipinos have presented a series of statements that conflict with those of the Americans as the two nations negotiate the meaning of the treaty.

American and Filipino policymakers agree that without American military bases, the Philippines is no longer of primary interest to the United States. Once the U.S. bases had been dismantled, the American navy and air force were able to find alternative staging areas that ensure a continuing strong American presence in Southeast Asia. Moreover, rather than declining economically as a result of the American ouster, the areas around Subic and Clark began to flourish as farsighted leaders transformed the former bases into economic export zones, significantly improving the Philippine economy.

## Conclusion

The contemporary Philippine political system is formally democratic, with structures and procedures conducive to an open polity. Informally, however, the system remains oligarchic, ruled by a self-perpetuating elite of landed families that has commanded the political and economic scene for centuries. Figuratively and literally, President Aquino symbolized this grand contradiction: commitment to democracy versus loyalty to her wealthy family. President Ramos has begun the long process of changing the political system into one that is more democratic.

In contrast to Thailand, the Philippines has not assimilated modern values with traditional ways in a coherent or harmonious manner. The Philippines also has not brought legitimacy to its government; there is no Philippine parallel to the Thai king. Moreover, until the 1990s, the Philippine polity did not meet the needs of the people. Indeed, the standard of living of most Filipinos deteriorated over the past several decades as a result of governmental mismanagement and the greed of the country's leaders. Philippine society has yet to develop an effective capacity to cope with changing demands and to assert the nation's destiny.

## Notes

1. This theme is the focus of David Wurfel's *Filipino Politics: Development and Decay* (Ithaca: Cornell University Press, 1988). Wurfel's book is the most comprehensive and balanced presentation of Philippine politics available.

2. William Overholt persuasively argues that, contrary to the established view that the assassination caused the collapse of the regime or even accelerated Marcos's decline, the assassination was a successful stratagem to delay the consequences of the Marcos regime's political, moral, and financial bankruptcy. See William Overholt, "The Rise and Fall of Ferdinand Marcos," *Asian Survey*, vol. 26, no. 11 (November 1986), pp. 1137–1163.

3. Justus M. van der Kroef, "The Philippines: Day of the Vigilantes," *Asian Survey*, vol. 28, no. 6 (June 1988), p. 630.

4. *Asian Wall Street Journal*, May 21, 1990, p. 18.

5. For a fascinating discussion of the lack of coordination among Philippine ministries, see Raul P. De Guzman, Alex B. Brillantes Jr., and Arturo G. Pacho, "The Bureaucracy," in *Government and Politics of the Philippines*, ed. Raul P. De Guzman and Mila A. Reforma (Singapore: Oxford University Press, 1988).

6. One of the best overviews of the evolution of political parties in the Philippines is Luzviminda G. Tancangco, "The Electoral System and Political Parties in the Philippines," in *Government and Politics of the Philippines*, ed. Raul P. De Guzman and Mila A. Reforma (Singapore: Oxford University Press, 1988). The following paragraphs are based on her analysis.

7. Felipe B. Miranda and Ruben F. Ciron, "Development and the Military in the Philippines: Military Perceptions in a Time of Continuing Crisis," in *Soldiers and Stability in Southeast Asia*, ed. J. Soedjati Djiwandono and Yong Mun Cheong (Singapore: Institute of Southeast Asian Studies, 1988), p. 169.

8. De Guzman, Brillantes, and Pacho, "The Bureaucracy," p. 180.

9. Ibid., p. 197.

10. Linda K. Richter, "Exploring Theories of Female Leadership in South and Southeast Asia" (paper presented to the Association for Asian Studies, Chicago, April 1990), p. 7.

11. David Joel Steinberg, "The Web of Filipino Allegiance," *Solidarity*, vol. 2, no. 6 (March-April 1967), p. 25.

12. Mary R. Hollnsteiner, *The Dynamics of Power in a Philippine Municipality* (Manila: Community Development Research Council, 1963), p. 75.

13. S. K. Jayasuriya, "The Politics of Economic Policy in the Philippines During the Marcos Era," in *Southeast Asia in the 1980s: The Politics of Economic Crisis*, ed. Richard Robison, Kevin Hewison, and Richard Higgott (Sydney: Allen and Unwin, 1987), p. 82.

14. Ibid., p. 83.

15. Ibid., p. 102.

16. Fred Greene, ed., *The Philippine Bases: Negotiating for the Future* (New York: Council on Foreign Relations, 1988), p. 4. Much of the material in this section comes from this comprehensive and balanced account of Philippine-U.S. negotiations over the bases.

17. Gregory P. Corning, "The Philippine Bases and U.S. Pacific Strategy," *Pacific Affairs,* vol. 63, no. 1 (Spring 1990), p. 6.

18. Ibid., p. 12.

19. Greene, *The Philippine Bases,* p. 94.

# 5

# INDONESIA

With over 200 million inhabitants, making it the fourth most heavily populated nation in the world and the world's most populated Muslim nation, Indonesia presents different challenges in its quest for economic and political development compared to its less populated, more homogeneous neighbors. Almost half of all Southeast Asians live in Indonesia, which is composed of thousands of islands and is populated by thirteen major and hundreds of minor ethnic groups. Two-thirds of all Indonesians live on the island of Java, one of the most densely populated areas of the world, while a minority lives in the larger outer islands. Although 90 percent of the population is at least nominally Muslim, the variety of religious beliefs within this Islamic ambiance suggests diversity more than unity. Indonesia is characterized by geographic, linguistic, ethnic, and social heterogeneity; thus, the population has overcome almost insuperable obstacles in achieving nationhood.

In contrast to Thailand and the Philippines, Indonesia experienced a daunting struggle for independence at the end of World War II. Having lived under Dutch colonialism for 350 years and then Japanese occupation during the war, in the postindependence period Indonesians looked for a leader who could forge unity within diversity. As spokesman for Indonesian independence, leader of the revolutionary struggle against the Dutch from 1945 to 1949, and first president of independent Indonesia, Sukarno became the charismatic "solidarity maker"—destined, it seemed, to forge a "new Indonesian person." Neither Thailand nor the Philippines needed such a leader because their societies had not been as devastated or torn asunder as Indonesia's.

Postindependence Indonesia can be divided into three periods: (1) parliamentary democracy, 1950–1957 (followed by a transition period, 1957–1959); (2) "guided democracy," 1959–1965 (followed by a transition period, 1965–1967); and (3) the "New Order," 1967 to the present. The first period featured multiple political parties, parliamentary government, and elections. These Western-style governmental forms—adopted to prove to Indonesians that they could govern themselves in a "modern" democratic manner—did not fit well with Indonesian culture, which traditionally placed little value on representation, group formation, and majority-plus-one governance. Eventually, the westernized institutions were blamed for the government's inability to meet the economic needs of the people.

As liberal democracy floundered, Sukarno moved toward a political system based on Indonesian traditions, with Western-style voting replaced by *musjawarah-mufakat*—a traditional method of deliberation-consensus—with Sukarno himself as the ultimate and unchallenged arbiter. The essence of this "guided democracy" was *gotong rojong* (mutual benefit), where in an environment of cooperation and tolerance (rather than competition) decisions could be arrived at with unanimous approval.

To rally support for his guided democracy, Sukarno made nationalism the cornerstone of his ideology. Nationalism was defined as the submergence of regional and ethnic loyalties in favor of national ones, allegiance to Sukarno, indigenous patterns of governance (free from the mentality of colonialism), and the annihilation of neocolonialism. After Sukarno banned most political parties, reduced the power of Parliament, and suspended civil liberties, he moved ideologically first to the left—embracing the Communist Party of Indonesia (PKI)—and then to the right—strengthening the armed forces—when the PKI became too dominant. Sukarno tried to balance the demands of numerous groups including the PKI, Chinese entrepreneurs, students, rightist Muslims, outer-island groups, and the army.

Although guided democracy was initially supported as an Indonesian antidote to a failed Western system, the deterioration of the economy and the administrative chaos that ensued undermined the unity Sukarno had established. Corruption was flagrant, and the cost of living index rose from a base of 100 in 1957 to 36,000 in 1965. Unemployment was rampant, and communists were gaining strength as peasants and workers were armed with Chinese weapons.

In 1965, in one of the seminal events in contemporary Southeast Asian history, a group of dissident army officers planned a purge of their high command, which led to an attempted coup d'état. The result fundamentally changed Indonesia's political structure, decimated the PKI, led to one of the worst bloodbaths in history, and swept into power a military government that has ruled ever since. The precise roles of the PKI, the army generals, the dissident army rebels, and President Sukarno himself in the September 30–October 1 Gestapu coup may never be known, as the evidence is inconclusive and contradictory. What is clear, however, is that

General Suharto, the commander of the Strategic Army Reserve, assumed command of the army and captured the coup leaders within hours. The coup failed when the army united against the rebels and the population failed to rise in their support.[1]

Within a year, hundreds of thousands of Indonesians—mostly suspected communists—were slaughtered, with the encouragement of the army. During this transitional time (1965–1967), Suharto reduced Sukarno's power, banned the PKI, ended the policy of confrontation *(Konfrontasi)* against Malaysia, brought Indonesia back into the United Nations, and by 1967 had taken all power for himself. Sukarno died on June 21, 1970, at the age of sixty-nine, while under house arrest.

Suharto proclaimed a New Order for Indonesia, ending the twenty-year postindependence charismatic, ideological, and ultimately catastrophic leadership of Sukarno and beginning a period of pragmatic, development-oriented, authoritarian, and stable rule that has endured to the present. The first task of the New Order was to create a stable and legitimate political system with control throughout the archipelago; the second task was to rehabilitate the shattered economy.

The military was portrayed as the savior against the communist threat that had existed before the coup. Indeed, to ensure that the threat would never again rise, Suharto and the military approved the mass killings of hundreds of thousands of suspected communists, carried out between 1965 and 1967. This massive slaughter was aimed primarily at Sino-Indonesians, who were despised by many for having a disproportionately large role in the Indonesian economy and who were suspected of being more loyal to their Chinese homeland than to Indonesia.

To counter the problems of inflation, corruption, and insurgency, Suharto instituted a bureaucratic authoritarian state where power was limited to the state itself, led by the military, his close friends, some Western-trained technocrats, and eventually his family members. Suharto has based his control primarily on co-optation and bureaucratic repression.

To enhance his nationalist credentials, Suharto mobilized the Indonesian army to occupy East Timor, after the territory had declared independence from the Portuguese in 1975. He feared that East Timor would be led by leftists and would become a beachhead for Soviet expansion. In 1976, East Timor became Indonesia's twenty-seventh province, but this was accomplished amid terrible carnage with fully 10 percent of the population killed in the invasion. In 1996, the Nobel Peace Prize was awarded to two East Timorese leaders, Catholic Bishop Carlos Filipe Ximenses Belo and exiled freedom fighter José Ramos Horta, for their "courageous" struggle against Indonesian aggression.

To achieve the task of consolidating power, Suharto purged the army of pro-Sukarno forces and made it the basis of his own strength. Suharto then set up a "government party" called Golkar (an acronym for *golongan karya,* or functional group), which was dominated by the military and administered by officials at every level of government, from national to village. All government officials had to become members, so Golkar developed a nationwide apparatus. Suharto further strengthened Golkar by forcing four Muslim political parties to merge into the United Development Party (PPP), while three secular parties and two Christian parties merged into the Indonesian Democratic Party (PDI). These two parties, which became the formal opposition to Golkar, did not have access to the resources available to Golkar and consequently were not able to challenge Golkar's political dominance. The appointment of retired military officers to leadership positions provided Golkar with greater clout.

To give legitimacy to his regime, Suharto agreed to elections for members of the People's Consultative Assembly (MPR), which in turn elected a president and vice president for five-year terms. In these elections, in 1971, 1977, 1982, 1987, 1992, and 1997, Golkar won 63, 62, 64, 73, 68, and 74 percent of the vote, respectively. Golkar's success has been due largely to its ability to mobilize the governmental bureaucracy on its behalf and to persuade voters that the nation's continued economic growth and political stability required the continuation of its rule.

Suharto was as successful in rehabilitating the economy as he was in stabilizing and legitimizing the political system. Following the advice of a group of Western-educated economic technocrats he had assembled, he cut government and defense spending and reaped revenues from the sale of oil. As a result, inflation was reduced (from several thousand percent annually during the Sukarno regime to less than 10 percent), per capita income was greatly increased, and per capita GNP grew by an average of 6 percent annually.

The availability of food improved in Indonesia more rapidly than in comparable developing countries so that the country is now self-sufficient in rice. An Indonesian born in 1985 can expect to live 23 percent longer than one born in 1965. Out of 135 million Indonesians in 1976, 54 million—or 40 percent—were below the poverty level. By 1987, out of 172 million people, only 30 million—or 17 percent—were below the poverty level. This figure had shrunk even further, to 11 percent of a population of more than 200 million people, by 1997. Per capita GNP in 1997 was $1,080, compared to less than $100 in the mid-1960s.

The success of the Indonesian economy (compared to its dismal performance in the Sukarno period) was the principal cause of widespread support for the Suharto administration. Economic growth brought Suharto legitimacy and undercut allegations made by his detractors about the authoritarian nature of his regime. The strength of the economy was integrally related to the regime's political stability.

Suharto became known as the "Father of Development" to Indonesians, many of whom give him high marks for ruling in a time when poverty decreased, the infrastructure improved, and inflation was reduced. Unfortunately, the gap between the rich and poor increased during this time of tremendous economic growth.

Because of his achievements and his domination of virtually the entire bureaucracy, Suharto has never lost control over the political system. Nevertheless, he has faced severe problems. He has been accused of nepotism and corruption for allowing his wife and children to control lucrative monopolies. After the death of his wife in 1996, his advancing age (seventy-seven in 1997) became an issue. Because the nation's youth and intellectuals viewed him as a leader from the old generation who could not understand the new international era of more open government, they demonstrated for increased democracy and against Suharto's autocratic rule. Human rights issues became central as living standards rose, a vibrant middle class emerged, and more and more Indonesians came to believe that military-dominated governments were anachronistic in an age of spreading democratization.

In 1997, the government-backed Golkar won a sweeping victory in Indonesia's national elections. The huge victory ensured that Suharto would be reelected president in 1998 (for the 1998–2003 term) when the MPR was scheduled to meet. (The MPR is made up of 425 elected legislators, 75 military appointees, and 500 people from various walks of life appointed by the president.) For the majority of Indonesians, Suharto was the only president they had known.

Because of Suharto's advanced age, the preelection period was characterized by much discussion about the shape that post-Suharto Indonesia would take. However, once Suharto announced his availability for a seventh term as president beginning in 1998, politics in Indonesia settled down to the stable routine of the past several decades. However, his choice for vice president, State Minister for Research and Technology B. J. Habibie, proved to be contentious. As a potential successor to Suharto, Habibie was scrutinized carefully and found to be wanting by military officers and International Monetary Fund (IMF) officials, who viewed his economic flamboyance as antithetical to IMF requirements for increased transparency and an end to the endemic corruption of Suharto's family and administration.

The major criticism of Suharto's leadership concerned his family's and friends' domination of indigenous business and industrial conglomerates. More and more areas of the industrial economy—television stations, toll roads, telecommunications facilities, oil tankers—were controlled by the children of Suharto.[2] Because these monopolies arose through personal contacts with the president, the business community became more and more cynical about the economy.

A second criticism came largely from intellectuals who chafed at the government's whims regarding openness in Indonesian society. Foreign newspapers were periodically censored, travel abroad was restricted, and freedom of speech was curtailed. This criticism reached a crescendo when the military committed human rights abuses against the people of East Timor. The worst abuse came in 1991 when soldiers killed about one hundred Timorese who were engaged in a peaceful procession. When Western governments threatened sanctions against Indonesia, Suharto initiated an official inquiry, which found that "excessive force" had been used. This admission was pathbreaking in its straightforward reproach of the formerly sacrosanct military.

Despite (or because of) the criticisms, Suharto has continued to use force to hold the country together. Many Indonesians remember the dire poverty and chaos of the former regime and are willing to give the New Order much slack. But with a growing middle class, widespread literacy, and access to radio, television, and the printed media, the new generation of Indonesians is quickly growing into a dynamic force for change. The severe economic crisis that struck Indonesia in mid-1997 became the greatest threat to Suharto's ability to maintain control. The crisis suggested that his time was over, that he no longer had the capacity to cope with the complex global conditions faced by Indonesia. The crisis meant that Suharto would have a more difficult time finding his way among the alternatives of coercion, co-optation, and cooperation, as he leads this vast nation.

## Institutions and Social Groups

### Constitutions

Contemporary Indonesia has been ruled under two constitutions: the 1945 constitution for the periods 1945–1949 and 1959 to the present, and the 1950 provisional constitution for the period 1950–1958. The present constitution establishes the People's Consultative Assembly as the highest governmental body in the land. The MPR elects the president and vice president, each holding office for a term of five years. The president, although responsible to the MPR, is the executive head of the government, in charge of its day-to-day administration. He has overall power over the armed forces, appoints ministers and governors, and promulgates laws.

The MPR consists of 1,000 members, including the 500 members of the Parliament (DPR). Twenty percent of the DPR is appointed by the government from the Indonesian military, ostensibly to ensure political stability by guaranteeing executive dominance of the legislature.[3] In brief, the constitution was fashioned around a centralized government led by a strong president. Suharto has been able to use the powers delegated to him by the constitution to dominate virtually every aspect of political life in Indonesia.

## Military

In no other Southeast Asian nation, with the possible exception of Burma, has the military so pervasively intervened in politics. Now enshrined in state doctrine, the military has set forth the notion of *dwi fungsi,* or dual function, ensuring for itself both a security and a sociopolitical role in Indonesian society. Through legislation, this dual role has legitimated the military's involvement as cabinet officers, governors of provinces, members of the legislative body, and leaders of Golkar. It is impossible to imagine in the short term an Indonesian administration without the active participation of army generals.

The Armed Forces of the Republic of Indonesia is characterized by a generational split between veteran soldiers who fought against the Dutch in the 1945–1949 war and younger soldiers who did not. The new generation was educated in Indonesia, and its military training stressed professional subjects. Younger officers, who have gradually taken over most of the top military positions, have supported Suharto (a 1945-generation officer) despite their ambivalence about the legitimacy of dual function. General Try Sutrisno is the first armed forces commander of the new generation, and he was elected vice president by the MPR in 1993.

Although the generational difference will be manifested most clearly when a succession decision occurs, these differences are muted while Suharto is in power because of the universal support he receives from his military subordinates. However, when he chooses not to remain president, both generations will attempt to replace him with a leader who supports their respective groups.

Military officers hold important civilian administrative posts at the national and provincial levels and sit on the boards of directors of leading corporations. This is dual function in action. The army's budget as a percentage of GNP is actually small by regional standards (1.96 percent of total GNP, compared with Singapore's 5.48 percent or Thailand's 3.26 percent).

Suharto has kept the highest military positions in the hands of his loyalists. Even in the waning years of his rule, his grip on the military remains total. Although there are periodic reshuffles, only the president's loyal followers are promoted to the top levels. Suharto works assiduously to make sure that no army generals can develop their own power base separate from his own. The generals are former presidential bodyguards, presidential adjutants, or members of the president's family; all are unswervingly supportive of his interests.

## Bureaucracy

Suharto's Indonesia has been characterized as a bureaucratic polity: "a political system in which power and participation in national decisions are limited almost entirely to the employees of the state, particularly the officer corps and the highest levels of the bureaucracy, including especially the highly trained specialists known as the technocrats."[4] Since the beginning of the New Order, the president, his personal advisers, selected technocrats, and top-level generals have exercised decisive control over national policymaking. This wielding of power has rarely been draconian (the period from 1965 to 1967, when suspected dissidents were executed, was an exception). Instead, bureaucratic leaders have relied on co-optation, manipulation of the electoral process, selective repression, persuasion, and success in meeting the needs of large numbers of Indonesians.

Initially after independence, the bureaucracy was weak because the Dutch had not trained an effective corps of Indonesian officials. However, the establishment in the 1970s of a new corps of civil servants known as Korpri made the bureaucracy far more efficient and eventually established its authority throughout the nation. Korpri is centralized, with the president appointing the governor in each of the twenty-seven provinces. In contrast to other Southeast Asian countries, the military holds the majority of bureaucratic positions, including most of the governorships.

Suharto has been responsible for seeing that a large number of Western-educated technocrats hold important positions in the civil service. They have been responsible, in turn, for much of the success of the economic development programs. A majority of ministers are also viewed as technocrats. As Indonesian universities improve, a new group of indigenously educated civil servants will play increasingly important bureaucratic roles as well. The economic downturn in mid-1997 dimmed the luster of some technocrats, although the decision to seek help from the IMF was blamed chiefly on Thailand, which had already sought and obtained IMF bailout funds.

## Political Parties

Since the late 1960s, no party has been able to compete with Golkar, the official party of the government and the military. Golkar functions simultaneously as the principal support of the government and as the representative of the Indonesian people. Golkar was originally established by the military to oppose communist organizations; thus, the party developed a national apparatus down to the village level.

The other important parties are the PPP and the PDI, two conglomerates of smaller parties that were banned by Suharto. By forcing Muslim parties into the PPP and secular parties into the PDI, Suharto neutralized them as threats to his regime, requiring the new parties to declare the state ideology of *Pancasila* (the five principles of nationalism, democracy, internationalism, social justice, and belief in one God) as their sole ideology. They could no longer set forth an ideologically unique program. Moreover, the government had the power to screen proposed leaders of political parties, exercising veto power over those found unacceptable.

The fifth election since independence and the fourth scheduled election since 1971 occurred in 1987 to choose members of the DPR, the mostly elected Parliament that forms half of the MPR. With 90 percent of the population voting, Golkar candidates won 73 percent of the vote, PDI 11 percent, and PPP 16 percent. Golkar candidates ran on a platform calling for the strengthening of democratization within the context of economic development. PDI candidates stressed the needs of the poor, whereas PPP candidates stressed education, the unequal distribution of resources, and bureaucratic corruption. Because of the requirement that *Pancasila* be the sole principle of the party, the PPP lost support because its claim to represent Muslim interests was diluted. Indeed, the Muslim faction, known as Nahdatul Ulama, defected from the PPP to become a nonpolitical educational organization and gave its permission to Muslim adherents to vote for Golkar.

The sixth election since independence was little different from earlier elections; the campaign was devoid of meaningful dialogue. Even though the candidates held diverse views, they expressed very few of these substantive differences. The PPP won 17 percent of the vote, the PDI increased its share to 15 percent, and Golkar received 68 percent, 5 percent less than in 1987. Eventually, each of the three major parties endorsed Suharto for the presidency.

Winning 74 percent of the vote in 1997, Golkar virtually knocked out the PDI, which won only 3 percent. The PPP increased its share of the vote from 17 percent in 1992 to 23 percent. The PDI loss resulted largely because one year before the elections the government had engineered the ouster of its popular leader, Megawati Sukarnoputri, daughter of Indonesia's founding President Sukarno. Because she had announced that she would boycott the election, the PDI's loss was actually interpreted as a moral victory for the party.

Golkar's overwhelming victories are explained by the party's access to unlimited government funds, which Suharto has distributed to his candidates. Also, the public sincerely supports Suharto's generally successful endeavors to bring economic stability and growth to Indonesia. Golkar candidates have persuaded the electorate that their ouster would jeopardize the country's economic growth. Golkar's victories are also attributable to the nation's civil servants, who have used their positions to mobilize the countryside. Further, a prohibition against opposition parties organizing in rural areas between elections and an injunction against certain criticisms of the government have limited open debate on the issues.

If these factors ever proved insufficient to hinder the opposition, Suharto had established the MPR in such a way as to ensure support for his retention of power. He retains the right to appoint a large number of the members (representing group interests), including military officials who owe their positions to Suharto. Thus, even if a majority of elected MPR members represented the opposition, they could never outvote the appointed members, who are unanimously supportive of Suharto. Having acceded to calls for democratizing his administration by means of this so-called vote, he enhanced his regime's legitimacy in the eyes of the Indonesian citizenry and the world community.

Although there are limitations on campaigning in Indonesia, there is not as much blatant voting fraud as existed in the Philippines under Marcos. Although the results of elections are clear before a campaign even begins, elections do influence government policy. If only for a short time, Indonesians participate in the political system, expressing their complaints, opinions, and aspirations through subtle forms of communication at campaign rallies, in letters to newspapers and editorials, and in public and private interaction.[5]

## Women

Indonesian women have rarely played major political roles at the top levels of the polity. Nonetheless, it would be incorrect to infer that women do not exert some influence on public affairs.[6] Like Malaysian women, Indonesian women are active in political party auxiliaries, but their influence appears to be more indirect than direct. As in most of Southeast Asia, women act as the overall managers of the family unit, whereas men dominate in the public sphere.

## Democratization

Liberal democracy has not flourished in postindependence Indonesia. The one attempt to fashion such a system, which lasted from 1950 to 1957, featured multiple political parties and a parliamentary government. However, that period was a time of great political unrest as the country moved from dependence on its colonizers, the Dutch, to independence. Sukarno, who was president during the transition, paid little attention to necessary day-to-day administrative tasks; nevertheless, the democratic system was blamed for the collapse of the economy and the country's infrastructure. Consequently, Sukarno's notion of a unique, indigenous form of democracy was readily embraced as more fitting for Indonesia.

Sukarno argued that "50 percent-plus-one" Western parliamentary practices exacerbated rather than solved problems. Therefore, he advocated a "democratic practice" of the villages for Indonesia, where deliberations are held until consensus emerges, in the spirit of gotong rojong, with himself as the trusted elder.[7] His notion of democracy appeared to fit traditional Javanese value systems in which power is bestowed on one person, usually a sultan. Indonesian political culture is essentially hierarchical and authoritarian: Central authorities cannot tolerate an opposition or any individual gathering power resources independently, as this will endanger the potency of the state.[8] From an Indonesian perspective, therefore, guided democracy is the most effective way to make policy, even if that process is not compatible with Western notions of representative and accountable government.

From a Western perspective, on the other hand, guided democracy ensured the perpetuation of Sukarno's power at the expense of the liberties and openness available under liberal democracy. From this vantage point, real democracy was not destroyed by a traditional culture but by corrupt, power-hungry politicians who established repressive policies and authoritarian institutions to retain their positions. Suharto's New Order is viewed from this perspective as the archetypal authoritarian administration that mouths the virtues of democracy but practices the politics of dictatorship.

Rejecting both of these extreme positions, a younger generation of educated officials has suggested that, indeed, Western-style democracy is difficult to sustain in a nation that has had virtually no experience with such practice except during a period of grave economic instability. Nevertheless, accountability and civil liberties are not exclusive values of the West, and as Indonesia's population becomes educated, informed, and economically developed, there is no reason why Western democratic institutions cannot be adopted. Officials who support Suharto have stated that during his thirty years as leader, Indonesia has evolved to a point where Indonesian-style democracy can begin to be meaningful. They argue that slow progress toward democracy, institutionalizing each step to make sure it holds, is the most effective way of ensuring the continuation of democratic processes.

Adding to the demand for a more open society are the numerous nongovernmental organizations (NGOs) in Indonesia, most of which are new, relatively unorganized, and trying to find their place in society. They represent women's groups, trade unions, student organizations, labor, and various other pressure groups. NGOs work to heal the nation's divisions and to present a progressive challenge to the status quo. Their growth represents rising disgruntlement with the lack of liberty and the suffocating restrictions they perceive throughout Indonesia.

Many of these NGOs are attempting to integrate Indonesia into the global economy on the assumption that the more Indonesia is tied into the global system, the more its government will be exposed to open institutions. For example, human rights activists use the Internet to get their stories out to the world. The global strategies of the NGO members have made it difficult for the government to control these organizations. Nevertheless, the Suharto regime has suppressed many groups, including the People's Democratic Party (PRD), a youthful organization led by students who demand an end to the military's involvement in civilian affairs. PRD leaders have been arrested.

Those who support an "opening" of the Indonesian system are reacting to the forces of democratization in the region from the Philippines to Burma as well as in Eastern Europe and throughout the Third World. The government does not want Indonesia to be viewed as having an anachronistic political system in an era of democratization. Hence, Suharto has allowed more and more discussion of the role of Parliament and political parties, of the press, and of developing a participatory culture.[9] These topics have complemented discussions on how to achieve a more open, stable economy. Such discussions have thus far taken place with the understanding that the military's role in the republic's political life will continue. Thus, contemporary Indonesia is a classic case of a nation seeking to balance the advantages of an open political and economic society with the advantages of an authoritarian system purportedly based on indigenous values.

## Economic Development

Although the Indonesian economy is the largest in Southeast Asia in terms of GNP, it ranks among the lowest of the original ASEAN countries in annual per capita GNP ($1,086). Having averaged over 6 percent growth each year since 1965 (7 percent in 1990 and 7.8 percent in 1997), the country's current per capita GNP reflects the strikingly low starting point of less than $100 at the beginning of the New Order. Sukarno's "revolutionary" economic system under his guided democracy was isolationist and xenophobic and was skewed to meet ideological goals rather than the needs of the citizenry. Suharto's New Order economics sought to provide order to replace disorder and rationality to replace irrationality so that economic development would become the yardstick by which the legitimacy of his regime would be measured.

For the most part, the yardstick measured steady although not spectacular growth, but it was enough to buy a substantial share of popular support and political stability. The means to this end were a series of five-year plans to improve the public welfare, a financial bonanza from oil revenues, the advice of economic technocrats, the repair of the infrastructure, and a reliance on the private sector for the necessary capital, structural change, and productivity.[10] Although the results were generally positive, some difficulties were encountered, including widespread income disparity, corruption, and mismanaged industries.

The most badly managed company was the government-owned oil industry, Pertamina, which went bankrupt in the 1970s. Led by President Suharto's colleague, General Ibnu Sutowo, Pertamina incurred huge debts from lavish spending on useless projects. When oil prices dropped precipitously from $34 per barrel in 1981 to $8 per barrel in the mid-1980s, economic growth in Indonesia fell correspondingly, ending a decade of greatly increased government outlays for education, infrastructure, and communications.

The importance of oil to the Indonesian economy in the early 1980s is evident in that oil exports accounted for 78 percent of export earnings and oil revenues for 70 percent of government income at that time.[11] In 1969, in contrast, oil revenues accounted for only 19 percent of government income. Development budgets grew 2,000 percent between 1973 and 1989 as a result of oil revenues. Oil, no longer representing the largest share of exports, has been replaced by manufactured items in this capacity.

When oil prices fell again in 1986, the government was forced to enact drastic reforms to keep the economy from slackening. Suharto mobilized his technocrats to bring order to the economy by making it less reliant on oil revenues, forcing austerity in budget expenditures so as to reduce the deficit, and opening the economy to foreign investment and joint ventures. A series of reform measures were established such as the creation of duty-free zones, the enactment of liberal investment laws, and the reduction of bureaucratic red tape, all designed to encourage foreign investment. Despite these reforms, foreign debt rose to about $70 billion in 1992, the largest in Asia, with a debt service ratio of about 38 percent. Debt servicing now constitutes a major portion of Indonesia's national budget.[12]

The policy of promoting exports and foreign investment replaced the former policy of import substitution, which had been characterized by protectionism and heavy government intervention in distributing capital. The success of the new policy is shown by the fact that foreign investment commitments rose more than threefold over a three-year period, from $1.4 billion in 1987 to $4.7 billion in 1989. However, foreign investment leveled off in the 1990s as China and Vietnam became cheap-labor competitors.

Part of the reason for the great increase in foreign investments was that Indonesia, like Thailand, has become a major assembly area for manufacturers from Hong Kong, Singapore, Taiwan, and South Korea. Most investments have been in labor-intensive, low-technology industries such as footwear, food canning, textiles, and wood processing where Indonesia's low wages attract entrepreneurs from higher-wage countries.[13] In addition, the indigenous Chinese, who have long been active in the economy (like the Chinese throughout Southeast Asia), have been given greater leeway in return for their support of Golkar. Officials and military officers have provided Chinese business executives with protection and useful legislation, while the Chinese in return have supplied capital and access to profits from their businesses. These Chinese businesspeople, called cukong (boss), are resented by Indonesian entrepreneurs, who view the cukong system as corrupt and exclusive.

The Suharto government initiated its fifth five-year plan in 1989, emphasizing income equity instead of economic growth that ignored the distribution of resources and wealth. These reforms have generally been successful, although income disparities continue to grow. Agriculture, which is still the slowest growth sector in the economy, accounts for 25 percent of the GNP and employs the greatest number of persons, fully 55 percent of the population. Indonesia has reached self-sufficiency in rice, partly as a result of the "green revolution," which provided fertilizers, new seed varieties, and pesticides, but more importantly because of the technological sophistication that farmers throughout the republic have learned from outreach programs.

The Indonesians' quality of life has improved in numerous ways. Life expectancy has increased significantly in just one decade: from fifty years in 1980 to sixty years in 1990. Infant mortality rates have also improved, and literacy is approaching 90 percent despite a weak educational system that is graduating far too few students with knowledge of science, engineering, agriculture, and other needed skills.

Still, there are significant problems with the economy. The growth has been paralleled by the growth of corruption and of monopoly control over key corporations and industries by the Suharto family. Although some money has trickled down to allow a small middle class to emerge, the rich have quickly become richer. Absolute poverty has declined markedly, but most Indonesians continue to live a subsistence existence. Suharto's children and grandchildren hold monopolies over large swaths of the economy, becoming fantastically rich and using their clout to keep other business elites from competing.

In the 1990s, the New Order administration has moved in contradictory directions, sometimes supporting market mechanisms and liberalization and other times state intervention and the protection of conglomerates controlled by Suharto's family or cronies. The overall strength of the economy and the high rates of economic growth have led to poor policies, such as the nationalist and protectionist policies Suharto set forth to protect those closest to him.

Suharto has responded to the national community when the pressure to do so has been particularly great. For example, in 1997 he stepped in to block a ministry recommendation that effectively would have forced parents to buy children's shoes from a company owned by the president's eldest grandson. The issue had been on the front pages of national newspapers since it was made public that the ministry had recommended that all elementary schoolchildren wear identical shoes, to be sold for $10.70 a pair. Indonesia's daily minimum wage is about $3.00. The shoes were dubbed "national shoes" by the public, in reference to the "national car" being manufactured by a company controlled by Suharto's son Tommy.

The clearest indication of the country's economic problems was provided in 1997 when drifting smoke from extensive forest fires in Indonesia spread across much of Southeast Asia, causing severe illnesses for millions of Indonesians, Malaysians, Singaporeans, and Thais. The fires resulted from the slash-and-burn farming techniques employed by many hill people in Kalimantan and Sumatra, and from brush fires set by large plantation owners in clearing new areas for crops. The fires were branded as one of the worst ecological disasters of the twentieth century, not only because of the pollution but because of the destruction of millions of acres of tropical rain forests. Weather patterns were negatively affected, and famine threatened the lives of many Southeast Asians as a result of the dramatic changes in the region's ecology. Although neighboring countries were infuriated, the Suharto government played down the disaster as an expected outcome of development.

Moreover, the 1997 economic crisis, which began in Thailand in June, spread to Indonesia like the Asian flu, causing the rupiah to lose value and forcing the administration to accept an emergency aid package from the IMF, the World Bank, the Asian Development Bank, and industrial powers. The loans came with a number of strings attached, including austerity measures that would prove painful for the Suharto family. The purpose of the loan was to contain the financial crisis, forcing Indonesia to deregulate its controlled economy and end corruption.

The total assistance package was estimated at over $40 billion. Indonesia had to present a reform package including the closure of private banks and more effective oversight of the financial sector. Other priorities were to stop the rupiah from continuing its slide and to reinvigorate the Jakarta stock market. During the entire New Order period, no economic crisis had so quickly jeopardized the foundations so meticulously laid by Suharto for ensuring his continued rule.

The Suharto family's involvement in the economy was viewed most negatively by the IMF, because the president's son Tommy was given rights to produce the "national car," the Timor (which is actually imported from South Korea). As a concession for receiving the bailout money, Tommy was removed as head of the company building the car. Prior to that decision, Tommy's exclusive tax exemptions and tariff concessions allowed him to sell the Timor at about half the price of competing vehicles. The United States challenged Suharto's support for Indonesia's national car on the grounds that to exempt it from taxes that other nations still had to pay for their cars to be sold in Indonesia was unfair. Domestically, many wealthy Indonesians refused to buy the Timor, citing its poor performance as an excuse that often masked their contempt for the family dynasty's use of its economic privileges to attempt to corner one of the most promising markets in Indonesia. All of Suharto's children, in fact, were involved in the nation's primary industries: automobiles, petrochemicals, computers, oil, toll roads, and satellite communications.

Tommy was also presented with lucrative contracts with the Burmese State Law and Order Restoration Council (SLORC). In 1990 Suharto awarded Tommy Indonesia's trade monopoly for cloves and named him head of the Clove Marketing Board, a position that provides him with the ability to generate tremendous revenue. His siblings have received similarly lucrative contracts. For example, his eldest sister, Tutut Siti Hadijanti Rukmana, has a controlling interest in a company that collects revenues from Java's principal toll roads, has held a senior post in Golkar, and is viewed as a potential successor to her father.

The generally strong economy has traditionally been a major factor in explaining the stability of the polity and the high level of legitimacy accorded the Suharto administration. Accordingly, contemporary Indonesia is a good example of a nation whose economic performance has been largely responsible for the legitimacy of the regime. At the same time, the 1997 economic crisis has left Suharto open to criticism that he and his followers cannot control the immensely complex Indonesian economy. However, he has cleverly seen to it that there are no obvious alternatives to his rule. At present, Indonesia's history of high levels of economic performance together with its recent financial crisis are both important forces moving the country toward a more open political system.

## The Indonesian State

The diversity of Indonesia's population and its demographic character make the country difficult to control. Nevertheless, a strong, autonomous state has emerged under Suharto. The state controls all aspects of political and economic life and has co-opted all institutions that could ever potentially challenge the state. Even so, the Indonesian state enjoys legitimacy because of its capacity to meet the economic needs of the citizenry and its ability to protect the country's security both internally and externally.

Suharto's New Order administration has intervened in the economy with generally positive results (at least until such interventions were carried out specifically to protect the Suharto family). This contrasts with the situation in the Philippines, where the Marcos administration brought the economy to ruin through corrupt and self-interested policies, and in Thailand, where the state intervened only minimally. Thus, the Indonesian model lies between the activist (but corrupt) interventionist Philippine model and the laissez-faire Thai example.

The Indonesian state, unlike that in the Philippines, is not subservient to particular societal forces. Instead, all potentially powerful groups have been integrated into the bureaucratic polity. However, the military plays the most important role in the bureaucracy in determining public policy. Most political institutions, such as the legislature and the primary political party, Golkar, are creatures of the bureaucracy and are led by President Suharto. Even the Chinese support Golkar in return for political protection and market monopolies.

The most prominent societal groups that are not integrated into the Indonesian state are the Muslim parties, although most of these have been emasculated under Suharto. The insistence that all parties adopt Pancasila was a successful effort to depoliticize Islamic groups. When a group of prominent retired generals submitted a petition known as the Petisi Kelompok 50 (Group of 50 Petition) criticizing Suharto and his administration for using Pancasila to undermine political opposition, the government-dominated Parliament ignored the petition.[14] This autonomy from societal groups is one characteristic that defines the Indonesian state as strong.

Indonesia has had a history of social dislocation, which is the first condition for the development of a strong state. Like the Philippines, Indonesia experienced a long colonial rule (350 years as the Dutch East Indies) during which its economy served Dutch interests through the exploitation of Indonesia's natural resources. The impact of the Spanish and Americans on the Philippines was greater than that of the Dutch on the Indonesians, perhaps because there had been powerful indigenous empires in Sumatra and Java before the arrival of the Dutch whereas there had been none in the Philippines before the arrival of the Spanish.

The Japanese occupation of Indonesia, while not as devastating as in the Philippines, was an important event. Indonesia and the Philippines present a striking contrast to Thailand, where there was neither colonialism nor occupation. Moreover, Indonesia waged a four-year war against the Dutch, who returned to retake their former colony after the defeat of the Japanese; thus, a revolutionary war led to rebellions and regional struggles between contenders for power.

More recently, the Indonesian state experienced a major bloodbath when, following the Gestapu coup of 1965, about half a million Indonesians were killed. Despite its enormity, the slaughter did not become the focus of international condemnation, perhaps because it occurred during the height of the cold war and because the new government in Indonesia was allied with the United States and was anticommunist. The violence spread as racial, religious, ethnic, social, economic, and political differences were judged to be sufficient cause for mass killings. What began as a political cleansing to oust communists became an orgy of killing and a breakdown of law and order. The PKI, which had once had 3.5 million members (and 23.5 million in affiliated organizations), was virtually annihilated. Together, these episodes suggest that Indonesia has had the necessary dislocations for the development of a strong state.

Strong states may also arise when external forces take advantage of crises to concentrate state control. For instance, the Indonesian state was strengthened during the era of the New Order when the United States and international agencies poured aid and grants into the country to ensure that it would not fall to the communists. Indonesia was often named as one of the "dominoes" that would be next to succumb to communism if Vietnam fell; thus, Western countries strengthened the state under Suharto to preclude such an outcome. Suharto himself often referred to outside threats as a justification for authoritarian rule.

Suharto brought various groups of people into his ruling circle who were independent of existing bases of social control yet skillful enough to execute the designs of his administration. The technocrats fit nicely into this category; they brought order to the economy and thereby managed to strengthen Suharto's claim to power. Even more important have been the military leaders who were loyal to Suharto and who consolidated their power around the regime. The prominence of these independent, skilled groups also led to a strong Indonesian state.

Clearly, Suharto qualifies as an able leader who brought Indonesia into the modern world, rationalized the economy, and secured over thirty years of political stability. His capabilities are not based on charisma, which he decidedly lacks. On the contrary, his strength has come from his capacity to provide effective government and economic development. In this sense he succeeded, at least until the economic indicators deteriorated. From all these perspectives, then, Indonesia has met the conditions for a strong state, but primarily because of its capacity to cope with changing demands and circumstances.

## Foreign Policy

As in other Southeast Asian nations, the primary goal of Indonesia's postindependence foreign policy has been to sustain the republic's security. Sukarno's means to this end relied on anti-Western nationalism; he was opposed to the old established forces (OLDEFOS) and allied with the newly emerging forces (NEFOS). OLDEFOS included the neo-imperialist nations and their allies, led by the United States. NEFOS, on the other hand, included the "progressive" Third World and communist nations, locked in struggle against OLDEFOS. Sukarno's *Konfrontasi* against Malaysia, which began in 1962 and ended in 1965, was described as a classic example of a NEFOS struggle against an OLDEFOS lackey. Supporting Sukarno's foreign policy against the agents of neocolonialism, colonialism, and imperialism was the PKI.

When his New Order was inaugurated, Suharto ended *Konfrontasi*, banned the PKI, and reentered the international arena with a pro-Western, anticommunist foreign policy. New Order Indonesia's quiet support for ASEAN and the Zone of Peace, Freedom, and Neutrality in Southeast Asia reflected its leadership's lower profile in international relations. During the Suharto regime, Indonesia has played only a minor role in international affairs, despite the fact that the nation is the fourth largest (in population) in the world and is of immense importance economically, geographically, and strategically.

The major exception to Indonesia's nonintrusive participation in foreign affairs was Suharto's decision to invade East Timor. This action exacerbated a vigorous guerrilla insurgency movement, which has continued since the annexation.

Indonesia, which has played a quiet role in attempting to resolve the Cambodian crisis, hosted the Jakarta Informal Meetings in 1989 and 1990. However, these talks proved unsuccessful in settling the many issues brought up by all the nations involved. Then, as relations between Indonesia and the People's Republic of China improved after two decades of tension following the Gestapu coup, Indonesian foreign policy moved closer to that of the other ASEAN countries. Thailand in particular had made accommodations with China, viewing Vietnam as the major threat to Southeast Asia's security. Indonesia, on the other hand, saw China as the primary threat and formed numerous ties with Vietnam. Its improved relations with China provided Indonesia with a more balanced regional foreign policy. In August 1990, the two countries formally established diplomatic relations, ending twenty-five years of hostility. The United States, Japan, South Korea, Taiwan, and the western European nations have continued to be Indonesia's primary markets and sources of investment and development assistance.

Indonesian-U.S. relations were temporarily strained when U.S. President Bill Clinton criticized Indonesia's violations of human rights. However, in 1994 the Clinton administration decided to cut the link between human rights violations and trade with China, Indonesia, and other violators. Even when two East Timorese leaders won the 1996 Nobel Peace Prize, the United States did not attack Indonesia's record or threaten to sever trade ties.

Indonesia made international headlines in 1996 concerning the scandal over huge contributions made to the Clinton presidential campaign by Indonesians connected to wealthy companies in Jakarta. In particular, John Huang, an official with the Lippo Group Corporation, solicited funds from wealthy Indonesian citizens including Mochtar Riady, who was accused of attempting to influence American foreign policy.

## Conclusion

President Suharto's Golkar won an overwhelming electoral victory in 1997, ensuring him a seventh term as president. Because Suharto has been the only leader most Indonesians have ever known, the succession question was of increasing interest and concern. In fact, succession discussions revolved around the issues of political stability, economic development, and democratization. Indonesians who have lived under Suharto's strong New Order state with its generally high capacity for effective governance (albeit under military-dominated authoritarian rule) have opted for performance over democracy.

Indonesia's modernization has facilitated the rise of a better educated and economically well-off middle class, which is generally informed about Western ways. This class therefore seeks a fit between its indigenous values and those of the Western world. Moreover, all Indonesians seek leadership that can cope with the problems of uneven income distribution, urban growth, the concentration of the country's population on the island of Java, the integration of ethnic minorities, corruption at all levels of the administration, and the rise of Islamic militancy. The military, of course, insists that it play a major role in resolving these problems. The crucial task for future governments is to create an environment that will allow democratic openness while ensuring political stability and continued economic growth. Suharto could always point to the strong economic performance of his administration, until mid-1997. Then, real questions arose about his capacity to handle the nation during a time of recession. The succession question has become even more important: When Suharto is no longer president, everything will change.

On May 20, 1998, after ten days of antigovernment demonstrations led by students, Suharto resigned as president. His vice president, Jusuf Habibie, was sworn in as president, receiving the support of the military. Because Habibie was viewed as a protégé of Suharto, he faced the problem of distancing himself from the former president and indicating his support for reform and democratization while setting forth economic policies designed to resolve the crises of currency devaluation, inflation, and unemployment.

## Notes

1. For a sampling of views of the Gestapu coup, see Benedict Anderson and Ruth T. McVey, *A Preliminary Analysis of the October 1, 1965, Coup in Indonesia*, Interim Report Series, Modern Indonesia Project (Ithaca: Cornell University Press, 1971); Arnold C. Brackman, *The Communist Collapse in Indonesia* (New York: Norton, 1969); Peter J. Dommen, "The Attempted Coup in Indonesia," *China Quarterly*, no. 25 (January-June 1966), pp. 144–170; John Hughes, *Sukarno: A Coup That Misfired, A Purge That Ran Wild* (New York: McKay, 1967); Justus van der Kroef, "Origins of the 1965 Coup in Indonesia: Probabilities and Alternatives," *Journal of Southeast Asian Studies*, vol. 3 (September 1972), pp. 277–298; Tarzie Vittachi, *The Fall of Sukarno* (New York: Praeger, 1967); and W. F. Wertheim, "Suharto and the Untung Coup: The Missing Link," *Journal of Contemporary Asia*, vol. 1, no. 2 (Winter 1970), pp. 50–57.

2. David McKendrick, "Indonesia in 1991," *Asian Survey*, vol. 32, no. 2 (February 1992), pp. 103–105.

3. Leo Suryadinata, "Indonesia," in *Politics in the ASEAN States*, ed. Diane K. Mauzy (Kuala Lumpur: Maricans, 1986), p. 120.

4. Karl D. Jackson and Lucian Pye, eds., "Bureaucratic Polity: A Theoretical Framework for the Analysis of Power and Communications in Indonesia," in *Political Power and Communications in Indonesia*, ed. Karl D. Jackson (Los Angeles: University of California Press, 1978), p. 3.

5. Harry Tjan Silalahi, "The 1987 Election in Indonesia," in *Southeast Asian Affairs 1988* (Singapore: Institute of Southeast Asian Studies, 1988), p. 98.

6. Ann Ruth Willner, "Expanding Women's Horizons in Indonesia: Toward Maximum Equality with Minimum Conflict," in *Asian Women in Transition*, ed. Sylvia A. Chipp and Justin J. Green (University Park: Pennsylvania State University Press, 1980), p. 187.

7. Ulf Sundhaussen, "Indonesia: Past and Present Encounters with Democracy," in *Democracy in Developing Countries: Asia*, ed. Larry Diamond, Juan J. Linz, and Seymour Martin Lipset (Boulder: Lynne Rienner Publishers, 1989), pp. 448–449.

8. Ibid., p. 455.

9. Gordon Hein, "Indonesia in 1988," *Asian Survey*, vol. 29, no. 2 (February 1989), p. 124.

10. Geoffrey B. Hainsworth, "Indonesia: On the Road to Privatization?" *Current History*, vol. 89, no. 545 (March 1990), p. 121.

11. H. W. Arndt and Hal Hill, "The Indonesian Economy: Structural Adjustment After the Oil Boom," *Southeast Asian Affairs 1988* (Singapore: Institute of Southeast Asian Studies, 1988), p. 107.

12. Gordon Hein, "Indonesia in 1989," *Asian Survey*, vol. 30, no. 2 (February 1990), p. 227. See also *Asiaweek*, April 7, 1993, p. 6.

13. *Far Eastern Economic Review*, April 19, 1990, p. 42.

14. Suryadinata, "Indonesia," p. 127.

# 6

# MALAYSIA

Malaysia has emerged as Southeast Asia's strongest open polity and economy. With an annual per capita income of $4,446, Malaysia has achieved the status of a newly industrialized country (NIC). Only the citizens of the city-state of Singapore have a higher standard of living than Malaysia's 19 million people. This is especially noteworthy because of the country's ethnic and geographic diversity. Malaysia consists of the peninsula (formerly Malaya), which is connected to southern Thailand, and Sabah and Sarawak on the island of Borneo, several hundred miles across the South China Sea.

There is no more powerful force in Malaysian society than communalism—the division of the country into ethnic communities, 48 percent Malay, 36 percent Chinese, 9 percent Indian, and the rest smaller minorities. The Malays are Muslim, mostly rural and agricultural *bumiputera* ("sons of the soil"), whereas the non-Malays are urban non-Muslim immigrants usually employed in industry, trades, and textiles.

Immigrants to Malaysia from 1860 to 1940 were mostly impoverished workers and peasants from southern China who came during the British colonial administration to work the tin mines and perform labor the Malays scorned. Their separateness was reinforced even as they expanded their economic roles, becoming money lenders, middlemen, contractors, and manufacturers. Their primary stress on education and ambition provided mobility so that at present the Chinese are the wealthiest businesspeople in every area of the economy. These conditions parallel those in other Southeast Asian nations, except they are magnified in Malaysia because the Chinese constitute almost 40 percent of the population in contrast to 10 percent for the rest of the region.[1]

Communalism has resulted in the stereotyping of Malaysia's ethnic groups. Malays view the Chinese as aggressive, acquisitive, unscrupulous in business dealings, ritually unclean, and politically suspect. Chinese, on the other hand, view themselves as hardworking, progressive, competitive, and faithful to their families. To the Chinese, the typical Malay is lazy and superstitious and without motivation for hard work or personal advancement, whereas Malays view themselves as scrupulous in their dealings with others and as more concerned with the quality of human relationships than with material acquisition.[2]

To mitigate ethnic differences, the British arranged the "Bargain" when they relinquished colonial authority over Malaya (not yet Malaysia) in 1957. The Bargain included such terms as constitutional advantages to the Malays; support for a Malay as head of state *(Yang diPertuan Agong)*, chosen from among the sultans of nine peninsular Malay states; Malay as the country's official language; and Islam as the official religion. Also, the constitution provided special privileges to Malays in land acquisition, educational assistance, and civil service employment.

To meet the terms of the Bargain, the leading Malay, Chinese, and Indian political parties formed an alliance with the understanding that non-Malays would prevail in the economic sector while Malays would control the political sector. As long as that formula was accepted by all groups, the Malaysian political system was stable. When the formula was challenged in May 1969 following a national election, rioting ensued, causing the deaths of at least 196 persons and precipitating the declaration of a state of emergency that lasted almost two years.

Great Britain continued to exercise influence over Malaya; over Britain's self-governing colony, Singapore; and over the dependencies of North Borneo (now Sabah), Sarawak, and Brunei (all situated on the island of Borneo). In 1963 Malaya joined with Singapore, Sabah, and Sarawak to form the Federation of Malaysia. All of these areas shared a common colonial heritage under Great Britain, and all feared that without collaboration, they could not function as viable and autonomous nation-states. To offset the integration of 3 million Chinese from Singapore into the federation, Sabah and Sarawak were brought in to maintain a favorable proportion of non-Chinese in the population. Singapore was given wide-ranging autonomy over its domestic affairs.

The federation lasted only two years until August 1965, when Malaysia's first prime minister, Tunku Abdul Rahman, expelled Singapore for many complex reasons inextricably bound up with communal problems. The prime minister of Singapore, Lee Kuan Yew, called for a "Malaysian Malaysia"—that is, for a Malaysia with equal participation from all areas and groups. His call opposed and contrasted with Tunku Abdul Rahman's design for a "Malayan Malaysia," with special privileges reserved for the dominant ethnic group. When Lee Kuan Yew attempted to influence the larger area of Malaysia, Tunku Abdul Rahman regarded the attempt as a direct threat to continued political dominance by the Malays.

The 1969 communal riots were a watershed event in Malaysia's postindependence era, and their immediate cause was the erosion of support for Abdul Rahman's Alliance Party in the 1969 elections. In the preceding two elections, in 1959 and 1964, the Alliance Party had won an overwhelming majority of the parliamentary seats. In 1969, for the first time the opposition parties won a majority (51.5 percent) of the votes against the Alliance Party's 48.5 percent. Although Alliance candidates still controlled a majority in the Parliament despite losing twenty-three seats, the 1969 election showed that the Alliance Party's capacity to govern was seriously impaired. To celebrate their "victory," anti-Alliance forces paraded in the streets of the capital, Kuala Lumpur. Later, on May 13, Alliance supporters paraded, which led to communal tensions to the point of provoking mob action that raged for four days.

The Malaysian government viewed the riots as a threat to the ethnic Bargain that had been the formula for civic stability. To ensure that Malays retained political power, a state of emergency was proclaimed, Parliament was temporarily disbanded, civil liberties were curtailed, and total authority was granted to a new body, the National Operations Council (NOC). The NOC worked to restore order and the eventual return to parliamentary democracy. The rights of Malays were extended by reserving for them a proportion of positions in higher education and certain businesses, and sedition acts were passed that prohibited discussion of such "sensitive issues" as the prerogatives of Malay rulers, special rights for Malays, and official status for the Malay language. This twenty-one-month period was a time of suspended democracy.

Believing that economic tensions were mainly responsible for the communal riots, Tun Abdul Razak, the new prime minister, proposed a new economic policy to promote national unity and a just society by attacking poverty and "reducing and eventually eliminating the identity of race with economic function." In essence, this meant that Malay participation in the economic sphere was to be increased by granting special privileges in terms of business ownership, tax breaks, investment incentives, and employment quotas.

By 1972 parliamentary democracy returned, albeit within the constraints of the sedition acts and the reworking of the Alliance Party into the National Front (Barisan Nasional). Tun Abdul Razak established the National Front to ensure dominance of the political system by Malays and to preclude upheavals such as the 1969 riots. His party, having co-opted most of the opposition parties, won 90 percent of the parliamentary seats in the 1974 election.

When Abdul Razak died in 1976 he was succeeded by Tun Hussein Onn who, like his predecessors, came from prestigious ancestry and great wealth and had a Western education. He continued National Front policies until 1981 when, following a serious illness, he resigned and was succeeded by Deputy Prime Minister Datuk Seri Mahathir bin Mohamad. Mahathir, the first commoner prime minister, with no aristocratic ancestry or family wealth and with a local education, symbolized the new Malaysian technocrat. His brash and confrontational style was the opposite of that of his refined predecessors.

Mahathir became an articulate spokesman in modern Malaysia's bid to develop economically. His "Look East" policy argued that Western nations were not appropriate models for Malaysia. He believed that Malaysia should emulate the methods of Japan, South Korea, and Taiwan, all Asian countries whose values were more in tune with those of Malaysia. He also introduced the concept of "Malaysia Incorporated," whereby business and government leaders would work together as in a modern corporation. His drive to privatize public utilities, communications, and transportation is an example of his attempt to encourage the profit motive and increased efficiency to the Malaysian economy.

In the 1982 parliamentary election, Mahathir and the National Front triumphed, winning 132 of 154 seats. Again in 1986, the National Front won a landslide victory, winning 148 of the 177 parliamentary seats, but this election marked the beginning of a period of political and economic difficulties. The leaders of the major parties in the Front fell into strife as the country underwent a major recession, which resulted in negative economic growth for the first time since independence.

The major problem was within the United Malay Nationalist Organization (UMNO), the dominant party of the National Front and the "home" of Mahathir (as well as all former prime ministers). Strife in UMNO led to the resignation of high-ranking officials, some of whom joined a faction known as Team B, who then challenged the leadership of Mahathir and his followers, known as Team A. In the elections for the leadership of UMNO in April 1987 (the most important elections in Malaysia because they determine the top party and government leadership), Mahathir barely beat his challenger, Team B leader and Trade and Industry Minister Tunku Razaleigh Hamzah, when of the 1,479 voting UMNO delegates he won by only 43 votes, 761 to 718. In a shocking display of internecine factionalism, Team B officials accused Mahathir of blatant abuse of power, authoritarian leadership, economic mismanagement, and corruption.[3]

Razaleigh had run against Mahathir following five years of a recessionary economy, including a 1 percent decline in the GNP, which disillusioned the Chinese and the new Malay middle class. Mahathir's confrontational administrative style had also become controversial. The challenge to Mahathir was especially noteworthy because it is the custom of Malays not to challenge their leaders; generally, Malaysians believe in *taat setia* (absolute loyalty) to their rulers. It is considered a case of *ku-*

*rang ajar* (impropriety) to question the leadership. The electoral challenge undermined this important custom in Malay politics.[4]

In response, Mahathir purged Team B members from his cabinet and from UMNO leadership, and he invoked the Internal Securities Act, ordering the arrest of persons critical of government actions. Also, three opposition newspapers were closed, and Operation Lallang was ordered: a sweep by the Malaysian police (on October 27, 1987) that took into custody 119 persons who had been accused of threatening internal security by provoking communal conflict. All those arrested were members of religious, political, and social organizations that, merely by criticizing regime policies, had qualified themselves as "thorns in [Mahathir's] side."[5]

In still another stunning incident related to UMNO factionalism, the Malaysian high court decreed that since unregistered regional branches had participated in the UMNO elections, UMNO was an illegal organization. The high court's decision was a shocking development because UMNO had won every election since independence. Immediately, there was a scramble to register a new party with UMNO in its name and to lay claim to the party's considerable assets. After the rejection of Team B's applications, Mahathir was able to get UMNO Baru (New UMNO) registered. A dissident faction, again led by Razaleigh, formed a new party, Semangat '46 (Spirit of '46, the year of UMNO's birth), and allied itself with other opposition groups to form an alternative party known as Angkatan Perpaduan Umnah (APU). Subsequently the National Front, led by UMNO Baru, won six of eight by-elections against the APU as well as winning the national election in October 1990.

Because of high-court decisions that Mahathir believed were against the interests of the National Front, he reduced the power of the courts by taking away their right to judicial review of executive decisions on internal security and matters concerned with the administration and operation of political parties. Indeed, in 1988 he forced a constitutional amendment through Parliament that eliminated the constitutional basis of judicial review and replaced it with "such powers as Parliament shall grant." Ostensibly, this reduction of the courts' power was to ensure that, in case of threat to the nation's security, an executive could move with dispatch rather than having to wait for the cumbersome courts to deliberate. Eventually, at Mahathir's instigation, a specially created tribunal removed a majority of court justices from office.

In early 1989 Mahathir suffered a heart attack and underwent a successful multiple coronary bypass operation. His rapid recovery restored him as the central figure in contemporary Malaysian politics, and he moved toward the 1990 elections with confidence as the National Front began to recover from factional struggles and as the economy recovered from recession.

The strong economy (with estimated growth of 9 percent in 1990) was the principal factor in the overwhelming election victory Mahathir and the multiracial National Front coalition achieved in October 1990. After only a ten-day campaign, the shortest political campaign in contemporary Southeast Asian history, he won a two-thirds majority, thus ensuring control over constitutional amendments. The National Front won 127 of the 180 seats in Parliament despite an exceptionally strong opposition campaign.

The primary political issue of the early 1990s concerned the role of Islam in Malaysian society. Islamization had made inroads into the state of Kelantan with the state assembly controlled by an Islamic-dominated coalition between the Partai Islam Se-Malaysia (PAS) and Semangat '46. Mahathir reacted against the notion of an Islamic state, which he deemed inappropriate for a multiracial society. The issue did not become a crisis because high economic growth rates provided a cushion that softened societal tensions.

In 1992–1993, a social reformation of great significance occurred when Mahathir decided to confront the nation's sultans, the traditional hereditary rulers of most of peninsular Malaysia's states, whose positions were largely ceremonial. The prime minister moved to reduce their power and prerogatives, notwithstanding laws and acts precluding discussion of the sultans' roles. By 1993, Mahathir had achieved the taming of the bureaucracy, political parties, judiciary, press, and sultans. Through confrontation and co-optation, he had successfully undermined the major forces once competing with him for political power.

The period from 1990 to 1996 was positive for the ruling National Front and for its leader, Mahathir. Winning its ninth general election in April 1995, with 64 percent of the popular vote, the Front enjoyed a two-thirds parliamentary majority. In addition, the Front won control of every state assembly except for one (that of Kelantan), and the opposition was left in disarray. Both the Democratic Action Party (DAP) and Semangat '46 were shut out throughout the nation. The Barisan Nasional coalition of UMNO, the Malayan Chinese Association (MCA), the Malayan Indian Congress (MIC), and Gerakan were united after the election. Malaysians supported the Front because of the strong economy, the disarray of the opposition, and the Front's monopoly of the mass media. Mahathir's position had never been more secure.

As Mahathir's health stayed strong (despite his age of seventy-one in 1997) and as his international stature increased, there were few politicians brave enough to question his preeminence. His main competition came from his deputy prime minister, Anwar Ibrahim, but Mahathir kept him off balance with intraparty rules that banned confrontations with the leader. Mahathir became Malaysia's longest serving premier and the only Front chairman to lead his coalition through four successive elections.

Mahathir's international reputation widened after a series of speeches in which he praised the virtues of "Asian values" and condemned "Western values." He often spoke passionately about his nation's sovereignty and, appearing to revel in the role of "West-basher," about the Americans whom he deemed to be neo-imperialist in their desire to control Malaysia and Malaysia's neighbors. Mahathir was responsible for backing the construction of the world's tallest building, the Petronas Towers in Kuala Lumpur (eclipsing America's Sears Tower in Chicago), in 1996. He has planned a gleaming high-tech research park, dubbed "technopolis," and a "Multimedia Super-Corridor" linking Kuala Lumpur with an immense new international airport. Mahathir has hosted numerous international conferences, including the 30th anniversary celebrations of the ASEAN, and was primarily responsible for bringing Vietnam, Laos, and Burma into the association.

Mahathir's Malaysia is a paradox: The nation has long enjoyed a rapidly improving standard of living for all classes of people. Simultaneously, Mahathir has brashly tamed the bureaucracy, political parties, judiciary, press, and sultans, all of whom had once dared to challenge his political power. He is known to be intolerant of pettiness, disdainful of opposition, and fervent in his commitment to Malaysian sovereignty.

In 1997, Mahathir was in his sixteenth year of tenure and in sole command of his country. A new problem arose when the Malaysian ringgit lost much of its value as a result of the Thai currency's devaluation. For the first time, Mahathir was in the midst of a crisis he could not control directly because the crisis was caused by international and not domestic factors. His first reaction was to blame outsiders, and he embarrassingly pointed his finger at "Jews," who had long wanted to undermine Malaysia because of its predominantly Muslim population. Mahathir later explained that he was referring to only one Jew, American financier George Soros, whom Mahathir accused of speculating with the Malaysian currency. Most of the world's press criticized Mahathir for his refusal to accept that a large reason for currency crisis was domestic, and not external.

Mahathir's focus is on "Vision 2020," a plan to lift Malaysia into the ranks of the developed nations in the next twenty-five years. His goal was blunted by the economic crisis, which may explain the depth of his anger and his shocking accusation against the Jews. He was furious that his plans could be undermined by an economic crisis that was beyond his control to fix.

## Institutions and Social Groups

### Political Parties

The Alliance (in the pre-1969 period) and the National Front are coalitions of parties, joined together by the common goals of winning elections and securing societal stability. These goals have for the most part been achieved. Three parties composed the Alliance: UMNO, the MCA, and the MIC. Representing the three major ethnic groups, these parties accepted the Alliance formula to legitimize the interests of these ethnic groups. The formula required that each group accept the basic societal division: Malays dominate the political sphere, and Chinese and Indians dominate the economy.

When the formula broke down in 1969, the Alliance was transformed into the National Front, which consisted of the three Alliance parties as well as a coalition of former opposition parties led by the PAS, the country's strongest Islamic party, and the DAP, the principal Chinese opposition party. In all, the Front is composed of eleven component parties, but UMNO is the senior partner and has the final say over coalition decisions.[6] Every Malaysian prime minister has been a member of UMNO.

In 1988, when the courts found UMNO unlawful on the grounds that the delegates sent to the assembly had not been properly chosen, the country was stunned. For most Malays, UMNO had embodied their culture, aspirations, and belief in their right to rule Malaysia. The rapid transformation of UMNO into UMNO Baru (with "Baru" subsequently deleted) was important to retain the country's legitimacy. For the first time since independence, UMNO was challenged by a party organization, Semangat '46, led by a Malay and strong enough to defeat the National Front. Having allied with the APU (which included the PAS and the DAP), the opposition provided the first viable alternative to the UMNO-dominated Front.

However, the APU's strength was found wanting in the 1990 elections, in which some 8 million registered Malaysians voted. For the first time, a multiracial opposition coalition led by a Malay (Razaleigh) was in a position to challenge the Front. Candidates representing the National Front capitalized on the issues of economic growth and political stability to achieve their electoral victory. They also warned the populace against the unwieldy alliance of the main Chinese opposition party (the DAP) with a fervent Muslim party (the PAS) that wanted Malaysia to become an Islamic state. The opposition's focus on issues of human rights, press freedom, lower taxes, and Mahathir's combative personality was not as credible to the voters.

The National Front also enjoys the advantage of UMNO's access to funds. UMNO has transformed itself into a huge business conglomerate with assets in numerous corporations. Although conglomerates throughout Southeast Asia rely on government patronage, no assemblage of companies owned directly by a political party appears to have benefited from government largesse to the same extent as UMNO's holdings.[7] Neither opposition nor allied parties in the Front have access to such funds.

Compared to political parties in Thailand and the Philippines, UMNO is highly institutionalized as a party, which makes it a potent instrument of government. Every Malaysian prime minister has reached that position because he has led UMNO, whereas Thai and Filipino leaders have reached the top governmental position in other ways, reflecting the lesser importance of their parties and weaker institutionalization of their party systems.

## Bureaucracy

In Thailand, the bureaucracy has been the core of political action; in Malaysia, however, politicians have dominated the decisionmaking process with bureaucrats in the role of implementers. There is no bureaucratic polity in Malaysia despite the bureaucracy's strength, which was built up under the British. The role of extrabureaucratic institutions, especially political parties, has impinged upon the centrality of the bureaucracy. Malaysia's bureaucracy employs Southeast Asia's most sophisticated and highly educated technocrats.

## State Royalty

Malaysia's means of choosing its monarch is unique. Nine states have hereditary rulers, the sultans, and the *Yang diPertuan Agong*, or king, is elected from this body (usually on the basis of seniority) for a term of five years. The king, who has ceremonial and religious duties and powers of appointment, can delay certain legislative bills (although this power has been circumscribed). The Malaysian king is not held in the same awe as the king of Thailand, who is venerated by virtually all Thais; nevertheless, he plays an important symbolic role as the head of state.

The role of the sultans changed dramatically in 1993 when Mahathir moved to place them under the law. The prime minister's actions were precipitated by an incident in which the sultan of Johore allegedly assaulted a hockey coach with whom he was displeased. Mahathir proposed to lift the hereditary rulers' immunity from legal action. He also moved to revoke their right to grant pardons to themselves and their families.

Mahathir's moves were accompanied by daily press reports on the sultans' rampant corruption, philandering, and high living. These reports were shocking to the citizens both because of the extent of the alleged debauchery and because the reports appeared to break sedition act regulations forbidding criticism of the sultans. Rural Malays were stunned to read such reports about their sultans, who had long commanded their loyalty and were viewed as their symbolic protectors.

Mahathir introduced amendments to the Parliament. However, amendments that concerned the "privileges, position, honors or dignities" of the rulers required their consent. The king eventually assented to a compromise bill that reduced the sultans' privileges. The compromise stated that the attorney general's consent was required before charges could be brought against the sultans and allowed for the creation of a "special court" that would rule on such cases. This measure would limit petty actions against the rulers. The larger point, however, was Mahathir's success in reducing the power and influence of one of Malaysia's oldest and most important institutions.

## Legislature

Malaysia's political system is based on the British model, with a bicameral Parliament that elects one of its own members to the prime ministership. The prime minister must sit in the lower House of Representatives (Dewan Ra'ayat) and must command majority support. The upper chamber, the Senate (Dewan Negara), has fifty-eight members, twenty-six elected and thirty-two appointed by the king after recommendation by the prime minister. Senators hold office for six years; representatives serve five years unless Parliament is dissolved sooner than that. Although representation is based on single-member constituencies, a weighting of constituencies in favor of rural areas enhances Malay representation—in effect almost guaranteeing Malay political power.[8]

## Military

In contrast to Thailand, Indonesia, and Burma, the Malaysian military has not played a major role in politics. In the early years of independence, priority was given to socioeconomic development rather than to building substantial armed forces.[9] When it gained independence, Malaysia had less than one army division, no air force, and no navy. Instead, it relied on a defense arrangement with the British, the Anglo-Malayan Defence Agreement, which was superseded by the Five-Power Defence Arrangement (with Singapore, Great Britain, Australia, and New Zealand). The average government expenditure for the military (13 percent of the budget) is lower than in most of the other nations of Southeast Asia.

The modernization of Malaysia's armed forces helped bring "the Emergency" to an end in 1960 after a twelve-year struggle between communist insurgents and government troops. Malaysian forces were also strengthened during the era of Indonesia's *Konfrontasi* policy in the 1960s, when Indonesian President Sukarno sought to bring down the "neocolonial" Malaysian government. It was not until Vietnam invaded Cambodia in December 1978 that the Malaysian military again perceived a threat to the nation's security. In 1996 Malaysia became a strong supporter of Vietnam's application for membership in ASEAN.

## Opposition Groups

In Malaysia, all Malays are Muslim by legal definition. Islam provides both legal and political privileges to Malays that if lost are tantamount to renunciation of the Malay way of life. Islam, which does not distinguish between secular and religious activities, is tightly organized from the village up to the state level; hence, Muslims can be easily mobilized. Proliferating Muslim youth groups *(Dakwah)*, which tend to be fundamentalist and anti-Western, call for rigid codes of conduct and the implementation of Islamic law, and this increase in Islamic militancy is viewed as threatening by the non-Muslim population. Mahathir has attempted to defuse the Islamic resurgence by a program of "absorption of Islamic values," but this issue fans the contentious flames of communalism.

The religious element is central to Malaysians' political party orientations. Since independence, parties have been defined almost exclusively in terms of their degree of Islamic orthodoxy. Although thus far moderate Islamic parties have been dominant in the ruling alliance, many opposition parties are made up of Islamic fundamentalists, and they use their religious doctrines for political objectives.

Chinese citizens also join political parties that reflect their ethnicity. Most Chinese have joined moderate parties such as the MCA (which has affiliated with the National Front), but radical parties have arisen among the Chinese in reaction to their fear of Islamic militancy and to economic policies that threaten their leading role in the economy.

Communist guerrillas fought against the central authorities beginning in 1948 when members of the Malayan Communist Party (MCP), having participated in the war against the Japanese, took up arms against a state they saw as fascist and anti-Chinese. Known as "the Emergency," this struggle threatened Malayan security until 1960, when the military prevailed, although sporadic fighting continued up to 1989. At that time, the MCP agreed to disarm. As the insurgency was carried out primarily by ethnic Chinese, their activities further worsened racial relations and raised questions about Chinese loyalty to the government. Currently, insurgency plays no role in Malaysia.

## Women

Women's roles in Malaysian politics have been subordinated to those of men because of Muslim teachings and traditional customs, which prescribe that women remain modest and stay in the background. Publicly active women are regarded with amusement and then indignation. Women have thus far not been able to occupy high public office.[10]

With the increasing influence of conservative Islam, women's roles in politics will continue to be circumscribed. Nevertheless, westernization has brought more women into professional and business positions. Moreover, the minister for trade and industry, Puan Rafidah, has been a highly visible woman in national affairs and an active representative of Malaysia internationally.

In party politics, women have formed auxiliary groups to ensure separate involvement. These auxiliaries have provided women with a way to involve themselves in the affairs of the parties while holding to Islamic customs that separate the public activities of men and women.[11] The separateness has guaranteed that women will not be brought into the internal workings of the political parties and that they will not participate in public activities.

## Democratization

As opposed to its neighbors, Malaysia has managed to sustain the institutions of democratic rule. The major exception, following the riots of 1969, was a temporary state of emergency, carried out less as a coup d'état than as an interlude during which parliamentary democracy could be rebuilt.

In contrast to the Indonesians and Vietnamese, the Malaysians had the advantage of not having to struggle against the return of their colonialist ruler after the defeat of Japan at the end of World War II. The granting of independence by Great Britain was carried out peacefully and was received with some reluctance by the Malaysians, who feared that their country's viability would be jeopardized without British support. Nevertheless, the Malaysians adopted the Westminster model of governance, including regularized competitive elections, a representative Parliament, the separation of powers, civilian supremacy, and civil liberties. This is especially noteworthy because Malaysian elites tend to hold a formalized view of democracy that crumbles when it faces more deeply held values; stability and security, for example, take precedence over democratic values.[12] The best example of this phenomenon is the universal acceptance of emergency rule in 1969.

Since independence, Malaysia has witnessed eight national elections—in 1959, 1964, 1969, 1974, 1978, 1982, 1986, and 1990. Opposition candidates won about 40 percent of the votes, although their numbers in the Parliament have been few. During the same period there have been four orderly successions of power. Despite this admirable record, Malaysia is generally regarded as a quasi- or semidemocracy because of limitations on civil liberties.[13] The country's Official Secrets Act, Internal Securities

Act, and Sedition Act have imposed a culture of silence on citizens and prohibited all discussion of "sensitive issues." Newspapers, television, and radio are government- or UMNO-controlled and are generally compliant vis-à-vis all communalism issues. Newspapers that raised "sensitive issues" after the 1987 split in UMNO were shut down when Mahathir invoked the Internal Securities Act.

The explanation for the necessity of quasi-democracy rather than full, Western-style democracy is that Malaysia's polycommunal situation is unique. Such a society cannot carry out its affairs in a fully democratic way if one segment of the society must be given special privileges of governance. For example, under full democracy the loss of an election would be tantamount to total defeat. In the context of communal issues, an election loss by the Alliance (later National Front) would mean the perceived end of the primary rights of the Malays. Emergency rule became necessary in 1969 once the leadership realized that the prospect of an election loss was possible.

The rules for Malaysian democracy, which had to be modified after 1969 to ensure the continuation of Malay political supremacy, were changed to include opposition parties in the Alliance.[14] Dividing the nation along ethnic lines between those in power and those not in power would only worsen communal issues. To mitigate divisiveness, the National Front was created to accommodate a wider range of parties. Even the Islamic-based PAS was initially included in the National Front, but it later withdrew to join the Chinese-oriented DAP in leading the opposition. The Front formula was uniquely Malaysian, reflecting the difficult ethnic sensitivities that have long been at the core of Malaysian politics.

In 1987 the formula broke down when factionalism arose in the National Front, and Prime Minister Mahathir responded harshly. The eruption of serious problems led to the end of the "Malay way." This Malay way, similar to conduct in Indonesia, emphasized the avoidance of conflict and direct confrontation and a reliance on courtesy, compromise, and broad consultation before decisions are made. Openings for reconciliation were always pursued. Mahathir's administrative style, however, has tended more toward confrontation than consensus, and his opponents have responded in kind, thereby departing from the traditional ways of leading the nation.

Malaysia's semidemocracy has been sustained by the continuing strength of the economy, which mitigates extremist demands; by the growing urbanized middle class, which favors moderate policies; and by the country's modern history of British-style democratic institutions. Mahathir's emphasis on "Asian values" has opposed such democratic tendencies, especially regarding the rights to protest and question governmental leaders. On the other hand, these same democratic values have supported the freedom of religion and the importance of education for a wide array of people. Malaysians have been content with the notion of semidemocracy, which they view as appropriate to their values.

## Economic Development

Malaysia has been one of the few success stories of economic development in the Third World. With a per capita GNP of nearly $5,000, Malaysia has surpassed Portugal and Hungary in the world rankings. However, the picture is not all positive. Large pockets of poverty, widening income inequality, and excessive dependence on world prices for primary products are major problems. The extent of Malaysia's dependence on the world economy became strikingly clear in the mid-1980s when the decline in the world price of primary products brought about a recession; and again in 1997 when the Thai currency crisis negatively affected Malaysia.

Despite these problems, there has been a clear improvement in the standard of living since independence in 1957. In 1966 only 18 percent of households in a typical Malaysian village had piped water. By 1978 the this figure was 71 percent and by 1993 close to 100 percent. Electricity was available to 45 percent of households in 1966; this increased to 79 percent in 1978 and 100 percent in 1987. In 1966 only 4 percent of Malay families owned a television; in 1997, the figure was just under 100 percent. During this period, dirt roads were paved, telephone lines were installed, and mosques were built.[15] These figures, valid throughout the country, indicate a rapid economic development achieved by few Third World nations.

In 1971, by means of an unprecedented "new economic policy" (NEP), the Malaysian government initiated an extraordinary twenty-year plan designed to eradicate poverty and eliminate race as a function of economic prosperity. The plan was meant to change Malaysia's fundamental structures and ethnic divisions by directing the increments of rapid economic growth disproportionately to the Malay sector without expropriating Chinese assets or weakening the vigor of Chinese enterprise.[16]

The NEP was the government's response to the 1969 riots and the perceived need for a dramatic attack on the ethnic divisions in the economy. According to government data, in 1971 the ownership of share capital was 63 percent foreign, 34 percent non-Malay, and less than 3 percent Malay. The goal was to raise the Malay share of capital ownership to 30 percent and reduce the foreign share to 30 percent, while allowing the Chinese share to rise to 40 percent.[17] The means to this end were tax breaks, investment incentives, employment quotas, and the granting of special privileges in business ownership. The government required all banks to earmark a significant proportion of their business loans to Malays.

The NEP was to end in 1990; however, as the target of 30 percent capital ownership by Malays had not been met (the estimate in 1989 was about 20 percent), the government appointed a commission to design a new twenty-year policy. The foreign share had fallen from 63 to 33 percent, and the difference was taken up by non-Malays, whose share increased from 34 to 47 percent. Other goals were substantially achieved, including the reduction of the poverty level, which had fallen from 30 percent in 1977 to 17 percent in 1987. Many more *bumiputera* Malays were engaged in businesses in which they had formerly been underrepresented. Investments in agricultural programs and rural development had increased manyfold during the twenty-year NEP.

Under Mahathir, Malaysia emphasized a market-oriented economy, featuring the privatization of public utilities, communications, and transportation; at the same time it also featured state-owned heavy industrialization. Mahathir's Look East policy stressed the adoption of the work ethic and other principles followed by companies in Japan and South Korea as well as increased trade with Asian neighbors. The success of these programs, including 8 percent economic growth in the 1980s and 1990s, led economists to claim that Malaysia had joined Singapore, Taiwan, South Korea, and Hong Kong as Asia's fifth "tiger."

As the world's largest exporter of semiconductors and one of the largest exporters of single-unit air conditioners, textiles, and footwear, Malaysia has become integrated into the world capitalist system. Manufacturing accounted for one-half of total exports in 1990, compared to just 20 percent ten years ago. These increases in manufacturing output, stimulated largely by export-oriented industrialization, have resulted in a much more broadly based economy.

In the 1990s, Malaysia's economic growth rate was one of the highest in the world, averaging 8.3 percent. With low unemployment and inflation rates, with manufacturing production increasing, and with high levels of foreign investment, Malaysia entered the ranks of the NICs, despite Mahathir's denials (he did not want to lose concessionary import tariffs under the generalized system of preferences).

Malaysia's economic success was mitigated, however, by continuing reports that the percentage of Malays sharing in the new wealth had not increased appreciably, despite the stated goals of the NEP. Hence, in 1991, Prime Minister Mahathir introduced a ten-year new development policy, which sought to achieve 30 percent equity for Malays in the economic system. Mahathir set forth his ambitious goal for Malaysia: full development by the year 2020, with the gross domestic product (GDP) eight times larger than that of 1990. Such a noteworthy goal would require an annual growth rate of 7 percent during the intervening thirty years. One measure of the program's success was the decrease in the number of Malaysians living below the poverty level in 1997.

Despite the country's remarkably high growth rates, several potential problems loomed. First, the growth rates required importing plantation workers from Indonesia and Sri Lanka. Second, as wage rates improved, foreign investors looked for alternative sites for their assembly plants. Third, Kuala Lumpur was suffering from rapidly increasing traffic congestion, pollution, and environmental degradation. Fourth, the 1997 currency crisis undermined Malaysian pride in their "miracle" economy and threatened to bring Mahathir's 2020 project crashing down.

## The Malaysian State

Malaysia was granted independence under peaceful circumstances and adopted and adapted British governmental institutions; thus, the country emerged from colonialism with a strong and stable political system. Because of the communal character of their society, Malaysian leaders adapted Western democratic structures in an attempt to provide Malays with dominance of the political realm. This required that the principal institutions of the society be merged with the state.

The clearest example of this close association is the integration of the Alliance (after 1969, the National Front) with the state. As in Indonesia, where Golkar is in essence a state institution, the National Front (led by UMNO) has merged with the state—dominating the bureaucracy, the Parliament, the media, and the courts. This sets Malaysia apart from Thailand and the Philippines, where political parties are relatively autonomous from the state and have minimal influence.

One characteristic of strong states is their ability to project their power into the countryside. Through the co-optation of local Malay elites and the provision of roads, financial credit, medical facilities, recreational programs, and other benefits, the Malaysian state has succeeded in tying local power brokers to the central authorities through either UMNO or local-level governmental agencies.

In economic affairs as well, the Malaysian state has asserted its control. No facet of the economy is excluded from governmental intervention, intended to ensure that the goals of the NEP are met and to provide resources to UMNO. The state has co-opted most of those who could challenge it. Indeed, oppositionists are established supporters of the state, differing only in terms of their desire to replace its political leaders. Thus, the Malaysian state is not subservient to societal forces, such as an autonomous military or insurgency, or to such external powers as a former colonial ruler.

Malaysia's status as a relatively strong state can be explained only partially in terms of its history of social dislocation (a major condition for the development of a strong state). In contrast to Indonesia, which experienced a traumatic colonialism and later had to struggle for independence, Malaysia's colonial situation led to less dislocation. However, the Japanese interregnum; the evolution toward independence; the federation with Singapore, Sabah, and Sarawak; the ouster of Singapore; and the May 1969 ethnic riots provided sufficient dislocation for the development of a strong state.

Dislocation is more likely to lead to a strong state if it occurs at a time in which external political forces favor control. For Thailand in the postwar period, the United States played the role of supporter in order to keep the country from becoming communist. The Thai military also played a primary role in state control, ostensibly to ensure Thai security, although an invasion of Thailand was never a real possibility. Malaysia, even less than many other Southeast Asian nations, was not endangered by external powers, nor did the nation rely on a particular foreign or domestic guarantor of its sovereignty. Thus, in terms of this condition, the Malaysian state was not strengthened.

As in Thailand and Indonesia, Malaysian bureaucrats, technocrats, and ethnic leaders identify their interests with those of the state. Chinese business leaders have joined groups and parties that have been integrated or co-opted into the state system through the National Front. These ethnic leaders have strong constituencies outside the bureaucracy, but they do not constitute a separate power base that opposes the interests of the authorities in power. Instead, they rely on the state to provide them with protection and access to needed resources. Even the NEP, ostensibly a plan to upgrade the status of Malays in the economy, did not attempt to usurp the dominant position of the Chinese; indeed, the Chinese flourished during the twenty years of the NEP. In this respect, Malaysia meets the condition of a strong state in that its societal groups can implement the designs of the state.

The last condition for strong state status is skillful leadership to take advantage of the prevailing conditions. Suharto in Indonesia clearly qualifies as such a leader. Malaysia has also experienced strong leadership, from Tunku Abdul Rahman, the father of Malaysian independence, to the present prime minister, Mahathir. Except for the brief period of the state of emergency in 1969 and the assault on the judiciary by Mahathir in 1988, Malaysian leaders have not undermined the institutions of the state in a manner similar to that of Marcos in the Philippines. On the contrary, each prime minister has strengthened state institutions as a means to promote political stability, economic development, and ethnic harmony. In short, all these perspectives provide a context for assessing the Malaysian state as strong.

## Foreign Policy

Malaysia has not been an interventionist country, nor has it participated prominently in international affairs since its independence in 1957. However, support for ASEAN has long been a first priority for Malaysia as a means to enhance both the nation's security and its economic objectives. Conflict with the Philippines over territory in Sabah has not precluded overall support for ASEAN. Thai-Malaysian relations improved in 1989 when communists in the border area ended their insurgency.

As the primary initiator of the Zone of Peace, Freedom, and Neutrality (ZOPFAN), a policy adopted by ASEAN to reduce intraregional confrontation in Southeast Asia, Malaysia has attempted to reduce its military involvement in the region. When Singapore offered to station U.S. air and naval facilities on its territory, Malaysia argued that the establishment of such a base was against the spirit of ZOPFAN. Nevertheless, Malaysia has supported U.S. military bases in the Philippines.

Malaysia's main adversary has been China because of the support the People's Republic gave to communist insurgents during the Emergency and because of distrust of Malaysia's indigenous Chinese. Nevertheless, in 1974 Malaysia normalized relations with China, although such ties are tenuous because of the domestic communal situation. Malaysia looked skeptically at Thailand's moves toward closer relations with China and Vietnam but then established diplomatic relations and engaged in economic ties with both nations. Economics in the end was determined to be more important than security concerns.

To gain greater international stature commensurate with its economic strength, the Malaysian government pursued and won a seat on the United Nations Security Council, and in 1989 Malaysia hosted the Commonwealth heads of government meeting. This latter event improved relations between Malaysia and Great Britain after a period of tension due to British policy regarding tuition rates for Malaysian students in Great Britain and London's refusal to impose sanctions on South Africa.

Mahathir has been a principal spokesman for the ASEAN Free Trade Area (AFTA) and for Asian trade groups, which, he argues, would counter the North American Free Trade Agreement (NAFTA) as well as the European Union. Mahathir's stance caused tensions with American officials, who argued that Asian groups that did not include Western nations would be regarded as protectionist. Mahathir also became a Third World spokesman against "Western values," which he viewed as inappropriate for Malaysia and other Third World countries.

Malaysia supported the admission of Burma, Laos, and Vietnam into ASEAN. In 1996, tensions with Singapore increased when Singaporean Senior Minister Lee Kuan Yew made the comment that if Singapore ever was forced back into Malaysia, it would be a catastrophe for Singapore's ethnic Chinese because the Malaysian system was "racist." Eventually, the issue was handled diplomatically, but the disagreement reminded many that racial differences in Southeast Asia are often not very deep below the surface.

## Conclusion

The April 1997 parliamentary election continued the established mode of authoritative decisionmaking, with the National Front leading an alliance of parties. These parties have upheld the Bargain, negotiated at the time of independence, which calls for Malay political dominance and non-Malay economic dominance. They have continued to support a refurbished NEP to end poverty and have provided Malays with special privileges.

After the decline of the "Malay way" in 1987, all leaders, including Mahathir, attempted to return to the traditional modes of political negotiation, emphasizing consensus rather than confrontation. The continued economic vibrancy of the country is important for providing a buffer for the Malaysian government, as an economic decline could bring ethnic tensions to the surface. That fear became especially troublesome when the Malaysian economy was hurt by the currency crisis that hovered over most of Southeast Asia in 1997. However, the universal desire for stability, especially now that a large number of citizens have an economic stake in the society, will help ensure the continued capacity of the state to cope with changes.

## Notes

1. Milton J. Esman, "Ethnic Politics and Economic Power," *Comparative Politics*, vol. 19, no. 4 (July 1987), p. 402.

2. Milton J. Esman, *Administration and Development in Malaysia* (Ithaca: Cornell University Press, 1972), pp. 20–22.

3. Diane K. Mauzy, "Malaysia in 1987," *Asian Survey*, vol. 28, no. 2 (February 1988), p. 214.

4. Hari Singh and Suresh Narayanan, "Changing Dimensions in Malaysian Politics," *Asian Survey*, vol. 29, no. 5 (May 1989), p. 517.

5. Stephen A. Douglas, "How Strong Is the Malaysian State?" (paper presented to the Association for Asian Studies, Chicago, April 1990), p. 2.

6. Zakaria Haji Ahmad, "Stability, Security and National Development in Malaysia: An Appraisal," in *Durable Stability in Southeast Asia*, ed. Kusuma Snitwongse and Sukhumbhand Paribatra (Singapore: Institute of Southeast Asian Studies, 1987), p. 125.

7. Doug Tsuruoka, "UMNO's Money Machine," *Far Eastern Economic Review*, July 5, 1990, p. 48.

8. Zakaria Haji Ahmad, "Malaysia: Quasi Democracy in a Divided Society," in *Democracy in Developing Countries: Asia*, ed. Larry Diamond, Juan J. Linz, and Seymour Martin Lipset (Boulder: Lynne Rienner Publishers, 1989), p. 373.

9. Zakaria Haji Ahmad, "The Military and Development in Malaysia and Brunei, with a Short Survey on Singapore," in *Soldiers and Stability in Southeast Asia*, ed. J. Soedjati Djiwandono and Yong Mun Cheong (Singapore: Institute of Southeast Asian Studies, 1988), p. 235.

10. Virginia H. Dancz, *Women and Party Politics in Peninsular Malaysia* (Singapore: Oxford University Press, 1987), p. 6.

11. Ibid., p. 226.

12. For an in-depth analysis of this point, see James C. Scott, *Political Ideology in Malaysia* (New Haven: Yale University Press, 1968).

13. Ahmad, "Malaysia: Quasi Democracy," p. 349.

14. Ibid., p. 358.

15. These figures come from Marvin Rogers, "Patterns of Change in Rural Malaysia: Development and Dependence," *Asian Survey*, vol. 29, no. 8 (August 1989), pp. 767–770.

16. Esman, "Ethnic Politics and Economic Power," p. 403.

17. Ibid.

# 7

# SINGAPORE

The quest for survival, order, and prosperity is a dominant theme of contemporary Singaporean politics. Surrounded by nations hundreds of times larger in area with populations twenty to nearly a hundred times greater, this island city-state is in many respects a speck in a region of giant nations. As a primarily urban entrepôt with virtually no agricultural base, Singapore stands alone, bereft of the resources and land of its neighbors.

Singapore's principal resource is its people. Multiethnic and multicultural, Singapore's 3.1 million citizens are about 77 percent Chinese, 14 percent Malay, 7 percent Indian, and 2 percent other minorities. Singaporeans, who live in a densely populated city, are the wealthiest (with an average per capita GNP of $30,500), best-educated, best-housed, and healthiest population in Southeast Asia. Literacy, for example, is over 90 percent, and among those under 30 years old it is 99 percent.

Singaporeans have access to the most westernized conveniences and public services of the region as well. Having achieved the highest standard of living in Southeast Asia, Singapore's leaders are now attempting to counter what they regard as the undesirable aspects of growing westernization (hedonism, materialism, and self-centeredness) by creating an Asian meritocracy.[1] The importance of creating a quality society is illustrated by the republic's concern about the emigration of almost 5,000 people each year. The primary reasons emigrants give for leaving Singapore are an overemphasis on work and competition, the restrictive regulations that permeate every facet of life, and the concern that their children will not pass the requisite exams to attain elite positions. Singaporean authorities are attempting to find the right formula that emphasizes order and merit while at the same time reducing the stress brought about by the pervasive competitive spirit.

No noncommunist society in Southeast Asia regulates its citizens' behavior as much as Singapore. For example, rules on traffic, street cleanliness, shops and markets, housing, gum chewing, landscaping, and food preparation are strictly enforced by the authorities and rigorously followed by the citizenry. Less corruption exists here than in any other Southeast Asian nation. Although a part of the political system, patronage is less salient in political recruitment and policymaking than is the case in the systems of Singapore's neighbors.

To achieve order, Singapore has fashioned one of the world's most effective and efficient governments. Characterized by democratic institutions but within the context of authoritarian order, Singapore's government has been controlled by a single party, the People's Action Party (PAP), since full independence was obtained in 1965. Until November 1990, Singapore had known only one leader, Lee Kuan Yew, who had led the island since 1957.

The themes of survival, prosperity, and order have become fused in Singapore to produce a unique style of politics and economic life.[2] The fusion stems from colonial times when the British controlled Singapore, making it dependent on British economic policies. After achieving limited independence in 1957, Singapore granted Britain control over its external affairs and security matters out of fear of a seizure of power by the communists or by external intervention. To achieve full independence, the Singaporean economic system established interdependence in the global economic system, and the country allied with its northern neighbor, Malaya, which complemented Singapore economically.

The concern for survival was the major impetus for the decision by Malaya and Singapore to forge the Federation of Malaysia in September 1963, which included Sabah and Sarawak as well. Tunku Abdul Rahman, Malaysia's founding prime minister, feared that Singapore might become communist, an "Asian Cuba." The solution was to accept the city-state as a member of the federation. From the Singaporean perspective, the agricultural resources of Malaya were necessary for their own development. Lee Kuan Yew did not believe that Singapore was viable by itself.

The federation lasted only two years, until August 1965, because the Alliance government in Kuala Lumpur perceived that the Chinese in Singapore were threatening the privileged political position of the Malays. Lee Kuan Yew had called for a "Malaysian Malaysia," with the implication that all Malaysians, regardless of race, could participate equally in all phases of life. This view was contrary to the Tunku's belief that a "Malay Malaysia" was in the society's best interest.

After being ejected from the federation, Singapore again faced the challenge of survival in an era of grave tensions, which stemmed mostly from the global cold war and the *Konfrontasi* threat from Indonesia. Rather than seek a complementary alliance to attain security, Singapore fashioned policies designed to achieve rapid and far-reaching economic development to ensure its sovereignty. By 1969 the government had consolidated the republic's independence, stability, and viability, a consolidation that has lasted to the present. This success has depended on continued economic development and the inculcation of values supportive of a unified, highly educated, quality-oriented Singapore in people from diverse backgrounds.

When Lee Kuan Yew stepped down in November 1990, he sponsored his protégé Goh Chok Tong to become Singapore's second prime minister. Just nine months after becoming the nation's leader, Goh called a snap election to legitimize his administration. Goh needed to step out of the shadow of Lee, who continued to act as Singapore's "senior minister." Goh did not yet have a popular mandate and wanted to take advantage of the country's excellent economy to ensure widespread support for the PAP.[3]

The August 1991 election resulted in a decisive victory for the PAP, although four of the eighty-one seats were won by the opposition Singapore Democratic Party, and the PAP's winning percentage was 61, down from 63 in 1988. Those who voted against the PAP were expressing their desire for an opposition in Parliament and sought to show their disapproval of the rising cost of living. Goh's more consensual approach to governing (in contrast to Lee's more authoritarian style) did not appear to be a factor in determining voter choices.

To shore up his administration even more, in December 1992 Goh stood in a by-election and received a significant victory, capturing 73 percent of the votes in his constituency. Goh's opponent, Chee Soon Juan, a professor at the National University of Singapore, was later charged with "dishonest conduct." Goh also took over from Lee Kuan Yew as the leader of the People's Action Party at this time. There was special poignancy in his victory because in the previous month he had informed the populace that his two deputy prime ministers were both suffering from cancer. The better known of these two was Lee Hsien Loong, minister of trade and industry, the son of Lee Kuan Yew and presumed heir apparent to the position of prime minister. Indeed, many commentators suggested that Goh was only an interim leader until Lee Hsien Loong was ready to assume the top position. The other deputy prime minister diagnosed with cancer was Ong Teng Cheong. Both deputies were immediately treated with chemotherapy and were soon reported to be recovering.

Indeed, in 1993 both men made remarkable comebacks. Ong Teng Cheong was elected for a six-year term as the country's first executive president in August and Lee Hsien Loong returned as the heir apparent to the prime ministership. Ong faced weak opponents, but he received only 58 percent of the votes cast (voting was compulsory). The PAP interpreted this as a rebuke from the public because candidates endorsed by the PAP are usually expected to win about 70 percent of the vote. The position of executive president was intended to be subordinate to the prime ministership, and it has not subsequently become more influential.

In 1995 and 1996, both Lee Kuan Yew and Goh Chok Tong engaged in a series of libel suits against their adversaries, winning every case and thus again demonstrating that the Singaporean judiciary has no autonomy from the executive branch. The PAP routinely wins multimillion dollar defamation awards against political opponents, and has even imprisoned some opposition candidates without charge. *New York Times* columnist William Safire described Singapore as a dictatorship in which students are denied basic freedoms. Goh challenged Safire to a debate, but the issue eventually dissipated. At the same time, the formerly impeccable Lee Kuan Yew and his son Lee Hsien Loong were revealed to have received discounts on two exclusive private condominiums. Lee explained that "it is an unfair world," which did little to mollify those who had supported the government's claim to meritocracy.

On January 2, 1997, parliamentary elections were held, but there was never any question about the outcome. The opposition contested only thirty-six of the eighty-three available seats, and the PAP won 63.5 percent of the total votes cast and eighty-one of the parliamentary seats. This strong showing reversed a downward trend that had reduced the PAP vote in 1991 to 59.3 percent. The Singapore Democratic Party lost every seat it had held. The victory was viewed as a vindication for Goh Chok Tong and his party's economic achievements. Goh interpreted the result as a sign that voters had rejected Western-style liberal democracy; he also saw the outcome as his liberation from the long shadow of Lee Kuan Yew.

The primary issue of the campaign concerned housing. The PAP campaign made it clear that those areas that did not support their candidates would be placed last in line for housing upgrades. Opposition candidates were ridiculed and then when they lost they were sued for slander (the courts determining in favor of the PAP). The election convinced Goh that authoritarian rule would continue in Singapore, with emphasis on economic development, technology, discipline, and international respect. The opposition, as insignificant as it was before the election, was effectively muzzled even more during and after the election.

## Institutions and Social Groups

### Lee Kuan Yew

Few leaders in Southeast Asia have had the impact on their societies that Lee Kuan Yew has had in some thirty years of dominating Singapore. Ho Chi Minh, Sukarno, Suharto, Ne Win, and Norodom Sihanouk had comparable influence, but none ruled a society with as much effectiveness as Lee. First in his class at both Cambridge and Oxford, Lee was a brilliant and pragmatic politician with more popular support than almost any other world leader.

By placing highly educated and technically proficient officials in charge of his development programs, Lee relied on his subordinates to establish effective policies free from corruption. By combining the advantages of Western-style democratic institutions with an Asian-style hegemonic political party system, Lee was able to dominate the country's politics and still achieve universal support and legitimacy.

In the late 1980s, Lee's consummate political skill lost some of its edge, as he moved toward authoritarianism and away from open and pragmatic policies. In a series of decisions concerning the jailing of dissident politicians and the restriction of newspapers printing articles critical of his administration, Lee veered from the careful balance he had achieved between civil liberties and order during the previous decades. Lee rationalized the new direction toward tighter order as necessary for the continued stability of the country and as appropriate for Asian culture.

Following his resignation as prime minister in 1990, Lee became senior minister and venerated statesman. He traveled extensively, advising developing nations on how to achieve the economic miracle he had overseen in Singapore. He stressed the importance of discipline and denigrated Western-style democracy as inappropriate for developing countries. He also gave up his position as secretary-general of the PAP in order to allow Goh to assume the legitimacy he needed to govern effectively.

In November 1991, the Parliament passed the Elected President Act, which provided for a stronger presidency but retained the cabinet, headed by the prime minister. Initially, it was believed that Lee would be nominated for the presidency, but he denied interest in a position that he judged too subordinate.

## Political Parties

The People's Action Party has been almost synonymous with Lee Kuan Yew and with governance in Singapore. The PAP has been in power since 1959; more striking than its uninterrupted rule, however, is the fact that since 1968 the PAP has won all but a handful of hundreds of parliamentary seats, garnering from 61 to a high of 84 percent of the vote.

The only party ever to provide credible opposition was the left-wing Barisan Sosialis (Socialist Front), which split from the PAP in the 1960s. Since that time, opposition parties have been allowed to function, but none have provided meaningful competition to the PAP. The reasons for the PAP's dominance include the factionalization of the opposition, the effectiveness and incorruptibility of most PAP politicians, the ability of the PAP to meet the needs of the people, and the rigid rules that circumscribe the activities of political parties and opposition groups, which were especially important in the late 1980s when newspapers were censored and suspected communists arrested. The other major reason for the success of the PAP is the reluctance of the electorate to risk undoing a system that has been working so well by voting in alternative leadership. To many Singaporeans, the PAP is indispensable for continuation of the extraordinary economic development and societal stability the city-state has enjoyed since independence.

Unlike most hegemonic parties, the PAP does not have a large staff to perform research and stage functions.[4] Instead, civil bureaucrats outside the party perform these functions, leaving the PAP visible only before general elections. To ensure its continued dominance, the PAP has prepared for succession through its self-renewal program, choosing young candidates who are more in tune with the electorate. In the 1988 election, virtually every PAP candidate was from the younger generation. Nevertheless, the percentage of votes won by PAP candidates decreased between 1980 and 1991. In 1980 the party won 77.7 percent of the votes; by August 1991, this figure had dropped to 61 percent. In the 1988 election, campaigning on a slogan of "more good years," the PAP won 80 of 81 parliamentary seats. In 1991, the party won 77 of 81 seats; and in 1997, with 63.5 percent of the vote, it won 81 of 83 seats.

## Legislature

Singapore's parliamentary system is a legacy of British colonialism, even though its practice is much different from that of today's Great Britain. In contrast to the British bicameral system, the Singaporean parliamentary system is unicameral and has presented no meaningful opposition to the administration. Legislators are elected to five-year terms, unless the prime minister dissolves Parliament before the term ends.

To ensure a semblance of bipartisanship, in 1984 the Parliament provided for three opposition seats, to be awarded even if opposition candidates did not win in any constituency. These three nonconstituency members would be appointed from among the highest-polling opposition candidates as long as they had won at least 15 percent of the votes cast in the constituency.[5] Nonconstituency oppositionists were not accorded full voting rights; they were prohibited from voting on motions relating to constitutional amendments, money bills, or votes of no confidence in the government. The opposition saw this change as tokenism rather than a meaningful commitment to open politics.

Another major change in parliamentary procedures is the "Team MP" scheme. Beginning with the 1988 election, in certain constituencies the electorate voted for a team of candidates instead of only one candidate. Certain constituencies are declared Group Representation Constituencies (GRCs), and each is represented by three members of Parliament. No more than half of the total number of constituencies can be GRCs. At least one of the three candidates in a GRC is required to be an ethnic minority (non-Chinese). The team that wins a plurality of the total vote is elected.[6]

The purpose of Team MP is to institutionalize multiracial politics by ensuring that minorities will be represented in Parliament by getting them elected on the coattails of others.[7] The PAP was confident that the change would not threaten its ability to win. Indeed, in the 1988 election the PAP won all but one parliamentary seat, and in the 1997 election all but two seats.

In another attempt to bring alternative ideas to Parliament while sustaining traditional values, six distinguished individuals from the community, academia, the military, the professions, and trade unions were selected to serve as nonvoting members. This innovation also did not imperil the PAP's dominance.

## Democratization

The case of Singapore raises the question of whether a one-party state can be democratic. From a Western perspective, the governmental system of Singapore does not meet the criteria of full civil liberties and competitive choices of leaders. From the Chinese perspective, the paternalistic nature of the government is appropriate, providing, as it does, law and order as well as economic achievement without relying on oppression. Lee Kuan Yew agrees with Sukarno's rationale for guided democracy in Indonesia and has said that Western-style majority rule leads to chaos, instability, dissension, and inefficiency.

Prime Minister Lee argued that in the Chinese tradition there was no concept of a loyal opposition. For example, it was not possible to support an opposition candidate without withdrawing total support from the government. This tradition stemmed from Confucian philosophy, which stressed the principles of centralized authority. Obligation to those in authority was the cement of the Confucian order. As long as the authorities were meeting the needs of the people and leading according to moral principles, the ruler was considered to have the mandate of heaven and was therefore deemed legitimate by the public. Singaporeans do not swing back and forth from opposition to support for the PAP. Given this cultural perspective, a strong one-party system is most conducive to effective rule.[8]

One-party systems can provide policy alternatives if there are differences in opinion among the party leaders. Moreover, if two-way communication between the government and the people is established, the citizenry can assert influence over public policy. In Singapore, a high degree of intraparty factionalism occurs, with varying points of view aired publicly. In addition, the PAP has established grassroots organizations, including Citizens' Consultative Committees designed to elicit ideas from the public. Singapore's semidemocracy has provided the republic with effective, but not always accountable, government, consistent with its traditions and history and supportive of the goals of development, order, and merit.

## Economic Development

It is impossible to make generalizations about Singapore's economic development because the nation's status as a city-state sets it fundamentally apart from its neighbors. With no agricultural base, Singapore is destined to become increasingly interdependent with the global economic system to ensure its survival.

Singapore is a mixture of capitalist and socialist economics, with emphasis on the former. The PAP leadership inherited a capitalist economic system from the British and has created state institutions such as the Housing and Development Board, which houses about 80 percent of the population.

With the exception of two years in the mid-1980s when the economy suffered negative growth, Singapore has consistently posted the region's highest growth rates. The 11 and 9 percent rates in 1988 and 1989, respectively, accompanied by an inflation rate of less than 3 percent, are indicative of this growth. These growth rates are largely the result of an outward-looking, export-oriented strategy begun after 1965 to accelerate the manufacture of consumer products, obtain needed outside capital, and reduce unemployment. Foreign investment increased from $0.3 billion in 1967 to $2.3 billion in 1972 and to $8 billion in the mid-1980s. Unemployment dropped from 13 percent at the beginning of the 1960s to under 3 percent in the 1980s. Singapore now hires foreign nationals to supplement its workforce.

Singapore's major export, electronic products, accounts for over 60 percent of domestic exports. Such a large percentage makes the Singaporean economy dependent on continued good prices for its products. Reduced global demand for personal computers and semiconductors could immediately undermine Singapore's economy. The republic has one of the highest trading-to-GDP ratios in the world; thus, an international recession could devastate Singapore, as almost happened for a brief time in

1985.[9] Today, Singapore's primary trading partner is the United States, followed by Japan, Malaysia, Hong Kong, Thailand, Australia, and Germany.

In anticipation of changes in the world economy, Singapore launched its "Second Industrial Revolution" in 1979, designed to restructure the economy toward high-tech industries. The plan was to manufacture exports of superb quality, win higher salaries for workers, upgrade job skills, and reduce dependence on foreign workers. The economy emphasized automotive components, machine tools, computers, electronic instrumentation, medical instruments, and precision engineering.

The revolution was a success until 1985, when the protectionist tendencies of developed countries hurt Singaporean exports. Low petroleum prices dealt a sharp blow to the ship repairing and shipbuilding industries (which made up one quarter of the manufacturing sector), and high wages were not matched by growth in productivity.[10] Finally, the continued high rate of national savings (42 percent of GDP) could not become a part of productive domestic investments.

After state intervention had corrected each of these difficulties, the economy responded rapidly, leading Singapore to a period of remarkable growth. As the economy diversified, financial and business services displaced manufacturing as the economy's leading sectors. Not content with the level of economic development, Lee Kuan Yew set forth a controversial program to improve the country's gene pool. He determined that the quality of the people was the most important factor responsible for a country's rapid development, and he arranged a program to encourage the marriage and procreation of the well-educated populace, giving incentives for educated mothers to have more children.

The early 1990s continued with solid 6–7 percent growth rates, although these percentages were down from previous years. Despite this record, several problems faced the economy. Seventy percent of domestic exports were produced by multinational corporations, perpetuating the nation's dependence on foreign-owned companies. Exports were not broadly based, with almost two-thirds of exports (in terms of value) in electronics and with the United States buying fully one-third of all exports. While Singapore lost its generalized system of preferences (GSP) rating in 1991 because it was named a developed economy, other less-developed Third World nations continued to reap the trade advantages of GSP status. The rising importance of China and Vietnam as potential economic rivals caused Singapore's leaders to place new stress on competitiveness and quality of output.

The Singapore economy is interdependent with the global economic system. With a diversified economy, one of the best infrastructures for transportation in the world, superb medical care, the highest standard of living in all Southeast Asia, a highly educated and technologically proficient population, and good relations with its neighbors, Singapore's prospects for continued high levels of economic development are excellent.

Given these achievements, it is surprising that many Singaporeans choose to leave the city-state. One explanation is that for many citizens Singapore's traditions and culture have been swallowed by the forces of economic development. Huge housing projects have undermined the traditional extended family. Modern glass-and-steel skyscrapers have replaced traditional Chinese architecture. Impersonal rules and regulations have supplanted personal relations as the arbitrator of behavior. For many Singaporeans, the city has become devoid of spirit, heart, and vitality, characteristics that have been displaced by a materialistic coldness symbolized by the nation's ubiquitous rules and prohibitions.

## The Singaporean State

By most reckoning, Singapore does not have the requisites for a strong state. Geographically, the country is minuscule and has no important natural resources. Although it boasts the highest per capita income in Southeast Asia (except for the anomaly of Brunei), its total GNP is far smaller than that of Indonesia, the Philippines, Malaysia, or Thailand. Singapore's military is capable of only minor defensive operations. Viewed in these terms, Singapore does not have the wherewithal to be a strong state.

Nevertheless, using different criteria, Singapore's state can be considered strong. Its leaders use the agencies of the state to get Singaporeans to do what they want them to do. In no other Southeast Asian society do the citizens follow the dictates of the state with the same regularity as in Singapore. Taxes are paid, young men accept compulsory military conscription, and traffic rules are followed. Few autonomous groups compete for influence in the society. Indeed, the state has co-opted the bureaucracy, the military, and interest groups, while the hegemonic PAP—itself a creature of Lee Kuan Yew—has co-opted the state.

In explaining or understanding the high capacity of the state in Singapore, it becomes apparent that the country's small size is a major advantage in strengthening the state. Although Singapore is heterogeneous in the ethnic sense, a more important fact is that its society is quite homogeneous culturally. All Singaporeans are urban and united in their goals for their society. Living in fewer than 225 square miles (smaller than the Jakarta metropolitan area), citizens have little room for nonconformity. One need simply compare Singapore with Indonesia—where 200 million people live across thousands of islands and speak hundreds of languages—to get a rough idea of the vast differences between the two countries.

A necessary condition for a strong state is massive social dislocation that has weakened the capacity of a people or a society sufficiently to inhibit or preclude state strength.[11] This condition, so clearly evident in Indonesia, has not occurred in Singapore. Singapore's post–World War II history has generally been stable, including its peaceful transition from colonial status to independence. Its expulsion from Malaysia was wrenching, strengthening the politics of survival, but it was not as traumatic as the anticolonialist wars fought by Indonesia, Burma, or Vietnam. Rather than massive dislocation, continuity characterized Singapore's transition to full independence.

States are strengthened when external forces favor concentrated social control. As in most of Southeast Asia, where the international modus operandi in the postwar era was cold war politics, Singapore was a recipient of Western aid to ensure that communism would not prevail. Also, in the period of the Vietnam War and in the 1980s, a tremendous growth in external investments occurred. The impact of aid and overseas investment was important for strengthening the role of the Singaporean state.

Serious military threats, whether they be internal or external, also facilitate the emergence of a strong state, and this condition was supportive of the strong state in Singapore. In the 1960s, when the PAP was factionalized into left-wing and moderate groups, Lee Kuan Yew's victory over the Left was interpreted as a victory over communism and, therefore, as a victory for the survival of the country's democratic system. Lee justified his "administrative state" as necessary for the concentration of power and for repressing internal and external enemies of the state.

Another condition conducive to state strength is the presence of a social grouping, independent of existing bases of social control, that is skillful enough to execute the designs of state leaders.[12] The technocrats in Singapore are among the most educated and skilled in Southeast Asia, and Prime Ministers Lee and Goh have turned policymaking over to these officials. Incorruptible and effective, they appear to be unbeholden to any particular societal groups. Instead, they are integrated into the state through the PAP or the ministries. Their lack of any mass political base reinforces their loyalty to the state.

The final condition for a strong state is skillful leadership, and here Singapore is the quintessential example. For many Singaporeans, Lee Kuan Yew *was* the state. His strength came less from charisma or repression than from his extraordinary capabilities to fashion an effective state. This condition alone appears to have moved Singapore into the ranks of the strong states, despite the absence of what was thought to be the necessary condition of massive state dislocation.

Singapore is the most disciplined society in Southeast Asia, in part because of its citizens' fear of being fined or punished and in part because these citizens genuinely believe lawful obedience to be in the public interest.[13] Certainly, the government has set forth strict and often ridiculed measures to ensure orderly behavior (such as installing urine detection devices in housing block elevators that, if the rider urinates, lock the elevator door until authorities arrive). Although the Chinese heritage is one of discipline for the common good, at the time of independence Singaporeans behaved no differently from their neighbors. The difference is that, since then, the Singaporean state has had the capacity to exploit that heritage to help it achieve its aims of survival, economic development, meritocracy, and order. The price it has paid is a lack of meaningful popular participation in the affairs of state and a sanitized society that has lost much of its soul.

## Foreign Policy

Singapore did not take charge of its foreign relations until 1965, when the republic was expelled from the Federation of Malaysia. Since then, the basic theme of foreign policy has been survival. As a small city-state with only minimal military capacity, Singapore has looked to Western powers and Japan to balance the influence of the Soviet Union (in the 1970s and 1980s) and China in Southeast Asia. Unabashedly anticommunist, Singapore supported the U.S. war in Vietnam and was a principal spokesman for a hard-line policy toward the Vietnamese government. More recently, Singapore has become a major investor in the Vietnamese economy.

Despite its pro-U.S. stance, Singapore has enunciated a policy of neutrality, avoiding embroilment in major power conflicts. Nevertheless, certain issues have strained Singapore-U.S. relations. In 1988 Singapore accused Washington of interfering in its domestic affairs and expelled a U.S. diplomat who allegedly encouraged a high-profile dissident to organize a group of opposition candidates. Bad feelings also arose when President Reagan removed Singapore from the GSP. The GSP had allowed selected goods to enter the United States duty free, but Singapore had attained the status of an NIC and was no longer eligible for this benefit. Relations improved when Singapore offered to host an increased U.S. military presence in response to the prospect that the United States would be expelled from the Philippines.

Relations between Singapore and the United States reached a new low in 1994 over the case of Michael Fay, an American teenager who was caned for an act of vandalism. U.S. public opinion polls indicated that most Americans supported Singapore's corporal punishment. The Clinton administration campaigned for a pardon for Fay, but Singapore's contemptuous response was to reduce his sentence from six lashes of the cane to four.

ASEAN was Singapore's primary instrument of foreign policy for trade matters and for security from outside aggression as well as internal subversion. Moreover, Singapore became China's fourth largest investor after Japan, the United States, and Hong Kong.

By 1997, Singapore had achieved its goal of survival. It was no longer threatened by internal insurgency or external intervention, and it was surrounded by large nations that had no capacity or desire to intervene in the affairs of the republic. As the cold war diminished and as regional and international ties improved, Singapore's security was strengthened accordingly.

## Conclusion

Singapore's singularity does not allow for meaningful comparisons with other countries. Indeed, Singapore is an exception in Southeast Asia in terms of culture, ethnicity, geography, state capacity, and level of economic development. Thus, the city-state is not a useful model for Southeast Asian nations to emulate because its conditions are so different from those of every other country in the region. The smooth succession from Lee to second-generation leaders bodes well as a sign of stability and continuing development. However, because of its persistently authoritarian nature, Singapore is becoming an anomaly in an increasingly democratic era.

## Notes

1. Thomas J. Bellows, "Singapore in 1989," *Asian Survey*, vol. 30, no. 2 (February 1990), p. 202.

2. Lee Boon Hiok, "Political Institutionalization in Singapore," in *Asian Political Institutionalization*, ed. Robert A. Scalapino, Seizaburo Sato, and Jusuf Wanandi (Berkeley: Institute of East Asian Studies, University of California, 1986), p. 202.

3. This section relies on Shee Poon Kim, "Singapore in 1991," *Asian Survey*, vol. 32, no. 2 (February 1992), pp. 119–125; and Hussin Mutalib, "Singapore in 1992," *Asian Survey*, vol. 33, no. 2 (February 1993), pp. 194–199.

4. Lee, "Political Institutionalization in Singapore," p. 207.

5. Chan Heng Chee, "The PAP in the Nineties: The Politics of Anticipation," in *ASEAN in Regional and Global Context*, ed. Karl D. Jackson, Sukhumbhand Paribatra, and J. Soedjati Djiwandono (Berkeley: Institute of East Asian Studies, University of California, 1986), p. 173.

6. Bellows, "Singapore in 1989," p. 146.

7. Lee Lai To, "Singapore in 1987," *Asian Survey*, vol. 28, no. 2 (February 1988), p. 203.

8. Far Eastern Economic Review, *Asia Yearbook, 1991* (Hong Kong: Far Eastern Economic Review, 1990), pp. 214–215.

9. Chan Heng Chee, "Singapore: Domestic Structure and Foreign Policy," in *Asia and the Major Powers: Domestic Politics and Foreign Powers*, ed. Robert A.

Scalapino, Seizaburo Sato, Jusuf Wanandi, and Sung-joo Han (Berkeley: Institute of East Asian Studies, University of California, 1988), p. 284.

10. Jon S. T. Quah, "Singapore in 1987," in *Southeast Asian Affairs 1988* (Singapore: Institute of Southeast Asian Studies, 1988), p. 249.

11. Joel S. Migdal, *Strong Societies and Weak States: State-Society Relations and State Capabilities in the Third World* (Princeton: Princeton University Press, 1988), p. 269.

12. Ibid., p. 274.

13. Donald K. Emmerson, "Beyond Zanzibar: Area Studies, Comparative Politics, and the 'Strength' of the State in Indonesia" (paper presented to the Association for Asian Studies, Chicago, April 1990), pp. 28–29.

# 8

# NEGARA BRUNEI DARUSSALAM

Negara Brunei Darussalam is the official name of the country known informally as Brunei. Overlooking the South China Sea, Brunei is located on the island of Borneo and is divided into two sectors surrounded by the Malaysian state of Sarawak. With a population of only 300,000 and one of the highest annual per capita incomes in Southeast Asia (estimated to be about $20,400), Brunei, together with Singapore, is unlike other nations in the region.

About 70 percent of the people of Brunei are ethnically Malay, and most of this group works in the public sector. The Chinese community, which makes up nearly one third of the population (but for the most part does not have Bruneian citizenship), supplies most of the nonpublic workforce. Islam is the state religion.

Brunei achieved internal self-government in 1959 when the sultan promulgated the country's first constitution, thereby ending British administration and ensuring that power would be transferred to the ruling dynasty rather than to the people. Foreign and military affairs were still handled by the British, however, until full independence was achieved on January 1, 1984. Ironically, the sultan was reluctant to accept independence because he feared his new nation would be vulnerable to attack from its larger neighbors, Indonesia and Malaysia.

Brunei's reluctance to assume full independence also stemmed from the monarch's fear that externally supported revolts could undermine the royalty's prerogatives. Therefore, British security was needed to shore up the royal family's absolute rule. The most threatening incident occurred in 1962 when a revolt led by A. M. Azahari, who favored popular representation, convinced the royal family that its continued rule was in jeopardy. (Azahari fled to Indonesia, where he remains in exile.)

Following independence, Brunei achieved political stability and economic development primarily because of enormous revenues from oil and natural gas. These funds allowed the government to establish a cradle-to-grave welfare system (facetiously known as the "Shellfare" state) that provided, among other things, free education and health care programs as well as subsidies for housing, cars, funerals, and pilgrimages to Mecca. Moreover, there is no income tax. These benefits are partially responsible for the high degree of legitimacy accorded the absolute monarchy and for the continuity of governmental institutions.

The national ideology of Brunei is *Malay Islamic Beraja* (MIB), which means Malay Muslim Monarchy. The ideology emphasizes Malay-style Islam, with the monarchy as the defender of the faith and the people. MIB also discourages westernization and secularism. All public ceremonies and the school curriculum include MIB teachings.

When the sultan celebrated twenty-five years on the throne in 1992, he strengthened the concept of MIB, drawing from traditional Malay kingship and binding with traditional Islam. MIB provides special status for Brunei's indigenous Malays and requires unquestioning deference to the throne. The purpose of MIB is ostensibly to keep unwanted foreign influences out of Brunei.

In honor of his jubilee year, the sultan built a new state mosque on the outskirts of Brunei's capital, Bandar Seri Begawan, at a cost of $30 million. Many Bruneians believed that the sultan would establish democratic institutions during the celebrations. Instead, he announced that political parties and elections were still proscribed and that the monarchy was the proper way to bring benefits to the people. He tightened internal security, increased defense spending, purchased jet fighters from Great Britain, and diversified the economy to end the nation's dependence on oil and gas. Very little dissident political activity has been allowed, and although democracy activists carefully push for a more open society, most Bruneians appear content with their Islamic monarchy.

## Institutions and Social Groups

### Sultanate

The sultanate is the embodiment of the state, and Sultan Sir Muda Hassanal Bolkiah—the twenty-ninth ruler in a dynasty that originated in the thirteenth century—is an absolute monarch whose legitimacy derives from his heredity, not from popular elections or accountability to Bruneians. He is the son of Sultan Haji Omar Ali Saifuddien Sa'adul Khairi Waddien, ibn Almarhum Sultan Mohammad Jamulul Alam, who was known as the Sultan Seri Begawan. Bandar Seri Begawan is named in his honor. Although the Seri Begawan abdicated in favor of his son in 1967, he attempted to keep ultimate power for himself so that the present sultan was not able to rule unconditionally until the death of his father in 1986.

At age 51 (in 1997), the sultan lives in a palace with 1,700 rooms and rules in the style of classic potentates. There is no distinction between the wealth of the state and the personal riches of the sultan; thus, he is reputed to be the richest man in the world (worth about $38 billion). All the state's revenues and reserves are his, and he alone decides what portion goes for state expenditures.[1] The sultan has attempted to shed his playboy image and to nurture a new image as a responsible, benevolent ruler. He has made three pilgrimages to Mecca to shore up his credentials as a devout Muslim.

However, numerous stories of the sultan's philandering have undermined his attempt to create a more positive image. In 1993, Filipino senators investigated reports that some of their country's best known actresses, models, and singers had engaged in prostitution while visiting Brunei. The senators reported a "high-class white slavery ring." Also, a former Miss USA made headlines with allegations of sexual abuse by Bruneian royalty. And in another case, the sultan eventually fired his brother from the position of finance minister after newspapers reported the brother's involvement in sexual orgies.

The sultan has ceremonial responsibilities and, as the nation's prime minister and defense minister, administrative duties through which he exercises total control over the day-to-day affairs of the state. There is no legislative body, the cabinet is made up principally of members of the sultan's own royal family, and there is no dissent from the populace because the sultan has absolute powers. His power is enhanced by the fact that he oversees the government bureaucracy, which employs an estimated two-thirds of Brunei's total workforce. The hierarchical nature of Bruneian society has made open communication with the sultan impossible for the common people. He is the head of state, the prime minister, the defense minister, and the leader of the faith.

Despite his announcement that Brunei would remain free from bourgeois decadence, Brunei has loosened up to some degree in an effort to attract tourism and Western business elites. New Western-style restaurants (including a McDonalds) have been established. Bookstores and movie theaters have opened and satellite TV is ubiquitous. Even hard liquor is available (although the nation is legally dry). In 1996, the American pop singer Michael Jackson presented a free concert for the sultan's fiftieth birthday, although he apparently was asked to swivel less than usual.

## Military

The Royal Brunei Armed Forces (RBAF), with about 4,000 members (the strength of a brigade group with support elements), is the smallest military force in ASEAN. This voluntarily recruited, highly paid national defense force represents a state that spends a higher proportion of its budget on defense than any other ASEAN nation. The RBAF is augmented by such mercenary forces as a battalion of British Army Gurkhas and is directly at the disposal of the sultan. This force helps to ensure that there will be no revolt against the sultan's rule.

## Political Parties

Brunei has no viable political parties, nor has the government mobilized its own party as is the case in Indonesia and Burma. In 1985 the Partai Kebangsaan Demokratik Brunei (Brunei National Democratic Party) was established, with a moderate platform based on Islam and liberal nationalism, with the aim of achieving a system of parliamentary democracy under a constitutional monarchy. In 1986 leaders of the party called for elections and for the sultan to give up his position as prime minister so that his royal position would not be sullied by involvement in politics. Not surprisingly, these leaders were arrested in 1988, and the party was deregistered by the sultan.

The Brunei Solidarity National Party was allowed to register in 1995 but folded almost immediately. Led by Haji Abdul Latif Chuchu, the party was not allowed to present alternative leaders, and members were not allowed to meet as a group.

## Democratization

There is no democracy in Brunei. The country's political system is an absolute monarchy, with no representative form of government. The 1984 constitution consolidated the power of the monarchy by suspending parliamentary institutions. All communications throughout the country are controlled by the sultan; for example, Brunei's only newspaper is strictly monitored by the royal family.

In the absence of democratic institutions, the sultan has initiated a "visit the people" program in which he encourages his subjects to voice their grievances. In 1989, more than a thousand residents attended a meeting at which they were allowed to express their views on government policy. However, it was not clear if this "town hall" meeting would become a regular occurrence or if the grievances would be addressed.[2] Eventually, the meetings fizzled out. Brunei remained under emergency decrees through 1997.

## Economic Development

Vast oil reserves make the dynamics of Brunei's economy different from the agriculturally based economies of other Southeast Asian nations. In 1996, oil and natural gas represented 40 percent of the GDP (down from 80 percent in 1985) and accounted for the great majority of export earnings. In view of the estimated twenty-year limit to Brunei's oil resources, the nation's Fifth and Sixth National Development Plans (1986–1990, 1991–1995) emphasized diversification of the economy by developing small industries based on agriculture, forestry, and fisheries. Newly discovered oil and gas have increased reserves to thirty to fifty years. The government has identified industries that could eventually offer employment and revenue in place of the oil industry as oil reserves are depleted. These alternative industries include pharmaceuticals, cement, steel, chemicals, ceramics, and high technology.[3] Garment manufacturing has increased as have cash crops.

The capital and technology for oil are acquired from abroad and have little impact on the other sectors of Brunei's economy. Most of the oil is exported, so the major result is that the state is provided with income; hence, any developmental effects that are derived from the oil sector depend on what is done with the profits. Brunei has chosen to use the profits to develop infrastructural facilities and a comprehensive welfare system.[4]

The recession in 1985—when Brunei, like Singapore, suffered negative economic growth—resulted from the cutback in oil production to conserve reserves and stop oil prices from falling. The recession also emphasized the need for alternative employment opportunities. Moreover, Brunei's dependence on other countries for its food had reduced the nation's autonomy. One of the priorities of the latest development plan was to boost rice production so that Brunei could meet 30 percent of its rice needs locally. Nevertheless, in 1997 Brunei was still importing over 90 percent of its foodstuffs. Brunei's welfare state mitigates the impact of recessions, as the citizens' basic educational and health care needs are provided free and their housing, religious, and cultural needs are subsidized.

## The Bruneian State

Brunei's small size makes governance far easier than in the larger and more diverse countries elsewhere in Southeast Asia. Moreover, the state has brought virtually all institutions into its fold, leaving no autonomous societal groups to compete with the state apparatus. There is an essential identity between the state and the person of the sultan. The welfare state provides all basic needs of most Bruneians; thus, there is little dissension with the absolute powers of the sultan. His lineage and royal aura and his leadership of Islam in Brunei further strengthen his position. Nevertheless, there have been moves to establish groups calling for the formation of democratic institutions and the relegation of the sultan to ceremonial rather than administrative functions.

Brunei has not experienced the massive social dislocation in the contemporary period that could explain its strong state status. The government has pointed to Indonesian and Malaysian support for past revolts as a major reason for the constraints imposed on the people's right to establish political groupings. However, the sultan's supreme role does not constitute a sufficient cause that clears the way for the installation of a new, state-sponsored strategy for survival. Brunei has experienced no event equivalent to the violent independence struggle in Indonesia, the destruction in the Philippines during World War II, or the Indochina war.

Brunei has received considerable aid and support from its former colonial ruler, Great Britain, and the presence of the Gurkhas has strengthened the state by intimidating potential dissidents. There is no major external threat to Brunei's security today, nor has there been since 1962 when Indonesia supported the Azahari revolt. No dissident groups have been allowed to grow to the point at which they pose a meaningful threat to the regime. Thus, Brunei's experience contrasts with that of Indonesia, where the internal communist threat was considered sufficiently dangerous to justify mass bloodletting and repression.

Every official, technocrat, and military officer in Brunei is related—directly or indirectly—to the sultan, his family, and his advisers. These persons do not have another base of social control independent of the state; the sultan is the state, and all officials are part of his entourage. The lack of any mass political base in Bruneian society has reinforced these officials' loyalty to the state. Nevertheless, they are skilled and highly educated. Even the Chinese community is loyal to the state, despite the fact that most Chinese in Brunei are not even citizens. However, their businesses depend on the sultan's continued largesse and support.

Sultan Sir Muda Hassanal Bolkiah has grown in his position. He was in the shadow of his father until 1986 and has only recently shown his leadership skills. His plan to diversify the economy in anticipation of the time when oil revenues will no longer be available is far-reaching. However, his unwillingness to move toward a more democratic government is effective in the short run but problematic in the long run, as increased communications and economic development bring the modern world to Brunei.

## Foreign Policy

Just one week after gaining full independence in 1984, Brunei joined ASEAN, strengthening its relationships with former adversaries such as Indonesia and Malaysia. Today, Brunei's foreign policy is pro-Western and anticommunist, and its central aim is security attained through international legitimacy. ASEAN membership has been the primary means to that end.

Since independence, Brunei's relations with the United States have been close. Indeed, according to media sources, Brunei channeled some

$10 million to help the U.S.-backed Contras in Nicaragua after depositing the money in a Swiss bank account in 1986, and the Bruneian government confirmed that "His Majesty the Sultan of Brunei Darussalam had made a personal donation to the United States to be used for humanitarian purposes in Central America."[5] This incident became part of U.S. President Ronald Reagan's "Irangate" imbroglio, and thus it was the first that most Americans had ever heard about Brunei. In keeping with the country's generally pro-Western foreign policy, Brunei supported the U.S. policy to liberate Kuwait (an allied sultanate) from Iraq in 1990.

To help defend the nation and to discourage any attempt to challenge the sultan's absolute rule, the Bruneian government pays the full costs of stationing a British Gurkha brigade in Bruneian territory. At present, however, perhaps because Brunei is not threatened by any external power, the country has adopted a low-key foreign policy that is more reactive than proactive. Its main concerns are participating in ASEAN programs and building its diplomatic missions abroad to ensure future investments in the Bruneian economy. In 1997, Brunei pointed to China's forward position in the Spratly Islands as a justification for acquiring new weapons systems.

## Conclusion

As is true of most other states in the region, there are discrepancies in the explanation of conditions for a strong state in Brunei, whose absolute monarchy is increasingly an anachronism in the changing world of Southeast Asia. As the world moves toward open societies and governmental accountability to the people, Brunei continues to more closely resemble a Middle Eastern kingdom. The country's capacity to sustain absolutism results from the great wealth brought in by the sale of oil and gas. In a country surrounded by agricultural societies in which most of the people are poor, the sultan has "bought" his legitimacy by providing his subjects with all of life's necessities and, indeed, with luxuries.

## Notes

1. D. S. Ranjit Singh, "Brunei Darussalam in 1987: Coming to Grips with Economic and Political Realities," in *Southeast Asian Affairs 1988* (Singapore: Institute of Southeast Asian Studies, 1988), p. 63.

2. Bruce Burton, "Brunei Darussalam in 1989: Coming of Age Within ASEAN," *Asian Survey*, vol. 30, no. 2 (February 1990), p. 198.

3. Far Eastern Economic Review, *Asia Yearbook, 1990* (Hong Kong: Far Eastern Economic Review, 1990), p. 91.

4. K. U. Menon, "Brunei Darussalam in 1986," in *Southeast Asian Affairs 1987* (Singapore: Institute of Southeast Asian Studies, 1987), p. 86.

5. Ibid., p. 99.

# 9

# BURMA

On June 18, 1989, the martial law government of Burma declared that the country's official name (in English) would henceforth be Myanmar.[1] Myanmar is a transliteration of what has been the country's official name in the Burmese language. The disadvantage of the name Myanmar (as well as of the name Burma) is that it has ethnic connotations, implying that the country is the land of the majority ethnic group—the Burmans. About a dozen non-Burman minority groups make up more than one-third of the total population of 50 million; thus, there has long been ethnic sensitivity to the dominant position of the Burmans. The name "Myanmar" has not been accepted by scholars of Burma who view the change as temporary until the illegitimate military government is overthrown.

As most of the nations of Southeast Asia moved toward economic development and democratization, Burma was a clear exception. Characterized by ethnic conflict, economic stagnation, and political oppression, Burma has been unable to achieve *pyidawtha*—the ideal peaceful, happy, and prosperous society. Failure to reach this goal has been all the more tragic because the nation is rich in natural and human resources and because the Burmese came close to securing their political rights in 1988 when they revolted against their military leaders. Carrying out their own version of "People Power," the Burmese exalted in a short "Rangoon Spring" before the military brutally quelled the uprising.

The 1988 revolt was not the first time the Burmese have struggled for their rights. In January 1948 the Burmese won their independence after several years of demonstrations and often violent opposition to British rule. The independence struggle was led by the Thankin movement, a group of anti-British nationalists headed by Aung San, the father of modern Burma and a fiery nationalist who received his training in Japan during World War II after the Japanese had occupied Burma. Subsequently, the movement turned against the Japanese as their occupation became increasingly repressive. Aung San, who was expected to be Burma's first head of state, was assassinated in 1947 and thus became the nation's martyred hero.

The Thankin movement became the core of the Anti-Fascist People's Freedom League (AFPFL), a united front group opposed to the Japanese. AFPFL forces cooperated with the British to oust the Japanese and then turned against the British in the struggle for independence. The AFPFL negotiated independence and formed the country's first parliamentary government in 1948 under the leadership of U Nu.

The period from 1948 to 1958 was known as the "Time of Troubles." The well-organized minority ethnic groups opposed the government's move toward a national state and instead supported the establishment of autonomous states for each group. The Shans and Karens in particular rose against the central authorities, precipitating a struggle that came close to becoming a full-scale civil war.

The second major postindependence problem concerned the poorly trained civil service, which was not able to carry out government programs effectively. U Nu's government had proclaimed a socialist policy that required a high degree of centralized administration, but the Burmese bureaucracy floundered, causing severe political and economic disturbances. By 1958 Burma's political condition was so chaotic that U Nu turned the functioning of the government over to the military, led by General Ne Win, a leader of the Thankin independence movement and a compatriot of Aung San. Following this "constitutional coup," a caretaker administration succeeded in stabilizing the cost of living and controlling the black market. Exports were increased and corruption was temporarily halted. Ne Win's government reorganized the bureaucracy to make it more efficient and restored a semblance of law and order.

Despite the success of the caretaker government in a number of areas, in 1960 the electorate chose to return to U Nu for leadership. Again, however, he was not able to control the economy. U Nu's leadership was based on his charismatic religious qualities and his reputation for impeccable honesty, but he was a poor day-to-day administrator. The nation was reeling from multiple rebellions among minority groups, and therefore a large share of the central budget was allocated to internal security, but U Nu concentrated on establishing Buddhism as the state religion. His efforts to conceptualize an idealistic vision of a Burmese welfare state based on the teachings of Buddha were not matched by a parallel plan for implementation and administration.

The military, which perceived that the civilian government was weak and dependent upon Western-style political institutions that were incompatible with Burmese culture, carried out a coup on March 2, 1962, led by Ne Win. This seizure of power, which was rapid, nonviolent, and without major challenge, began an era of military rule that has continued for thirty-five years. Ne Win disbanded the Western-style Parliament, banned political parties, and restricted civil liberties. He also devised a program of radical economic and political policies called the "Burmese Way to Socialism," which included the nationalization of major industries, schools, rice mills, small and large businesses, and financial institutions. His program to install a centralized state monopoly of the means of production was designed to ensure control of a united Burma.

To mobilize support for the socialist program, Ne Win established the Burmese Socialist Program Party (BSPP), organized to reach down to the village level along hierarchical lines but with all power remaining firmly at the party's military-dominated top echelon. The party's main function was to legitimize army rule. To keep Western "bourgeois decadent" ideas from infiltrating into Burma, Ne Win arrested those who opposed his policies, restricted travel to Burma by foreigners, and ended academic freedom at the universities. His move toward a neutralist foreign policy took the form of isolationism. By rejecting all forms of westernization, Burma—unique in Southeast Asia—has not accepted or encouraged the Western model of development.

In January 1974, Burma became the Socialist Republic of the Union of Burma after the new socialist constitution had been passed by the electorate. Although Ne Win discarded his military uniform in 1971 and became the "civilian" president of the new government, the military continued to be the dominant political force. Ne Win stepped down as president in 1981 but retained his more powerful position as head of the BSPP. In that position he was able to continue his dominance over political and economic policymaking. In the summer of 1988, hundreds of thousands of farmers, urban workers, students, monks, and civil servants took to the streets of Burma's major cities to demonstrate against their government leaders.[2] This revolt was the culmination of years of frustration and disgust at the failures of the military government to bring development to Burma. Although rich in natural resources, Burma had been humiliated by the U.N. decision in 1987 to declare it one of the world's least-developed nations. The revolt was also a response to the pervasive suppression of the people's political rights since 1962, when the military had assumed all political power.

A more immediate cause of the revolt was the decision of Ne Win's administration to declare valueless some 80 percent of the Burmese money in circulation. Any kyat note over $1.60 in value became instantly worthless. This demonetization, justified as a measure to undermine black marketeers and to control inflation, adversely affected the entire population, rich and poor. The bulk of the working economy was sustained by the black market (the government's socialistic economy having collapsed), so the demise of this unofficial market was seen as a great catastrophe. Moreover, no recompense was given to holders of kyat notes above the maximum allowed; in effect, then, the savings of the entire population were wiped out.

The precipitating incident of the revolt occurred in a tea shop, where students and other patrons squabbled over the choice of music tapes being played. When the police arrived, a student was killed. Thousands of his schoolmates later returned to avenge their colleague's death, but they were met by weapons and security police. In a particularly dreadful incident, forty-one students were herded into a police van, where they suffocated in the intense heat. The head of the security police, General Sein Lwin, was held responsible by the students and their sympathizers for these and other killings. More and more demonstrations and deaths occurred in the ensuing weeks. Unofficial estimates of student deaths from beatings, bayonet stabbings, and suffocation were in the hundreds, but the government blandly announced a total of only two student deaths.[3]

To defuse the threat to the army's continued political domination, Ne Win announced his resignation as BSPP party chairman and advocated a popular referendum for a multiparty system, implicitly admitting the failure of the Burmese socialist experiment. The party rejected the idea of the referendum but agreed to accept his resignation. In an incredible decision, the BSPP appointed as chairman Sein Lwin, the head of the despised security police *(lon htein)*, who was known as "the butcher" for his role in violently quelling student demonstrations in 1962, 1974, and 1988. His appointment set off even more demonstrations and more killings by the police.

After only a period of weeks as leader of the country, Sein Lwin was replaced by the civilian Dr. Maung Maung, an academic scholar and biographer of Ne Win. His appointment, however, came too late to stop the growing power of the people. In fact, his toleration of a free press and free assembly encouraged newspapers to criticize the government and swelled the ranks of the demonstrators in what became known as the Rangoon Spring. The U.S. government was one of the first to protest the military and police violence and was also a visible symbol of democratic government; thus, the grounds of the U.S. embassy in Rangoon became an important site for antigovernment demonstrations. Demonstrations in Rangoon and in Mandalay involved more than a million people.

With the knowledge that the military's dominance was in jeopardy, army commander in chief General Saw Maung, ostensibly on orders from Ne Win, crushed the revolt and restored the military (Tatmadaw) to power on September 18, 1988. The military's coup was not against an opposition government, as none existed, but was against the civilian facade government under Maung Maung that the army itself created. The violent coup was followed by the arrest of demonstrators, the censorship of all forms of communication, and the flight of tens of thousands of students to the nation's borders to escape the military and to organize for a future rebellion. Altogether, some 3,000 Burmese lost their lives in their attempt to end military rule.

Saw Maung, taking his orders from Ne Win, established the State Law and Order Restoration Council (SLORC) to endure "until anarchy and demonstrations could be brought under control." SLORC consisted of generals who were loyal to Ne Win and who were given responsibility for administering the state. Ruling by martial law, SLORC brutally suppressed all dissent. At the same time, but only for brief periods, SLORC allowed more open politics than during the Ne Win years. For example, political parties were able to apply for official recognition in anticipation of an election to be held in May 1990. However, when opposition party leaders spoke out against the regime, they were arrested.

SLORC argued that its harsh policies were necessary because of an alleged collusion between the Burmese Communist Party and the U.S. Central Intelligence Agency, which was the cause of demonstrations and antigovernment dissidence. For example, Aung San Suu Kyi, the highly respected daughter of Aung San and head of the major opposition party, the National League for Democracy (NLD), was placed under house arrest for having been "manipulated" by communists and foreign intelligence agencies. SLORC also argued that a highly centralized, military-oriented administration was necessary to ensure the country's continued unity in the face of potential rebellion by minority ethnic groups. None of these explanations were accepted by the vast majority of Burmese, who were extremely angry that their people's revolt had been crushed. The Tatmadaw, once a symbol of stability in Burma, became a hated organization.

Reports from Burma were few during 1989 and 1990 because SLORC did not allow foreign journalists or scholars into the country. However, sketchy reports suggested that SLORC was violating the human rights of the Burmese people by silencing writers, banning assemblies, and forcefully moving some half a million people from their homes with the aim of breaking up pro-democracy neighborhoods. The relocation of urban residents in late 1989 from cities to satellite towns was particularly egregious but was justified, according to SLORC, as a "beautification measure." A large number of people were also moved from constituencies believed to be favorable to opposition leader Aung San Suu Kyi.

Despite these violations of human rights, SLORC organized the May 27, 1990, election to choose legislators in the Pyithu Hluttaw (People's Assembly), the sole organ of legislative authority. Under the election law, each constituency was to elect one representative to the Pyithu Hluttaw. Some 492 constituencies, defined by population, were to choose representatives; seven constituencies of ethnic minorities, however, were not allowed to vote because of "security" threats in their regions. SLORC believed that the election could be controlled to ensure that pro-government forces would prevail. In fact, the government was given the power to censor the speeches and publications of parties and candidates. Television time was limited to one ten-minute period per party during the entire campaign, and statements had to be submitted for approval seven days in advance. Candidates who gave speeches that had not been scrutinized and approved by the authorities were imprisoned.

Popular opposition leaders were harassed and kept from participating in the election. Aung San Suu Kyi, for example, was disqualified, as were former Prime Minister U Nu and another prominent opposition leader, former General Tin U. All of these leaders were placed under house arrest. Pro-government candidates who joined the successor party of the BSPP, the National Unity Party (NUP), received government funds for campaigning, but funds were not available to oppositionists. The authorities banned outdoor assemblies and relocated citizens from their voting constituencies to ensure a pro-government vote.

In spite of these measures and in an extraordinary display of independence, the oppositionist National Democratic League won more than 80 percent of the seats (396 of 485) in the Pyithu Hluttaw. The NUP won only 10 seats, losing even in areas dominated by the army. Such a sharp rebuke of the martial law government was unexpected. Even months after the election, the military still refused to turn the government over to the newly elected legislators, even though the latter were ready to install a new constitution based largely on the country's last democratic constitution of 1947. Although the Burmese had expressed their anger toward the military government and their support for democratic rule through their vote, the regime in power was unwilling to act in compliance with the people's will.

Although world reaction to SLORC's oppression was strongly critical, the military continued to jail opposition leaders, to dominate every facet of society, and to isolate the regime from global currents. When in December 1991 Aung San Suu Kyi received the Nobel Peace Prize in absentia for standing up to the military junta, many believed that SLORC could not withstand the negative worldwide publicity. However, despite global condemnation and economic sanctions, SLORC dug in even deeper, claiming that freeing the Nobel laureate would threaten the peace and tranquillity of the nation. By 1997, she had been under house arrest for seven years (she was formally released from house arrest in 1995 but not given freedom to travel).

In 1992, General Saw Maung stepped down as chairman of SLORC and was replaced by General Than Shwe, who was the nation's military commander and minister of defense. The new leader released some five hundred political prisoners, although the principal oppositionists were not freed. Colleges and universities were opened, and a constitutional convention was called. The latter was viewed as a sham by both the Burmese people and foreign observers, who pointed out that the convention was dominated by the military and that the leading oppositionists were still in jail. The convention met in January 1993 but did nothing to undermine military rule. Indeed, the conference specifically approved a leading political role for the army in the future governance of the country.

During the postelection period, numerous opposition groups consisting of members of Burma's minority peoples formed along the Thai border. The National Coalition Government of the Union of Burma, for example, called for the release of Aung San Suu Kyi and all other political prisoners, the transfer of power to those elected in 1990, and a halt to the civil war. But the military rulers did not listen.

The generals eventually realized, sometime in 1994, that SLORC's policy of isolation had brought devastation to Burma. They allowed small openings in the economy, but the lack of capital, the poor infrastructure, and the disdain of much of the world made change difficult. Nevertheless, in 1994 Burma's economic growth rate improved, ending the total stagnation of previous decades. Foreign entrepreneurs began setting up investments, and a "Visit Myanmar Year" promotional campaign was launched. New hotel projects changed the face of Rangoon. The opening did almost nothing to improve the standard of living of the people, among the world's poorest, most of whom led subsistence lives. Corruption, an inflated bureaucracy, political mismanagement (the military were more effective as warriors than as governors), and the continued imprisonment of the democracy leaders were all reasons for the ongoing economic problems.

In July 1995, Aung San Suu Kyi was "released" from house arrest. In reality, she was guarded closely to ensure that she and her followers would not jeopardize SLORC's control over the nation. The government felt compelled to release her because of foreign pressures stemming from her extraordinary international reputation as a democrat. She was also released as an inducement to convince foreign nations to invest in Burma, and because her National League for Democracy had been decimated by the generals, the party's leaders jailed or executed. Finally, she was released because the "constitutional convention" had mandated that Burmese who had married foreigners could not rule the nation. Aung San Suu Kyi's husband, Michael Aris, is a British citizen. Although thousands of Burmese citizens came to hear her speak, Aung San Suu Kyi was effectively silenced. Her talks were not allowed to be broadcast or printed in the government-controlled press. Indeed, the press attacked Aung San Suu Kyi daily.

SLORC allowed no discussion of the key issue: Which was the more legitimate institution, SLORC or the NLD, which had overwhelmingly won the fair elections of 1990? In 1997 SLORC continued to be led by Senior General Than Shwe, the prime minister, who was omnipresent. The "man behind the throne" was General Khin Nyunt, in charge of all intelligence agencies. These leaders touted the Tatmadaw as the "savior" of Burma. When the crowds at the home of Aung San Suu Kyi grew to many thousands, she was placed under house arrest, her NLD colleagues still at large were jailed, and the universities were again closed. In an attempt to improve its international image in 1997, SLORC officials renamed the ruling council the State Peace and Development Council (SPDC). The new acronym could not be pronounced as a word. However, SPDC policies remained virtually the same as those of SLORC.

## Institutions and Social Groups

Since independence, the Burmese military has played the central role in governmental affairs. No other institutions or social classes have even been allowed to compete with the military. With the exception of Brunei, where the monarchy controls every aspect of society, no nation has been ruled by a single institution to the same degree as Burma.

### General Ne Win

Eighty-six years old in 1997, Ne Win has been commander of the armed forces, deputy prime minister, prime minister, minister of defense, chairman of the Revolutionary Council, president, and chairman of the state's only legal political party. He is now in semiretirement and holds the title "Patron of the War Veterans' Organization." Ne Win's power has been so great because power is personal in Burma; loyalty within the government is to the person holding office, not to the institution. As the supreme patron in a land of patron-client relationships, Ne Win received the undivided loyalty of government officials and common citizens.[4] Only when his abuse of power went beyond acceptable limits did his clientele rise against him. Even after the 1988 revolt, when he became more reclusive, Ne Win continued to wield power as he had for the preceding thirty years. In September 1997, after a long and enigmatic absence, Ne Win was seen publicly during a personal visit to President Suharto in Indonesia. He had been in Singapore for medical treatment.

### Legislature

The Pyithu Hluttaw, a unicameral body, was elected by the people in single-member constituencies. Prior to 1989, the only legal party was the

BSPP, which controlled the nomination of candidates so that there would be no deviation from party policy. Twenty-nine members of the legislature were chosen to the Council of State, the supreme executive authority, whose chairman, Ne Win, served as president of the republic. The Council of State nominated a Council of Ministers for the Pyithu Hluttaw to approve. The council chose the prime minister and carried out day-to-day governing responsibilities. The role of the legislature under SLORC was negligible. When the new legislature elected in 1990 was won overwhelmingly by democratic forces, the military promptly shut it down altogether. In 1997, the Pyithu Hluttaw had yet to be re-formed.

## The Military

In the early 1960s, the 190,000-member Tatmadaw, which began as a popular pro-independence force, was the only credibly unified force in the country. Ne Win, identified as the leader of the military, took over state power as a guardian who was above party politics. He ran the government by assigning leading governmental positions to military comrades.

In the postindependence period, the army has intervened to take power on three occasions. In 1958 the army was asked by U Nu to step in temporarily, but in 1962 it took power without an invitation. The military then dominated Burmese politics until demonstrations in 1988 threatened to oust it, whereupon the army intervened once again, this time under Saw Maung, who was fronting for Ne Win. Since 1988, the military has dominated every aspect of Burmese life.

## Political Parties

The only party allowed to function during the period of military dominance until 1989 was the BSPP. Committed to socialist policies, the BSPP became a national mass organization dedicated to supporting Ne Win as leader. In 1988 the BSPP was reborn as the National Unity Party, which—with its symbol of a rice stalk—inherited a strong organization and generous funding from its parent organization. The NUP had access to government resources, including transportation, and to government officials who supported the party. During the 1990 election campaign, NUP candidates were the only ones not harassed by government and military bureaucrats.

When political parties were sanctioned in 1989, more than two hundred parties registered. Most political parties were ethnically or regionally based and supported a particular person. Many small parties were formed, however, in order to qualify for access to telephones and rations of gasoline provided by the government to political parties. Registration as a political party conferred the right to display a signboard, hold gatherings of fewer than five persons, and obtain extra gasoline. Nevertheless, governmental decrees made it impossible to hold meetings of more than five persons, print and distribute party literature, and say anything that might be construed as criticism of the military.[5]

The most important opposition party was the NLD, with its symbol of a farmer's hat. Initially, the party was led by Aung Gyi, Tin U, and Aung San Suu Kyi. Aung Gyi had become famous in Burma for a series of letters he wrote to Ne Win deriding the military regime, which he argued had brought great suffering to the people. Aung Gyi later alleged that communists and procommunist elements had infiltrated the NLD. When he could not substantiate the charge, he was asked by the other party leaders to resign.

Aung San Suu Kyi, the daughter of independence hero Aung San, was schooled in Burma during her first fifteen years. A member of a prominent family, she was then sent to India where her mother was ambassador and to England to study politics, philosophy, and economics at Oxford University. She later published books on Burmese history and literature. Prior to 1988, she had no direct political experience and was known primarily as the daughter of Aung San.

Shortly before the beginning of the rebellion, Aung San Suu Kyi returned to Burma from England to care for her ailing mother. She joined the opposition and, because of her name and superb oratorical ability, began to draw large crowds to her speeches. Burmese women imitated her hair and clothing style. She was cheered for her straightforward attacks against the government and against Ne Win. Her military adversaries, frightened by her mounting popularity, suggested that she was manipulated by communists. On July 20, 1989, the military placed her under house arrest and cut off all communications between her followers and the outside world. While still under arrest, she was awarded the Nobel Peace Prize in December 1991 for her courageous struggle against the military dictatorship. Aung San Suu Kyi has remained the symbol of the Burmese democracy movement. The U.S. Congress approved a resolution stating that if SLORC harms Aung San Suu Kyi, the U.S. president will prohibit American businesses from investing in Burma.

## Minority Ethnic Groups

During the postindependence period, Burma's minority groups have continued to view themselves primarily in terms of ethnicity rather than nationality. The Karens, Shans, Kachins, and other groups that fought for state autonomy do not trust the government. In their struggle for minority rights, these groups have joined the National Democratic Front (NDF), an organization of nine groups, in revolt. The NDF assumes, first, that the peoples of Burma are members of ethnic-linguistic communities that came together in 1947 and formed a voluntary Union of Burma.[6] In this union, equality of communities was to be reflected in their organization as political units, each having power to govern itself, claim to a reasonable share of the nation's resources, an equal right to develop its land and society, and equal representation in the national government.[7] The states were to be strong and the central government weak. In reality, however, and despite promises to state leaders at the time of independence, the central government became strong and the separate states weak.

In order to achieve their goals, the minority ethnic groups have organized armed insurgencies to protect their territories and to pressure the central government to accept a federated Burma, with ethnic states having autonomy under a federal umbrella government. Many opposition parties in the 1990 elections supported a federal system of government.

Another problem has been opium, which represents a traditional form of livelihood in areas where it has grown for more than a century but which now has attracted criminal elements. The insurgents as well as the Burmese Communist Party rely on opium profits to finance their guerrilla activities. Also, the illicit drug trade is lucrative for Thailand, which is the marketing channel for opium grown in Burma. If the opium trade were to dry up, Thailand would sustain an economic loss. Some reports estimate that Burma's export of opiates is worth as much as all legal exports.

## Women

Aung San Suu Kyi is the first woman in contemporary Burma to be seriously considered for national leadership. Like Corazon Aquino in the Philippines, she is the relative of a martyred hero. Because she is the daughter of Aung San, the nation's founder, Aung San Suu Kyi is not a typical Burmese woman. In addition to having instant name recognition, Aung San Suu Kyi has qualities that explain her immense popularity. She is an eloquent orator, has impeccable character, is brilliant, and has the courage to oppose the military government. Like Aquino, her incorruptible character stands in striking contrast to that of the leaders in power. Her house arrest at the hands of Burma's autocratic military leaders resulted from her growing influence and her commitment to democratic values.

Women have experienced a large degree of equality with men at the family level. They are household managers, have equal inheritance rights, and retain their own names during marriage. However, at the national level women have played subordinate roles compared to men, who have held virtually every position of political power. No woman in contemporary Burma has held a major military position or served in the cabinet.

## Democratization

For almost all of its history, Burma has been ruled by autocratic monarchs, colonial administrators, or military leaders. Burma's only experience with democracy was a brief period under the 1947 constitution after independence, when U Nu supported representative institutions, free elections, and civil liberties. The ineffectiveness of U Nu's rule was used as a rationalization for the military takeover of the government in both 1958 and 1962. Since that time, democratic institutions and behavior, said to be "foreign to the traditions" of the Burmese and a rejected legacy of Western imperialism, have been suppressed.

Burmese political culture, with its emphasis on hierarchy and status, is not conducive to democracy. Paternalistic authority is inconsistent with democracy's reliance on equality of opportunity, freedom of speech and assembly, and representative institutions. Burmese leaders, like those in Thailand during periods of military rule, argue that the quest for modernization and for security from outside aggressors demands strong, effective government.

The inability of the Burmese government to develop the nation economically together with its oppression of human rights led to the people's rebellion against their leaders. The "supreme patron," Ne Win, was not fulfilling his obligations to his clients to meet their economic needs and to provide them with security. He lost his *pon* (grace) and therefore the respect of the Burmese people. The government became the problem rather than the solution.

Events in the summer of 1988 suggest that despite their isolation from world events, the Burmese desire the same freedoms and opportunities demanded by the peoples of Eastern Europe, East Asia, and the Third World, many of whose nations have moved from authoritarian to democratic regimes in the past decade. Hearing about the higher standard of living in Thailand, the Burmese know that their government's claim that authoritarianism is necessary for economic development is false. Throughout Burmese history, at the moment when the nation's leaders could no longer meet the people's needs, they were believed to have lost their unquestioned authority and their supposedly magical powers. That moment occurred again in the summer of 1988.

## Economic Development

The similarities between Burma and Thailand are striking. Both nations have had histories of absolute monarchy; both have practiced Theravada Buddhism; and both have comparable natural resources and fertile soils for agriculture. In the 1950s, Burma and Thailand also had similar GNPs. In view of these similarities, why has Thailand had success in its quest for economic and political development while Burma has failed?

One answer stems from the most obvious difference between the two nations: The Burmese were colonized by the British, whereas the Thais have been independent throughout their history. The Thais, who did not develop an inferiority complex toward the West or antipathy to Western ways, were therefore more flexible about adopting and adapting westernization. In contrast, the Burmese consciously eschewed Western ways, including the materialism and commercialism of Western culture, which the Burmese believe have ruined Bangkok.

Another answer is that the postindependence governments of Burma chose to isolate their nation from the global economic system, relying on indigenous government-controlled socialistic economics. Thailand, on the other hand, opened its economy through a policy of free enterprise and export-driven growth. The results are dramatic: Thailand's per capita GNP rose from $100 in the 1950s to almost $3,000 in 1997, whereas in the same period Burma's rose from $100 to just over $700. This latter figure does not take into account Burma's unofficial black market, which involves about 80 percent of the economy and acts as a safety valve for an otherwise explosive level of economic underdevelopment. This large "free market" within the socialist system has helped check the Burmese people's frustration.

Burma's economy reached its nadir in 1987 when the United Nations granted the once prosperous nation the ignoble status of Least Developed Country, placing Burma in the same category as Chad, Ethiopia, Nepal, and Bangladesh. Whereas Burma once controlled 28 percent of the world's rice trade, by 1970 the figure had decreased to 2 percent.[8] The brutal suppression of demonstrators in 1988 ended the few ongoing Western development projects, reducing the external capital that had been available to the government. To counter this cessation of aid, in November 1988 Burma promulgated its most liberal foreign investment law to date. It permitted foreign investors to form either wholly owned enterprises or joint ventures in which the foreign partner was required to hold a minimum 35 percent stake. However, little investment was induced by the government's policy because of the country's political instability.

SLORC opened the economy slowly, hoping to rejuvenate the private sector. Civil servants were given large pay raises, but much of those were wiped out by an annual inflation rate of 60 percent. Burma also opened its border trade with Thailand and China and granted oil exploration agreements to South Korean, Japanese, Australian, and U.S. firms. (It was believed that Burma possessed significant oil reserves.)[9] However important these changes were for achieving higher levels of economic development, they were limited by the continuation of a closed and tightly controlled political system.

Following the 1990 election, the authorities continued to liberalize the economy, allowing some foreign investments and beginning tourist development. However, few foreigners were interested in visiting a country whose leaders were so scornful of human rights. Moreover, Burma's crumbling infrastructure and chronic corruption remained an obstacle to implementing economic programs. Transportation within the country, which had been comparable to that of Thailand or Malaysia forty years earlier, had fallen far behind. Inflation rates were about 60 percent per year, stemming from the government's printing of money to finance the budget deficit and to pay for imports of mainly military matériel and luxury goods. Tourists and foreign business executives were forced to exchange their money at the official rate of six kyats per dollar, whereas the unofficial rate was closer to one hundred kyats per dollar (and in 1998 three hundred per dollar).

In the early 1990s, Burma's annual economic growth rate was about 1.5 percent, and the overall standard of living, especially among rural people dependent on agriculture, had fallen. Only the presence of a black market made the economy tolerable. In the mid-1990s, economic growth rates improved to the 4 to 6 percent level, as more foreign nations agreed to invest capital. International pressure forced some companies (Pepsi-Cola, Levi Strauss, Apple) to leave Burma on the grounds that human rights were systematically being violated. Tourists in 1995 numbered 30,000 (compared to 5,000 in 1989) but few tourist-oriented projects improved the lot of the Burmese people.

Thailand's "constructive engagement" policy became the norm for the other ASEAN nations, all of which began investing heavily in Burma and taking advantage of the country's rich natural resources sector such as forestry, fisheries, and mining.

It is difficult to be precise about economic development in Burma because government figures are unreliable. For example, SLORC boasted an 11 percent growth rate in 1995, whereas international specialists noted a 4 percent rate. Moreover, so much of the economy is pegged to the black market that accurate statistics are impossible to gather. The informal economy is as large as the formal economy. The government's highly touted "Visit Myanmar Year" campaign was a dismal failure as hotels remained largely empty. Tourists held back because of the country's widely reported human rights violations and the extortion of dollars from foreign travelers at Rangoon's airport. The isolation of Burma from the global capitalist system kept the nation from directly feeling the impact of the 1997 currency crisis in the rest of Southeast Asia.

## The Burmese State

The Burmese state has been dominated by a small number of rulers and institutions. Absolute monarchs and British administrators followed by a military general have made the authoritative decisions that have affected the entire Burmese citizenry. In the postindependence period, General Ne Win and the state became one and the same. Ne Win and his subordinates constituted the officials who decided public policy that is binding on the society. His domination of the state was impressive, but his capacity to meet the needs of the people was weak.

Burma has not developed institutions outside the military and its subsidiary organization, the BSPP. Essentially, the many political parties established in 1989 were all tailor made for the individuals who led them; they had no institutionalized structure. External institutions, such as a parliament, established political parties, and interest groups, have had little influence over the state's policy decisions. In this sense, the Burmese state has been strong and autonomous, independent of societal organizations.

Whereas in Thailand the integration of the military into the political process increased governmental capacity, in Burma the integration reduced capacity. In Thailand, the military worked in conjunction with the bureaucrats, the monarchy, and interest groups to meet the demands of the citizenry. The military-dominated state managed the political-economic affairs of the kingdom effectively, thereby co-opting opposition groups and reducing challenges to the authorities. In Burma, on the other hand, the military used force rather than co-optation and coordination to retain its power.

In Thailand, the state authorities managed to achieve one of the highest economic growth rates in the world, primarily by allowing the nation's entrepreneurs to promote economic development. In Burma, however, the state authorities intervened in every aspect of the economy—nationalizing public utilities, industries, and agribusinesses and placing numerous obstacles in the path of entrepreneurs. The Burmese state has shown little adaptability to changes in the international and regional spheres and to the worldwide movement toward democratization. This lack of adaptability has undermined the legitimacy once enjoyed by the Tatmadaw and by Ne Win himself. The military is no longer the respected unifier of the nation; instead, it has become a symbol of stagnation and oppression. In this regard, the Burmese state at present is viewed as weak. It is a patronage operation with low capacity and legitimacy levels.

Like the Thai state, the Burmese state can be viewed as strong or weak. Burma, like all the other Southeast Asian nations except Thailand, underwent colonialism and Japanese occupation, both of which caused severe social dislocations. These experiences favored concentrated social control to ensure that the nation would be secure from similar aggressions in the future. Surrounded by strong nations, Burma has accepted its centralized rule as a means to thwart foreign invasion. Under similar circumstances, Thailand strengthened its state by receiving large amounts of foreign aid, especially from the United States. Burma fashioned its state primarily with its own resources. Those resources were few, and the strength of the state withered.

Burma's postindependence government has not invited technocrats, politicians, intellectuals, or socioeconomic elites to participate in state affairs to the same degree as has Thailand. The few outsiders brought into the polity have no autonomous political base or constituency. The economically powerful Chinese minority has not participated in Burmese politics, and the ethnic minorities have struggled against the state for decades. In contrast to Thailand, where there are no strong autonomous groups whose primary loyalties are to regional or ethnic sects, fully one-third of Burma's population has such loyalties. In this respect, Burma does not meet the condition for a strong state requiring the presence of groups that are willing and able to execute the grand designs of state leaders.

## Foreign Policy

There are many good reasons why the Burmese have emphasized the importance of national security. Their colonial heritage and the Japanese occupation are reminders that Burma has been a victim of both imperialism and aggression. Burma is surrounded by nations with far greater populations and military strength, sharing a thousand-mile-long border with both China and India as well as with Thailand. Burma's ethnic minorities, who mostly live in the northern half of the country, have been supported by outsiders and are linked with the drug trade and with elements of the Burmese Communist Party. Moreover, the nation's Indian and Chinese minorities have an influence in the Burmese economy disproportionate to their numbers. Finally, the government views westernization as a threat to Burmese traditional culture.

The government's response to this insecurity has been a policy of nonalignment. Burma has attempted to maintain a quasi-isolationist foreign policy by refusing to participate in the Indochina conflict, eschewing aid from various nations, and, until recently, forgoing membership in ASEAN. However, this policy did not prevent China from providing military and political support to rebels along the border, although that support apparently ceased under China's more pragmatic post-Mao administration, which was more concerned with economic relations. Burma was one of the few nations in the world that expressed support of the Chinese government for its handling of the Tiananmen Square demonstration, possibly because Burma's 1988 rebellion was quelled in a similarly brutal manner.

Relations with Thailand have always been tense because of the history of conflict between the two nations. However, relations improved following the 1988 revolt when General Chavalit Yongchaiyut visited Burma to negotiate logging and fishing deals for Thai companies. Desperate for foreign capital, Burma acceded to Thai requests to exploit its teak forests. Thai firms could no longer log in Thailand due to new environmental regulations; these restrictions did not apply in Burma. Concessions to Thai companies in Burma permit extraction of 1.2 million tons of logs annually.[10] For the first time in decades, official and legal border trade was established between Thailand and Burma. The two nations resolved another obstacle to improved relations when the Thai military granted the Burmese military permission to use Thai territory to attack ethnic minority camps from the rear.

Relations with Burma's other major neighbor, India, remained cool, especially when the Indian government expressed support for the Burmese people's resolve to achieve democracy. India's support for Burma's opposition movement was shared by most Western democracies, and Japan, West Germany, the United States, Great Britain, and Australia suspended their aid programs after the mass killing of demonstrators in 1988.

The United States has protested human rights violations in Burma but has not broken relations after the 1988 rebellion, at least partially because of the need to continue coordinating policies to stem the narcotics trade. However, more recently the Clinton administration condemned Burma's oppressive system, especially following the death in custody, in June 1996, of Leo Nichols, an honorary consul of Norway, Sweden, and Denmark. He had been charged with possessing a fax machine and was sentenced to three years in prison, where he died after interrogations. In response, the United States imposed visa restrictions on SLORC members and their families. Several municipalities in the United States passed legislation forbidding trade with Burma.

Burma's policy of modified isolationism will be tested as the cold war recedes and international interdependence becomes the means by which economies grow. As economic development becomes the primary goal of successor regimes to the military, Burma will have to expand its international involvement.

That new involvement began in 1997 when Burma was formally accepted into ASEAN. Burma's neighbors argued that membership in ASEAN would encourage Burma to approach economic development and political liberalization constructively. The ASEAN leaders argued that international sanctions would only serve to further isolate Burma and that democratic reforms in the country would come about most readily through constructive persuasion. In addition, ASEAN leaders hoped that Burma's membership in the organization would help pull the nation away from its most important ally, China. China has been Burma's major weapons supplier, and several ASEAN countries have sought to reduce this dependence.

## Conclusion

Burma's future is unclear because the state is in a period of traumatic transition. Although the move from socialism to capitalism appears to have begun, the move from authoritarian military rule to democracy is still problematic. Most significantly, the Burmese will continue to resolve their problems at their own pace, refusing to become dependent on outsiders. While the authorities' first goal is to perpetuate their power, they maintain that Burma's development will be based on indigenous values and not on crass westernization. In the post–Ne Win era, the state has been freer to broaden its constituencies. At the same time, the country has not had the stabilizing force of a known leader. The remarkable support accorded Aung San Suu Kyi suggests that the Burmese are willing to accept the notion that the military is not indispensable.

The Burmese polity will not lose its personalistic character overnight, nor will Western-style democracy immediately flourish. Patron-client politics, factionalism, and oligarchy have been essential elements of Burmese politics and will continue to be important factors. A politically balanced democracy is not the sole alternative for Burma. Military control, however, is no longer acceptable to the Burmese people.

## Notes

1. The "r" in Myanmar is not pronounced but serves to lengthen the "a" sound. The word is pronounced approximately as "Bamah." As "Burma" was the universally accepted English-language name for the country until 1989, as the government that changed that name may be temporary, and to reduce confusion resulting from the use of two names, this chapter will use the name "Burma" throughout.

2. Maureen Aung-Thwin, "Burmese Days," *Foreign Affairs*, vol. 68, no. 2 (Spring 1989), p. 143.

3. Burma Watcher, "Burma in 1988," *Asian Survey*, vol. 29, no. 2 (February 1989), p. 174.

4. David I. Steinberg, *The Future of Burma: Crisis and Choice in Myanmar* (Lanham, Md.: University Press of America, 1990), p. 1.

5. Josef Silverstein, "Aung San Suu Kyi: Is She Burma's Woman of Destiny?" (paper presented to the Association for Asian Studies, Chicago, April 1990), p. 10.

6. Josef Silverstein, "National Unity in Burma: Is It Possible?" in *Durable Stability in Southeast Asia,* ed. Kusuma Snitwongse and Sukhumbhand Paribatra (Singapore: Institute of Southeast Asian Studies, 1987), p. 80.

7. Ibid., pp. 80–81.

8. Aung-Thwin, "Burmese Days," p. 150.

9. Robert H. Taylor, "The Evolving Military Role in Burma," *Current History,* vol. 89, no. 545 (March 1990), p. 108.

10. James F. Guyot and John Badgley, "Myanmar in 1989," *Asian Survey,* vol. 30, no. 2 (February 1990), p. 191.

# 10

# VIETNAM

Stretching some twelve hundred miles from its border with China to its southernmost point in the South China Sea, Vietnam is shaped like two rice baskets at either end of a pole. The bulk of the population lives in the two baskets: the Red River Delta in the north and the Mekong River Delta in the south. The "pole" is the mountainous stretch of territory in the central, sparsely populated part of the country.

The majority of Vietnam's 72 million people work in agriculture. Eighty percent are Mahayana Buddhists and 7 percent are Roman Catholics, a religion to which they converted during the French colonial period. Many indigenous minority religions exist in Vietnam, including the Cao Dai and the Hoa Hao sects, each with about one million adherents. Since independence, Vietnamese society has been secularized so that most residents do not actively practice or pursue their religious beliefs. Confucianist principles from the nation's Chinese heritage stress centralized political authority and the notion of duty and subordination to superiors: ruled to ruler, son to father, and pupil to teacher.

Nationalism has been the key concept for understanding Vietnamese politics. Indeed, Vietnam's search for a national identity received its greatest impetus during the thousand-year Chinese domination (111 B.C.–A.D. 939). The ability of the Vietnamese to emerge from that period with many of their traditions intact is a clear indication of the nationalist urge that has pervaded the country's history. Similarly, the struggle against French colonialism, Japanese occupation, and U.S. intervention reflects the importance of that nationalism.

Vietnam has not always been united. During the era of French colonialism, the country was divided into three areas: Tonkin in the north, with Hanoi as the capital; Annam in the middle, with Hue as the capital; and in the south, Cochin China, whose capital was Saigon. Traditionally, the northerners have seen themselves as modern, progressive, and efficient, and they have viewed the southerners as lazy. The Annamese have seen themselves as highly cultured, the northerners as grasping, and the southerners as rustic. Southerners have regarded themselves as pacifistic and their northern neighbors as aggressive and violent.

In addition to these differing regional perceptions, national unification had to overcome the cultural and political dichotomy between the rural areas and the cities. Such interaction as there was consisted largely of the exploitation of the peasantry by the mandarin class. Moreover, Vietnam is populated by minority groups that have traditionally been treated with disdain by the Vietnamese majority.

Despite the divisiveness that has characterized much of Vietnamese history, a nationalist continuity has remained in the form of anticolonialism and anti-neoimperialism. Following the Japanese defeat in 1945, Ho Chi Minh—the leader of the League for the Independence of Vietnam, known as the Vietminh—proclaimed the country's independence and set up a provisional government headed by himself. The French and the representatives of the newly established Democratic Republic of Vietnam led by Ho initially agreed that a new independent state existed and that the French would not move to reclaim their former colony. However, the agreement broke down, and a series of clashes ignited the France-Indochina War, which lasted eight years.

The military defeat of the French led to the Geneva Conference of 1954, which sought to separate the rival French and Vietminh forces by setting up a temporary military demarcation line at the seventeenth parallel. This line was not intended to be a political or territorial boundary. In addition, the Geneva agreements called for eventual national elections for the purpose of establishing a single administration throughout the country. During the Geneva Conference, an anti-Vietminh administration emerged below the seventeenth parallel, led initially by the former Annamese emperor Bao Dai and subsequently by the strongly anticommunist Catholic mandarin Ngo Dinh Diem. On October 26, 1955, Diem proclaimed the Republic of Vietnam, better known as South Vietnam, with his capital in Saigon and with himself as the first president; he had the support of the United States. He repudiated the Geneva agreements, specifically the provision for national elections.

Ho Chi Minh had agreed to the Geneva agreements at least partly because he believed that national elections would ensure reunification under communist Vietminh leadership. Ho, who was both a nationalist and a communist, saw the two ideologies as inseparable. His goal of a united Vietnam was scuttled when it became clear that Diem had no intention of merging with the north.

During Diem's increasingly repressive rule in the late 1950s, South Vietnam became the site of a guerrilla insurgency against his government. The political arm of the guerrilla activity was the National Liberation Front (NLF), which was initially an autonomous southern-based movement. The military arm was known as the Viet Cong (Vietnamese Communist). A large number of northerners who had moved to the south following the Geneva Conference joined these guerrillas. In the early 1960s the North Vietnamese provided increasing military support to the NLF. The People's Revolutionary Party—South Vietnam's communist party, which was controlled by the north—gradually came to dominate the NLF until ultimately the two organizations were indistinguishable.

To counteract the insurgency, Diem relied on U.S. advisers, weaponry, money, and soldiers. U.S. support began in 1954 with one thousand advisers, which increased to five thousand by 1960 and half a million advisers and military personnel in 1968. Despite this support, Diem's own position deteriorated until U.S. President John Kennedy acquiesced to a coup d'état against Diem by South Vietnamese generals. The coup, which took place in October 1963, and Diem's concurrent death paved the way for a dozen ineffective and unstable military governments, which were less interested in economic or social reforms than in a military victory over the Viet Cong and the North Vietnamese.

U.S. involvement continued to escalate. In February 1965 the United States began massive bombing of the north in order to interdict North Vietnamese supply lines, erode morale, and provide time for the south to strengthen its forces. None of these purposes was achieved. The massive 1968 Tet offensive by the north, which involved coordinated attacks on all major cities and towns in the south, clearly showed the ineffectiveness of the U.S. bombing policy and led to President Lyndon Johnson's decision not to run for office again.

South Vietnam had increasingly become a client state of the United States. To reduce this dependency and to blunt rising U.S. protests against the war, in the early 1970s President Richard Nixon began a policy of "Vietnamization"—the gradual withdrawal of U.S. troops from Vietnam—while escalating the bombing against the north. In May 1970, U.S. and South Vietnamese troops invaded Cambodia, ostensibly to halt Viet Cong use of Cambodian "sanctuaries." The result, however, was a massive escalation of the war to all of Indochina, unparalleled demonstrations against the war in the United States, and the unification of insurgent forces in Cambodia.

Following the 1972 Christmas bombing of Hanoi (in which 40,000 tons of bombs were dropped), the Paris Peace Accords were signed by the contending powers in January 1973. North Vietnam agreed to a cease-fire, while the United States agreed not only to a cessation of bombing in the north but to withdrawal of its troops. The Paris Peace Accords were essentially a victory for the north because North Vietnamese troops were able to stay in place. Without U.S. bombing support and financial aid (the United States had spent over $112 billion in Vietnam since the 1950s), South Vietnam could not withstand the pressure from the north.

The rationale for U.S. intervention in Vietnam had several foundations. The first concern was the perceived national interest of the United States itself. Most U.S. policymakers saw the fall of Vietnam to communism as one more stage in the growth of a cancer that could eventually spread to America itself. Thus, South Vietnam became a testing ground for communist wars of national liberation. It was believed that anything less than a committed stand against communist aggression would be tantamount to an invitation for further aggression in other parts of the world. American policymakers cited the commitment of four presidents, the terms of the Southeast Asia Treaty Organization (SEATO), and agreements with South Vietnam as proper sanctions for U.S. involvement; they believed that American credibility as a world power was at stake.

Decisions regarding Vietnam were also a function of internal pressure. Each president feared a political backlash if he were seen to be responsible for the defeat of South Vietnam. Therefore, Vietnam became the test of presidential strength, especially for Presidents Johnson and Nixon, both of whom articulated the need for total victory.

U.S. policy in Vietnam was also the result of several small steps, each insignificant in itself but in sum representing a giant leap. In this sense, U.S. intervention was almost inadvertent, a policy of gradual escalatory moves that by themselves seemed restrained but that in sum committed the United States to a war in which over 2 million soldiers fought and 58,000 died; in which over 2 million Vietnamese were casualties; and in which more bombs were dropped than in all past wars combined.

In April 1975 North Vietnamese troops moved swiftly through the south, conquering province after province and eventually capturing Saigon. A war that had endured for three decades came to a swift close. The immediate causes of the communist victory included the corruption of the South Vietnamese army and the end of U.S. support. Longer-term reasons for the communist success included the artificiality of the south's political system. The South Vietnamese government, which did not meet the needs of the people, was viewed by northerners as well as many southerners as a lackey of the United States. The war was also never fully understood by U.S. policymakers, who underestimated the importance of nationalism and the tenacity of the Vietnamese people to withstand great pressure. Moreover, the war never received the wholehearted support of the American public or of even a large element of the government. As the war continued, more and more Americans became convinced that the means used by the U.S. government were disproportionate to the stated goals.

The North Vietnamese moved swiftly to consolidate their power. The newly united nation was named the Socialist Republic of Vietnam. Ho Chi Minh's goal of a united Vietnam under communist rule was reached, and in his honor Saigon was renamed Ho Chi Minh City (although local residents continue to call the city Saigon). Hanoi became the nation's capital. Plans were carried out to transform the south's economy from capitalism to socialism, and "reeducation camps" were established to indoctrinate former partisans of the South Vietnamese government with socialist values. An estimated 2.5 million Vietnamese have been sent to these camps and been released following "rehabilitation."

The southerners did not take well to the economic programs of their new rulers, and many fled the country in a first wave of refugees. They resisted efforts to collectivize and redistribute the land. Moreover, the Vietnamese economy deteriorated, worsened by drought and the diversion of resources to its military in Cambodia and along the Chinese border. Poor management and planning by the central authorities were also responsible for the economic catastrophe faced by the new revolutionary government.

As the Vietnamese government ended the traditional free-market system in the south, the indigenous Chinese, long the mainstay of entrepreneurship in Saigon (now Ho Chi Minh City), fled the country. The government's reform of the monetary system had wiped out the savings of these shop owners. The result was a second wave of refugees, this time ethnic Chinese who fled by sea and thus became known as "boat people." During 1978 and 1979, 75,000 refugees per month fled Vietnam, arriving on the shores of Thailand, Malaysia, Singapore, and Indonesia and finally overwhelming those countries' resources.[1] Close to one million Vietnamese of all ethnic backgrounds have left the country since the communist takeover. Ho Chi Minh City in particular has suffered from the loss of its Chinese shopkeepers and the resulting inflation and unemployment.

On December 25, 1978, with the concurrence of the Soviet Union, Vietnamese troops invaded Cambodia and established a new government led by an unknown Vietnamese-trained Cambodian named Heng Samrin. The Vietnamese claimed that they launched their invasion to restore order and security in border areas by punishing Cambodia for a long series of border incursions and for intransigence in negotiations. The Vietnamese also insisted that they were liberating Cambodians from the genocide and repression of the Pol Pot regime. The invasion acted as an impetus for the subsequent Chinese invasion of Vietnam in February 1979. The Chinese hoped that their own offensive would force Vietnam to withdraw its occupation force of 200,000 troops from Cambodia. China desired to "teach Vietnam a lesson," to convince the Vietnamese that China was not a paper tiger, to punish the country for its harsh treatment of overseas Chinese, and to send a signal to the Soviet Union that China would not acquiesce to growing Soviet influence in Southeast Asia. Neither country was able to claim a clear-cut victory.

Vietnamese expectations that independence from foreign exploitation for the first time in over a hundred years would bring them a better life were dashed by the continued deterioration of the economy. In the 1980s, a decade after their defeat of the United States—the world's mightiest and most technologically sophisticated nation—the Vietnamese people's standard of living was worse than before the war. Indeed, the economy had advanced little since the French colonization of Vietnam in the late nineteenth century.[2]

The Sixth Congress of the Communist Party of Vietnam (CPV) realized the seriousness of the economic malaise and met in December 1986 to implement a plan to remedy the problems. Nguyen Van Linh, a prominent reformer, was named CPV general secretary. His appointment and the retirement of such old-guard communist revolutionary leaders as President Truong Chinh, Premier Pham Van Dong, and Foreign Minister Le Duc Tho signaled a significant turn in Vietnamese politics. The leadership shift to the more pragmatic, social welfare–oriented, reform-minded younger officials from the ideologically conservative, security-minded party leaders was the first major break in leadership patterns since Ho Chi Minh came to power after World War II.

The succession to Nguyen Van Linh was carried out smoothly, just as a smooth succession had occurred in 1969 when Ho Chi Minh died. After Ho's death, a collective leadership had arisen with Le Duan the first among equals. No one could replace Ho, for his stature was too vast to be inherited by a single person. When Le Duan died in 1986, the succession to Linh again proceeded without purges, despite the desperate state of the nation's economy.

At the December 1986 party congress, Linh set forth a policy of renovation *(doi moi)*, a plan publicly approved by the CPV leaders, all of whom agreed that the policies of the previous eleven years—since the end of the war—should not be continued. Renovation called for major economic and political changes with the proviso that the party-led dictatorship of the proletariat remain sacrosanct.

Nevertheless, renovation was difficult because a strong coalition of conservative party leaders felt threatened by the changes. CPV leaders feared that the party's dominance would be lost, and military leaders— who played an important role in the politburo—believed that renovation threatened national security because it diminished the importance of military strength in favor of economic development.[3]

The changes included rapid movement away from the centrally planned economy and development of a more market-oriented model. The shift built upon the economic reforms that had begun in the late 1970s when a contract system was introduced and decentralization of various sectors of the economy carried out. The contract system had allowed peasants to sell a small portion of their crops after meeting their obligations to the government. That system had stagnated when peasants refused to cooperate because their profits were so small that they had no incentive to produce more. The new plan provided greater incentives, including ownership of land formerly nationalized by the government.

Renovation also called for more public debate and more power for the National Assembly, the main legislative branch of the government. Political prisoners were released and corrupt officials ousted from their positions. The press was allowed to criticize government policies more aggressively.

Although initially popular, renovation met with sharp criticism when the new policies failed to improve the economy. In 1988, for example, famine was barely averted in the northern provinces, and inflation increased to almost 1,000 percent. In response, hard-liners insisted that a conservative, Do Muoi, be named prime minister. Uncharacteristically, the National Assembly members demanded that two candidates be permitted to run, for the first time challenging the CPV central committee's nominee for a key government post. Do Muoi, who was unpopular in the south because of his role in introducing repressive socialist policies, won only 64 percent of the assembly's votes against his reform-minded opponent, Vo Van Kiet, an unprecedented rebuke to the CPV. The reformers lost the vote, but the dissent allowed in the National Assembly reflected the new openness of the regime.

Renovation was also threatened by the remarkable changes in Eastern Europe, as country after country brought down communist rulers. Of most concern to the Vietnamese party leaders was the fall of Romania's dictator, Nicolae Ceausescu, who most had believed was invincible. The people's revolt against the military in Burma also worried Vietnamese leaders, as there were many parallels between the two countries' bleak economic conditions. These international changes, however, only strengthened the position of the hard-liners. Vietnam was one of the few nations in the world that condemned Poland's change to a noncommunist government and praised China's crushing of its democracy movement.

Also jeopardizing renovation was the reformers' decision to disengage from Cambodia, withdrawing all troops by September 1989. The conservatives argued that Vietnam received no visible benefit from the disengagement, not even expressions of gratitude let alone offers from the

United States to move toward normalizing diplomatic relations and ending the trade embargo that had been in effect since the war. This lack of positive response from the United States caused the reformers to be more orthodox and to take fewer risks.[4] Also, the reformers were more careful about making public claims regarding the benefits that would be forthcoming to Vietnam as a result of their more pragmatic policies.

Despite renovation, human rights violations continued in Vietnam. Amnesty International documented cases of detention without trial of former civil servants and members of the South Vietnamese armed forces in reeducation camps. Also documented were unfair trials of alleged opponents of the government and prisoners of conscience and reports of torture and ill treatment of prisoners in police custody and in prisons. Amnesty International concluded that the treatment of dissenters had improved since renovation but that the record was still unacceptable.

As Vietnam entered the 1990s, the government was in transition from the old-guard revolutionary forces, who had held power in the north since independence, to younger (although still elderly) reform-minded communists, who were more willing to try new means to achieve their aims. These means fluctuated between hard-line and more open policies. Although the zigs and zags of government policy remained unpredictable, the ultimate goal remained constant: perpetuating the central power of the CPV.

From 1992 to 1997, the CPV opened much of its discussions to public scrutiny, leading critics to complain that the party was introducing only half-hearted reforms and allowing second-rate officials to run the economy. Adding to the CPV's problems was the growing irrelevance of the party in the minds of many Vietnamese, who had grown intolerant of the reactionary, incompetent, and corrupt party leadership. The CPV launched a major drive to increase party membership after years of shrinking support.

Conflict also continued between dissident Buddhist monks and communist government officials. The Buddhists wished to establish the Unified Buddhist Church in place of the Vietnam Buddhist Church, which had long been under the dominance of the CPV. Human rights issues continued to arise, forcing officials to stress that Hanoi's concept of human rights differed from that of the West, which the officials claimed overemphasized individual rights and absolute individual freedoms. The government also spoke harshly against the rise of licentious behavior, especially in Ho Chi Minh City, where there were an estimated 50,000 prostitutes and 30,000 drug users.

Dramatic and far-reaching changes in Vietnam occurred in 1995, when the country became a member of ASEAN, and Washington and Hanoi normalized diplomatic relations. The stumbling block for diplomatic relations had been the American perception that not all U.S. soldiers from the war classified as missing in action (MIAs) had been accounted for by the Vietnamese. Once that barrier was overcome, the process moved smoothly, especially when conservative American politicians and business leaders decided to support new ties. They had seen the advantages to American business from the 1994 lifting of the U.S. embargo against Vietnam. There was virtually no negative reaction by Americans to the new policy, except for minor complaints against President Clinton himself for not having participated in the war thirty years earlier.

There is great irony in the acceptance of Vietnam as ASEAN's seventh member because the alliance was originally formed principally to oppose "Vietnamese intervention" in noncommunist Southeast Asia. By 1996, ASEAN members no longer believed that Vietnam had aggressive intentions. Instead, they believed that economic ties were more important to the area than security arrangements.

The three most important positions in the contemporary Vietnamese political structure have been the CPV secretary general, the prime minister, and the president. Since the death of Ho Chi Minh, these positions have been held by elderly leaders who were participants in Ho's revolution. In 1997, at the National Assembly (whose members had been selected at CPV party congresses), seventy-six-year-old Le Duc Anh and seventy-five-year-old Vo Van Kiet resigned and were replaced by younger, more reform-minded leaders. Secretary General Do Muoi remained in his position. Choosing Vietnam's leadership is always complicated because balance must be achieved between regions, between civilians and the military, and between conservatives and reformers. Phan Van Khai, a sixty-three-year-old Russian-trained economist from the south, became prime minister, and Tran Duc Luong, sixty, became president.

## Institutions and Social Groups

### Ho Chi Minh

On May 19, 1990, the people of Vietnam celebrated the one hundredth anniversary of Ho Chi Minh's birth. As the founding father of independent, communist Vietnam; the victorious leader over the Japanese, French, and Americans; and the founder of the CPV, Ho is the most important Vietnamese of contemporary times and perhaps the most important leader in recent Southeast Asian history. He was and remains a central institution—the symbol of united, nationalist, communist Vietnam. Pictures of Ho are ubiquitous in the northern half of the country, and millions of people have viewed his embalmed body in the Soviet-built mausoleum in Hanoi.

Ho was the son of a Confucian scholar who was active in anticolonial activities. His mother died when he was ten. Throughout his life he used numerous pseudonyms (the name Ho Chi Minh means "he who enlightens"). In his youth, he traveled to the Soviet Union, China, New York, London, and Paris. He became a committed communist and founded the forerunner parties of the CPV, including the Indo-Chinese Communist Party in 1930 and the Vietminh in 1941. His tastes were simple, even ascetic, yet he was tenacious and sometimes ruthless in the means he used to achieve his goals.

Ho died six years before the nation was reunited. His last testament requested that at his death there be a one-year moratorium on farm taxes and that his ashes be placed in urns in the three parts of Vietnam: Cochin China, Annam, and Tonkin. However, these requests were not heeded by Ho's successors. Instead, taxes were raised, and his body was embalmed in a massive building similar to Lenin's mausoleum in Moscow. No Vietnamese leader has subsequently received the adulation Ho received during his life, although every leader has attempted to wrap himself in Ho's mantle.

## Communist Party of Vietnam

Although the communist parties of postwar Eastern Europe were imposed from without by Soviet arms, the communist party is indigenous to the Vietnamese and was the vehicle for the independence struggle against the French colonialists and, later, the Americans. In modern Vietnamese history, the CPV has had an almost exclusive claim to represent the broader ideals of nationalism and patriotism. For many Vietnamese, the CPV and nationalist struggle are identical.

Total membership in the party has stagnated at about 1.8 million, or 3 percent of the population. In effect, the party controlled the state until the era of renovation, when the state was given more authority. Vietnam's constitution of 1980 gave the party the leading role in society, enforcing a unified Marxist-Leninist policy line for the state and society.

However, the party is not unified. Vietnamese politics as practiced in the politburo is best understood by analogy to the great game of *bung-di*, or faction bashing.[5] Factions, long prevalent in Vietnamese society, form around individuals but traffic in issues. They are enduring but not permanent, and they can divide and re-form to meet changing needs. Despite attempts to contain factionalism, they remain ubiquitous. The present politburo can be divided into four major factions: reformers, neoconservatives, bureaucrats, and the military.[6] In a sense, these categories are misleading because all thirteen politburo members are "reformers"; that is, all agree that the status quo is and has been unworkable. All are "conservative" in being cautious about taking risks; all agree that national security is a top priority, and all have bureaucratic constituencies that they control.

The CPV's Seventh Congress met in Hanoi in June 1991 to set forth its development plan focusing on free-market mechanisms and the continuation of one-party rule. The congress was momentous in that it institutionalized capitalist economics, an inevitable change following the worldwide rejection of socialism, while insisting on the total control of the CPV. Nevertheless, the CPV granted new powers to the National Assembly, turning the legislature into a more meaningful lawmaking body rather than just a rubber stamp. The assembly was to have more power to implement policies set forth by the party.

Vietnam's new constitution, promulgated in 1992, created the post of president and strengthened the positions of prime minister and the National Assembly. The prime minister would head a cabinet and would have to be an elected member of the assembly. Private property was enshrined as a citizen's right. Although subsequent National Assembly elections involved more candidates than available seats, the CPV continued to dominate the electoral process, with noncommunists kept off the ballot.

In 1993, the major positions of power were held by two elderly leaders who were moderately progressive: Secretary General Do Muoi (seventy-nine years old at the time) and Prime Minister Vo Van Kiet. (As mentioned above, the prime minister, along with President Le Duc Anh, retired in 1997.) However, the party politburo was made up of younger members than ever before, was more concerned with technology than ideology, and was no longer dominated by the heroes of the revolutionary struggle against the French and the Americans.

The CPV's Eighth Congress was held in June and July 1996. The congress resolutions appear to have been unanimously approved by the delegates. In reality, there was much difference of opinion behind closed doors in the months preceding the congress. The Eighth Congress was particularly contentious because reformers were in conflict with conservatives. The conservative character of the congress was clear when it was announced that 60 percent of GNP, rather than 40 percent, should come from the state sector. The congress appeared to be torn by the many conflicts facing Vietnam: reform versus state control, factional disputes among politicians and military generals, state enterprises versus privatization, northern domination versus southern domination, and the older generation versus youth. Given these dilemmas, it is not surprising that the Eighth Congress chose to keep the country in a holding pattern.

## Military

The Vietnamese army is the creation of the CPV, and the leading generals are members of the party leadership. After 1975, the 1.2 million–member

People's Army of Vietnam (PAVN), initially given the mission of reunifying the nation, was charged with defending Vietnam from external attack, such as when the Chinese crossed Vietnam's northern border in 1979. In contrast to the armies of Thailand, Burma, and Indonesia, the Vietnamese army has not threatened a coup against the communist leadership. Its role remains subordinate to that of the party.

## Mandate of Heaven

Traditional Confucianist thought remains an important institution in Vietnam; according to Confucianism, each person must carry out his or her duty by fulfilling the obligations of a subordinate to a superior, and vice versa, in order to maintain a universal, harmonious moral order. The emperor is as obliged to rule according to moral principles as the peasant is to follow his commands. When harmony does not exist or when there are wars, pestilence, or natural calamities, the ruled may perceive that the emperor has lost the "mandate of heaven." In other words, the emperor's personal virtue is lacking, for otherwise the cosmos would not be out of harmony.

The "mandate of heaven" is an important concept for illuminating authority relationships in Vietnam. On the one hand, one can interpret the cosmological beliefs of the Vietnamese as essentially conservative, for the mandate of heaven is lost or gained by means that are beyond the control of individuals. On the other hand, the cosmological view can provide a rationale for rebellion, for if the emperor is lacking in virtue—with a consequent disharmonious effect on the cosmos and society—his mandate is perceived as lost and his rule is called into question. The rise of a new government is proof that the new revolutionary regime has assumed the mandate. Accordingly, the ruled have transferred their allegiance to the new government with a renewed sense of community.

The Vietnamese had sensed the changing of the mandate during the post–World War II struggle, first against the French and then against the Americans. According to Confucianist interpretation, Ho Chi Minh inherited the mandate when he declared Vietnam's independence in 1945, and the communist triumph shifted authority relationships rapidly and traumatically to the new communist rulers. In April 1975, the communist mandate spread southward to encompass the former South Vietnam. The Marxist view of collective discipline is not incompatible with the Confucianist concept of societal order, and the centralized, hierarchical nature of the command structure under a vanguard class is compatible with a Confucianist mandarin state. For these reasons, and because the communist government took total control of the society, the Vietnamese are likely to carry out their duty to obey the sovereign leaders until they sense that these leaders have lost the mandate.

## Democratization

In 1989 the central committee of the CPV, alarmed by developments in Eastern Europe and Burma, rejected appeals for political pluralism in Vietnam. President Nguyen Van Linh stated that the party rejected calls for "bourgeois liberalization, pluralism, political plurality, and multi-opposition parties aimed at denying Marxism-Leninism, socialism, and the party's leadership."[7]

From the Vietnamese perspective, Western democracy represents all that their own leaders have rejected: unstable regimes led by bourgeois leaders for their own interests against the interests of the masses. The Vietnamese also reject the "arrogance" of the Western world (and now the Eastern European nations as well), which is critical of the Vietnamese government. The Solidarity movement in Poland was condemned by the Vietnamese as counterrevolutionary when it replaced Poland's communist government. Vietnamese leaders have stated that Vietnam is not prepared for democracy, that conditions in the country are not appropriate for democracy. In what Linh characterizes as a period of restoration and economic travail after a destructive war, the strong leadership of the party is necessary to ensure the nation's stability and progress.

In the economic domain, democratization is not such a pejorative term. Decentralization and accountability are accepted as necessary for an effective economy. Economic principles of the market and competition, once viewed as decadent bourgeois concepts, have become the centerpieces of renovation.

Vietnam has no history of democracy. Its traditions are Confucianist, stressing hierarchy and order, and more recently communist, emphasizing the unquestioned supremacy of the party. There have been few popular demonstrations for democratic rights, and the Vietnam War was never a struggle for civil liberties and representative government. The movement of the Eastern European communist governments toward democracy has not impelled the Vietnamese leadership or the people to initiate a similar transformation of their own government.

## Economic Development

After the end of the war in 1975, the Vietnamese economy declined for a full fifteen years. Inflation rates were astronomical, and unemployment hovered at about 20 percent. Infrastructural essentials such as ports, roads, and electricity were primitive, and housing abysmal. Vietnam's banking system was barely viable, partly because there was so little managerial expertise. Annual per capita income was estimated to be $200, making Vietnam one of the poorest nations in the world. Famine, which threatened the northern provinces in 1988, affecting 10 million farmers, forced Vietnam—a country once self-sufficient in rice—to appeal for international food aid. Ho Chi Minh's favorite aphorism, emblazoned on red banners strung across streets throughout Vietnam—"Nothing is more precious than independence and freedom"—was interpreted in an ironic and sardonic sense. In unguarded moments, Vietnamese stated that "nothing" was exactly what they had.

Given Vietnam's superb natural and human resources, the country's poverty was all the more shocking and embarrassing to Vietnamese leaders. However, there were important reasons why the country was unable to develop in parallel fashion to the neighboring ASEAN nations. A major reason is the extensive war damage, which required tremendous resources to repair. In the south alone, the war produced 20,000 bomb craters, 10 million refugees, 362,000 invalids, 1 million widows, 880,000 orphans, 250,000 drug addicts, 300,000 prostitutes, and 3 million unemployed. Two-thirds of the villages and 5 million hectares of forests were destroyed.[8]

The U.S. involvement in South Vietnam created a dependent economy, and the billions of dollars spent on the war brought a surfeit of capital that ended abruptly when the United States disengaged. Hanoi had expected to receive some $3 billion in reparations aid, which had been promised by U.S. Secretary of State Henry Kissinger but was later refused when the United States maintained that North Vietnam had not carried out the terms of the Paris Peace Accords. Soviet aid did make up for the loss of Western aid and trade lost to the Vietnamese because of the U.S.-sponsored trade embargo. Moreover, the Soviet Union's technological aid was insufficient in many ways.

Adding to Vietnam's woes was mismanagement by its leadership. Alternating between reform and orthodoxy, Vietnam's leaders "displayed a paranoid world view, a low adaptability level, perfidy consistently perceived in the motives of others and perpetuation of a cult-type leadership capable of believing the illogical, the irrational, even the absurd."[9] Nationalization and collectivization, thrust upon the south after reunification, were unfailingly disastrous, largely because of the refusal of southerners to adhere to socialist policies. Peasants refused to meet their obligations to the state when the state's prices for their crops did not cover even the costs of production.

To overcome the crisis, the CPV's Sixth Congress in December 1986 proposed major reforms and initiatives. Rice output in 1986 was far below that in 1942, and northern farmers, who were members of cooperatives, produced 52 percent less than private farmers from the south. To alleviate this situation, land laws were modified to guarantee farmers a ten- to fifteen-year tenure on land they cultivated, although the expectation was that land could henceforth be owned in perpetuity and be inherited. This policy change signaled the end of efforts to collectivize agriculture in the south.

The 1986 reforms gave farmers the legal right to sell their produce on the free market after each paid a tax based on his or her output. Approximately 10 to 20 percent of the tax went to the state for the farmers' use of cooperatively owned machinery and for fertilizer and other necessities. Under the new system, farmers could keep a far larger percentage of their output than under the former contract system. Although it took several years for the policy to make a positive impact, Vietnam reemerged in 1989 as a major rice exporter for the first time since the 1950s. Vietnam became the world's third-largest rice exporter after the United States and Thailand; most of its rice was exported to West Africa, the Philippines, India, Sri Lanka, and China.

Vietnam's foreign investment code was also revised to attract more foreign investors. To draw joint ventures, the government liberalized tax policies and extended guarantees that investment capital would not be expropriated or joint ventures nationalized.[10] The 1987 investment law offered a two-year tax moratorium for joint ventures and established export processing zones in which foreign companies could import materials, use low-cost local labor for assembly, and export final products. A large proportion of the new investors were overseas Vietnamese.[11] The new code increased trade with Japan, Singapore, Hong Kong, France, Indonesia, and India but did not bring in the amount of capital hoped for because of the continuing U.S. trade embargo. More and more countries, however, broke the embargo to take advantage of the liberalized trade and investment opportunities, especially regarding offshore oil exploration.

The reforms made a dramatic difference in Vietnam's everyday economy. Construction of homes, buildings, bridges, roads, and schools, for example, burgeoned throughout the country, even in the north where the economy had been stagnant for many decades. Privately run restaurants and shops opened and flourished. Inflation dropped to more manageable levels as a result of the devaluation of the dong to the free-market rate, and government austerity measures—recommended by the International Monetary Fund, with which Vietnam hoped to restore relations—were adopted in order to attract investment, credit, and technology from the West.

Vietnam remained impoverished, but for the first time since the end of the war there was economic development. In a sense, however, the country remained divided because development was more rapid in the south than in the north (partly as a result of the millions of dollars sent back to relatives from the one million southern Vietnamese living abroad). Unemployment remained high, especially among those considered "unreliable" because of their involvement with the former Saigon regime. Peasants who continued to farm within a small margin of error risked devastation by natural disasters, such as drought or flooding, or by the possible imposition of orthodox socialist economics less favorable to small-scale agriculture under a new administration.

Having faced up to the nation's abysmal economy, in December 1990 the CPV set forth a plan called the "Draft Strategy of Socio-Economic Stabilization and Development up to the Year 2000." The plan's goals were to double the country's per capita income, raise rice production by 50 percent, triple electricity output, and achieve a fivefold increase for exports—all by the year 2000. These goals were thought to be unattainable without significant investment from the West, which would be an impossibility until the trade and aid embargoes were lifted.

As a sign of confidence in the future, Vietnam proclaimed 1990 the "Year of the Tourist" and began building hotels and increasing airline traffic to Ho Chi Minh City. (In 1989 only 50,000 tourists visited Vietnam, whereas in the same year 5 million tourists visited Thailand.)

It was initially believed that the loss of the Soviet Union as a major financial supporter would undermine the Vietnamese economy irrevocably. However, by 1992 the economy had improved, with increased rice production and controlled inflation. Both exports and imports increased dramatically, and trade with Japan as well as Singapore and the other ASEAN countries more than made up for the Soviet loss. Manufacturing, which rose 14 percent in 1992, centered on textiles and light industrial products. The U.S.-led embargo continued to undercut investment capital, and infrastructure problems discouraged many foreign investors. Nevertheless, Vietnam's economy in 1993 showed some signs of progress after decades of disaster.

The ending of constraints on the International Monetary Fund's assistance to Vietnam in 1993 and the lifting of the American embargo in 1994 were responsible for a huge increase in foreign direct investment. These openings represented the breakdown of the last external barriers to Vietnam's goal of becoming an Asian "Tiger." GNP growth rose to an annual 8.2 percent with progress in all economic sectors. The politicians remained committed to *doi moi*, so that the 1994–1996 period became an era of fundamental economic change. Ho Chi Minh City's economy grew by an astonishing 15 percent, and the new free-market system inexorably affected every sector of the economy. Vietnam was increasingly viewed as the "new economic frontier," capable of achieving extraordinary growth rates because of its disciplined workforce, cheap labor and materials, and zealous goal to join the global capitalist system.

Not even catastrophic natural disasters could ruin Vietnam's progress toward "Tigerhood." In 1995 and 1996, annual economic growth rates stood at 9.5 percent, the highest in the world. Inflation stayed below 10 percent during these years. Vietnam had become a major rice exporter; indeed, total exports grew by 27 percent in 1995–1996. Although the CVP was still dominated by a gerontocracy, the party continued its program of economic liberalization with surprising unanimity.

Given the country's remarkable growth and the enthusiasm of the world community for the "new" Vietnam, the subsequent difficulties of 1997 were surprising. Suddenly the economic boom hit a plateau, and growth rates actually declined to 7 percent (still high in comparison to growth rates in industrialized nations). Foreign entrepreneurs reduced their investment by about one-third from the total for the previous year. The number of tourists also declined precipitously.

The major source of disenchantment was the bureaucratic waste and corruption that made it almost impossible for investors and entrepreneurs to move forward with dispatch. Even low-level policy decisions required the approval of those highest in the CPV hierarchy, wasting a tremendous amount of time and talent. Also, the banking system remained primitive, virtually incapable of making or collecting on loans. The dong was overvalued, especially during the 1997 currency crisis that struck the rest of Southeast Asia. Vietnamese exports were becoming more expensive even though the products were often of low quality. Foreign companies shut down their factories in the absence of legal contracts and to protest against the emphasis on under-the-table payments demanded by both private business elites and public officials.

The nation's new leaders, including the economist, Prime Minister Phan Van Khai, understood the depth of the crisis and called for more reform. However, as long as the CPV retains control over every aspect of society, reform will be slow and the downturn of the once flourishing economy may continue.

## The Vietnamese State

Until recently, the Communist Party of Vietnam has been the state. All authoritative decisions were made by the party, then disseminated to the populace through a tightly controlled organization that allowed no dissent. Civil liberties have been curtailed to ensure that the party is uncontested. Only since 1986 have new institutions emerged that have real power, such as the National Assembly.

Vietnam is the archetypal example of a nation that endured major social disturbances that uprooted the traditional bases of social control and cleared the way for new state leaders. For Vietnam, a succession of wars and revolutions led to fundamental organizational changes in everyday life, concentrating social control into a single agency—the CPV.

These social dislocations occurred at a time when support and shelter for Vietnamese state leaders were provided by the world communist movement. Since World War II, Vietnam has never been free of either potential or actual aggression by outsiders. The Japanese, French, Americans, and Chinese have all intervened, compelling state leaders to mobilize their forces and concentrate their power and capabilities. Vietnam is therefore a classic example of a country in which war and the threat of war induces state leaders to take risks to consolidate social control and thereby create a strong state.

Vietnamese rulers have no constituencies except their party leaders, and state bureaucrats identify their ultimate interests with those of the state as an autonomous organization. Loyalties lie with the state rather than with autonomous religious, ethnic, or class interests.

Whether Vietnam has prospered from skillful top-down leadership is debatable. In many respects, the Vietnamese state has not had the capacity to meet the everyday economic needs of its people. Except for Burma, Laos, and Cambodia, no country in Southeast Asia is as poor. On the other hand, Ho Chi Minh stands out in modern history precisely because of his skills in using given circumstances to concentrate social control. His successors, who have had to deal with more difficult issues than nationalism, have had to meet the needs of 72 million persons whose expectations have been high, especially since achieving victory over foreign aggressors and the reunification of the country. Thus far, the state's capacity to meet these needs has been weak.

## Foreign Policy

The major goal of Vietnamese foreign policy has been unchanged: to secure the sovereignty of the nation against all aggressors. To meet this goal, Vietnamese foreign policy has sought to ensure a cooperative, non-threatening Indochina firmly allied with Vietnam; to prevent an anticommunist front from threatening Vietnamese interests; to limit the role of the United States, China, and (until 1991) the Soviet Union in Vietnam's sphere of influence; and to establish working relations with neighboring ASEAN countries. These latter, more specific goals have met with varying degrees of success.

Since at least 1975, Vietnamese foreign policy has been framed by fundamental Marxist-Leninist principles. The nation's reliance on socialist solidarity versus the interventionist, exploitative capitalist world has narrowed its options and reduced the flexibility that the conduct of foreign relations requires in a world of fast-moving change. Until the mid-1980s, foreign policy was carried out in *dau tranh* (struggle) terms, in which diplomacy was treated strategically—like protracted military conflicts—

over an extended period of time.[12] This approach made negotiations with allies and adversaries difficult because Vietnam's arguments were presented as statements of superior virtue, not as expressions of national interest.

After 1986, ideological fundamentalism decreased, and policymakers stressed the need for Vietnam to play a greater role in the global economic system. Vietnam's leaders saw that communist governments were falling around the world, that Vietnam was economically isolated, and that the nation was increasingly dependent on the Soviet Union; thus, they moved in fundamentally new directions in foreign policy.

Vietnam's military withdrawal from Cambodia in 1989 was one major change. Politburo liberals argued that keeping Cambodia as a friendly neighbor was important but not to the point of threatening Vietnam's economic collapse. These reformers argued that withdrawal from Cambodia would end Vietnam's international isolation by leading to the normalization of ties with the United States, halting the multilateral trade embargo against Vietnam, and inviting Western aid.[13] Adding to pressure to withdraw was the restiveness of Vietnam's armed forces, demoralized by the military stalemate in Cambodia that had cost some 55,000 Vietnamese lives.

However, the withdrawal in September 1989 did not bring the expected international gratitude. Instead, ASEAN and the United States faulted the troop withdrawal for not being part of a comprehensive peace plan for Cambodia and for not allowing monitoring by an international control mechanism. It was not until July 1990, when U.S. Secretary of State James Baker announced that his government would begin direct negotiations with Vietnam relating to the Cambodian situation, that the withdrawal elicited a positive response from the United States. Meanwhile, no moves were made toward normalization of relations, and the trade embargo continued.

Vietnam also moved to improve relations with Asian and Western nations interested in developing economic ties. Hundreds of trade and investment delegations from Japan, Taiwan, South Korea, Thailand, and various European countries arrived to set up business ventures. Relations with China also improved, partly because of the vast border trade between the two nations.

For the United States, Vietnam and the rest of Indochina had been a low foreign policy priority since the end of the Vietnam War. The United States was no longer concerned about Chinese aggression in Southeast Asia; nor did the United States see itself as the guardian of the region, once thought to be vulnerable to conquest by a monolithic communist empire. The ASEAN countries were flourishing and no longer viewed themselves as potential victims of Vietnamese aggression. In many respects, U.S. goals in Southeast Asia had been attained sufficiently to allow the United States to focus more on Japan and China than on Indochina.

Nevertheless, in 1988 U.S. interest in Indochina increased as the withdrawal of Vietnamese troops from Cambodia and the threat of a new Khmer Rouge takeover in that country again brought Vietnam into the news. Memories of the war the United States had lost were fading, and Vietnam had become more cooperative on POW-MIA issues. Hanoi had accepted a standing U.S. offer to conduct joint U.S.-funded searches in provincial areas where the remains of MIAs were thought to be located. As these difficult problems were moving toward resolution, the question of normalizing relations between the United States and Vietnam was brought to the fore.

A longer-term argument favoring normalization concerned the need to balance the presence of the Soviet Union in Southeast Asia. The development of Soviet naval bases at Cam Ranh Bay and Da Nang was particularly troubling to ASEAN, Japan, the United States, and China, all of whom viewed the Soviet military buildup in Vietnam as a security threat. The Cam Ranh base provided potential control over the vital waterways of the Pacific Ocean, the South China Sea, and the Indian Ocean, which were deemed indispensable for U.S. trade, Japan's access to oil, and the security of ASEAN.

As Soviet aid to Vietnam decreased and as President Mikhail Gorbachev confirmed the USSR's intention to give up its military bases there eventually, Vietnam became vulnerable to potential Chinese aggression. Russians were not liked in Vietnam, and there was a surprising feeling of warmth for Americans in both the northern and southern areas. Moreover, it was not in the best interests of the United States to have the Soviet Union and China make the crucial decisions affecting Vietnam's present and future status. Normalization would allow the United States to act as a counterweight to Soviet and Chinese influence.

A different argument for normalization suggested that American support would help the cause of the reformers in Vietnam against the hardliners. By expanding aid and trade relations, Vietnam's economy would be strengthened, thereby strengthening political liberalization as well. In noncommunist Southeast Asia, economic growth and prosperity were the underpinnings of political stability and the movement toward democracy, and the same pattern might apply to Vietnam. By balancing pressure for reform with normalization, the United States would help the Vietnamese end their political isolation.

Supporters of normalization noted the parallel cases of Germany and Japan, two nations the United States had fought in World War II. U.S.

support of those nations in the postwar period encouraged them to become the closest U.S. allies in Europe and Asia, respectively, and opening diplomatic relations with Vietnam could produce a similar outcome.

Normalization would also enable the United States to better monitor the Orderly Departure Program (ODP), which was designed to give Vietnamese nationals who had worked with the U.S. government prior to 1975 an opportunity to move to the United States as refugees. In 1989, when approximately 19,500 ODP refugees came to the United States, Vietnam agreed to resettle more than 300,000 former prisoners, most of whom had been officials associated with the U.S.-backed government in South Vietnam and had subsequently been detained by the invading North Vietnamese. In addition, a U.S. presence would encourage Vietnam to repatriate refugees.

Vietnam shifted its policy slightly in 1989, agreeing to repatriate some refugees in order to remove an obstacle to improved relations with its neighbors that had been a source of friction since the first wave of refugees in 1975.[14] As countries of "first asylum" for Vietnamese refugees, many of Vietnam's neighbors—including Thailand, Malaysia, the Philippines, and Hong Kong—had been unduly burdened by the obligation to provide refuge over the years to the enormous numbers of people fleeing Vietnam. Normalization of ties with the United States would facilitate discussion of this and other humanitarian issues.

The last argument for normalization related to the perceived best interests of the United States. Vietnam was viewed by other Asian countries as the next economic frontier, and Japan, South Korea, Taiwan, and Thailand were already investing heavily in the country, taking advantage of its inexpensive labor and disciplined workforce. With its liberal new foreign investment code, Vietnam had become more enticing to business ventures. As their economy strengthened and their infrastructure improved, the Vietnamese could become an economic power in Southeast Asia. U.S. business interests were increasingly supportive of normalization so that the trade embargo could be lifted.

Arguments against normalization stressed that diplomatic relations with Vietnam would legitimate a repressive government. Indeed, many Vietnamese refugees in the United States opposed normalization for that reason. In their view, the North Vietnamese had brutally and illegally taken control of the south, and they should not be rewarded for that action. Moreover, normalization would provide incentives to international organizations to aid Vietnam, thereby providing its communist government with resources for further repression.

Normalization could also remove the major lever the United States had to influence Vietnamese behavior. Because Vietnam desired normalization, some argued that it was more willing to accede to U.S. demands in order to encourage the United States to end its boycott. From a geopolitical perspective, some analysts argued that normalization would cause China and the Soviet Union to seek a greater role in Southeast Asia to counter the new U.S. involvement in Indochina. Also, the U.S. alliance with Vietnam might cause China to provide greater support to the Khmer Rouge forces in Cambodia.

From a Vietnamese perspective, normalization was desirable, notwithstanding the government's negative view of past U.S. involvement in Indochina. Vietnamese leaders believed that the United States helped France attempt to restore its colonial control over Indochina, helped divide the country in the Geneva Conference in 1954, bombed their nation indiscriminately during the Vietnam War (causing 2 million casualties), punished them with a worldwide trade embargo, allied itself with Vietnam's traditional enemy, China, and condemned Vietnam for its intervention in Cambodia despite its role in ending the horrific regime of Pol Pot. Notwithstanding these negative perceptions, Vietnam made clear its desire for normalization in order to end the blocking of U.N. aid and World Bank loans as well as to reverse U.S. opposition to investment from Japan and western Europe. Vietnam also desired a counterbalance to its overdependent relationship with the Soviet Union.

Most observers believed that Vietnam and the United States would establish diplomatic relations in 1992 before the end of President George Bush's administration. Because Vietnam had withdrawn its troops from Cambodia, had supported the Cambodian peace process, and had cooperated on POW-MIA issues, officials in Hanoi believed that the embargo would be lifted and diplomatic relations restored. Indeed, the Bush administration began the process by softening the terms of the embargo and allowing the resumption of telephone links with Vietnam. U.S. firms were allowed to sign contracts, which could quickly be executed once the trade embargo was lifted. U.S. companies could open offices in Vietnam and carry out feasibility studies. President Bush announced that "we can begin writing the last chapter of the Vietnam War." Nevertheless, the Bush administration did not follow through.

Bill Clinton announced early in his presidency that diplomatic relations would not be restored until "every MIA and POW is accounted for." This impossible condition discouraged supporters of improved ties between the two nations. They surmised that Clinton might be more hesitant than Bush to open relations with Vietnam, given allegations during the presidential campaign that Clinton dodged the draft during the Vietnam War. Meanwhile, virtually every other Western nation was involved in various economic relationships with the Vietnamese. Japan soon joined Singapore, Taiwan, and South Korea to become Vietnam's leading trade and investment partners. It was not until 1994 and 1995 that the embargo was lifted and diplomatic relations established, respectively.

The demise of the world's socialist nations undercut Vietnamese foreign policy, which was based on solidarity with the Soviet Union and its allies. This dramatic change made improving Vietnam's ties with the Western capitalist world the only possible means of future economic aid and trade. At the same time, Vietnam mended fences with its traditional adversary, China; leaders of the two nations attended a summit and restored many crucial ties. Although these improved relations were damaged by Chinese claims of sovereignty over the Spratly Islands in the South China Sea, the positive aspects largely outweighed the negative ones.

Vietnam basked in its new status as ASEAN's seventh member; the country's recent foreign policy moves indicate that the development of economic ties has become far more important than the security considerations of the past. The language of Vietnam is increasingly about markets, investments, intellectual property rights, trade, and credits. Few can remember that just three decades ago the vocabulary was about weaponry, bombings, military bases, refugees, and the escalation of war.

## Conclusion

Vietnam's future is linked to the outcome of factional struggles between reformers and conservatives. With rich natural resources, a disciplined workforce, and a long tradition of entrepreneurial activity, Vietnam has the capacity to become Asia's new economic frontier. Until 1986, the communist government undermined Vietnam's advantages with its oppressive policies and mismanagement. The regime's realization of this fact has brought about major economic reform, which bodes well for the nation's future, but only if the nation's leaders understand that political liberalization must accompany economic renovation.

## Notes

1. Frederick Z. Brown, *Second Chance: The United States and Indochina in the 1990s* (New York: Council on Foreign Relations, 1989), p. 39.

2. David G. Marr and Christine P. White, eds., *Postwar Vietnam: Dilemmas in Socialist Development* (Ithaca: Southeast Asia Program, Cornell University, 1988), p. 2.

3. Ronald J. Cima, "Vietnam's Economic Reform," *Asian Survey*, vol. 29, no. 8 (August 1989), p. 789.

4. Douglas Pike, "Change and Continuity in Vietnam," *Current History*, vol. 89, no. 545 (March 1990), p. 119.

5. Douglas Pike, "Political Institutionalization in Vietnam," in *Asian Political Institutionalization*, ed. Robert A. Scalapino, Seizaburo Sato, and Jusuf Wanandi (Berkeley: Institute of East Asian Studies, University of California, 1986), pp. 49–51.

6. Pike, "Change and Continuity in Vietnam," p. 118.

7. Far Eastern Economic Review, *Asia Yearbook, 1990* (Hong Kong: Far Eastern Economic Review, 1990), p. 241.

8. Marr and White, *Postwar Vietnam*, p. 3.

9. Pike, "Political Institutionalization in Vietnam," p. 43.

10. Ronald J. Cima, "Vietnam in 1988: The Brink of Renewal," *Asian Survey*, vol. 29, no. 1 (January 1989), p. 67.

11. Cima, "Vietnam's Economic Reform," p. 797.

12. Douglas Pike, "Vietnam and Its Neighbors: Internal Influences on External Relations," in *ASEAN in Regional and Global Context*, ed. Karl D. Jackson, Sukhumbhand Paribatra, and J. Soedjati Djiwandono (Berkeley: Institute of East Asian Studies, University of California, 1986), p. 240.

13. Ronald J. Cima, "Vietnam in 1989: Initiating the Post-Cambodia Period," *Asian Survey*, vol. 30, no. 10 (January 1990), p. 89.

14. Cima, "Vietnam's Economic Reform," p. 794.

# 11

## CAMBODIA

The many names under which Cambodia has lived in the past two decades reflect the turmoil this country has undergone. Cambodia was once known as the Kingdom of Cambodia, but the country became the Khmer Republic when the military came to power in 1970. From 1975 to 1979, the period of fanatic Khmer Rouge leadership, the country's name was changed to Democratic Kampuchea, followed by the People's Republic of Kampuchea when the Khmer Rouge was overthrown. In 1989, the country became the State of Cambodia.

Cambodians trace their heritage to the great Khmer civilization, which culminated in the twelfth century when the Khmers ruled over most of modern-day Cambodia, Laos, Thailand, and Vietnam. This magnificent civilization, symbolized by the great temples at Angkor, lasted over five hundred years and reached a level of military, technological, political, and philosophical achievement that was unmatched at the time in Southeast Asia. Angkor eventually fell, and the kingdom suffered from domestic instability and external invasions until 1864, when the French took over a weak Cambodia as a protectorate.

The great Khmer civilization has now become the State of Cambodia, with about 9 million residents—mostly rural farmers—almost all of whom are Buddhists who live in deep poverty. As a nation, Cambodia personifies tragedy, its people having suffered unspeakable horrors during the Khmer Rouge era from 1975 to the beginning of 1979. Indeed, neither the people nor the nation have fully recovered from these horrors.

Cambodia's search for identity and nationhood once freed from French colonialism was dominated by Prince Norodom Sihanouk, whom the French had placed on the throne in 1941. In 1955, one year after Cambodia's independence was granted, King Sihanouk abdicated and entered politics as Prince Sihanouk. His unrivaled dominance of Cambodian life from the end of World War II to 1970 was due to the way he had achieved leadership, which was by plebiscite, and to the unsurpassed loyalty of rural Cambodians. He was revered as a god-king in the tradition of the Angkor kings, and his authority rested on charismatic, traditional, repressive, and legal foundations.

Sihanouk, who controlled all important policymaking institutions, exhibited a remarkable capacity to keep each major sector of society in check, thereby maintaining political stability. His overthrow on March 17, 1970, was therefore a surprise to most analysts of Cambodian politics. On that date, while Sihanouk was in the Soviet Union, the Cambodian National Assembly—charging Sihanouk with abuses of office—unanimously condemned him to death for treason and corruption. His position was assumed by General Lon Nol, the premier in Sihanouk's government.

Sihanouk's downfall stemmed from the presence of North Vietnamese and Viet Cong forces in the so-called Cambodian sanctuaries. Against his army's wishes, Sihanouk had allowed the Vietnamese to use this territory, although his trip to Moscow was to request Soviet aid in ousting the Vietnamese. The Vietnamese presence in Cambodia had become so permanent that by mid-1969 they had built a base of support in a region that encompassed nearly one-fourth of Cambodia's total area. Sihanouk had also allowed shipments of Chinese arms across the country from the Cambodian port of Sihanoukville.

Sihanouk's relations with the United States during this time were both acrimonious and supportive. He opposed U.S. involvement in Vietnam, although as the North Vietnamese established themselves in Cambodian territory, he reversed policy and argued the need for an American force in Asia to provide a balance of power to the communist nations. From the U.S. perspective, Sihanouk was mercurial and untrustworthy, but there is no evidence that the U.S. government ever approved the Cambodian military's plan to overthrow Sihanouk.

From Sihanouk's perspective, his short-term changes in policy were consistent with his overall objective of keeping his country neutral and sovereign. Cambodia's history has been characterized by the attempts of more powerful neighbors as well as Western imperialists to dominate the country's political life. Therefore, Sihanouk's neutralism reflected his appreciation of historical precedents and his awareness of the rising influence of China and a communist Vietnam in Asia as well as the declining influence of the United States.

The Cambodian National Assembly nevertheless deemed Sihanouk's apparently ambivalent and inconsistent policies regarding the Vietnamese intrusion as an act of treason. It charged him with allowing the North Vietnamese and Viet Cong to operate in sanctuaries on the border.

It also charged that the prince had engaged in corruption and had ruined the economy by nationalizing Cambodia's few industries.

These charges used to justify the coup must be seen, however, in a larger context. Before his fall, Prince Sihanouk had lost the loyalty of elite groups in Cambodia. The army united around General Lon Nol and agreed with his view that Sihanouk was not moving strongly enough to remove the Vietnamese from Cambodian territory. Bureaucrats resented Sihanouk's total control over policymaking and personnel decisions; intellectuals opposed his policies of press and speech censorship; and university graduates were frustrated by the lack of job opportunities. Although Sihanouk retained the loyalty of the rural masses, that group wields little influence in Cambodian politics.

Sihanouk's major failure was his inability to institutionalize a political system in which power relations were not exclusively a function of his own desires and whims. Initially his charisma was the country's primary integrating force; subsequently, however, his total dominance of Cambodian political life undermined the nation's major institutions. The army became the dominant institution in Cambodian politics in March 1970, and for a short time Lon Nol had the support of many Cambodians. There was greater freedom of speech and the press than under Sihanouk, and the economy showed signs of opening and expanding. However, after a few months it became clear that the new government was not only inefficient but corrupt. At the end of April 1970, U.S. President Richard Nixon, without first informing the Cambodian government, announced an American invasion of Cambodia to protect the lives of U.S. soldiers, to ensure the success of his Vietnamization program, and to gain a decent interval for U.S. withdrawal from Vietnam. He announced that the intervention would clear Cambodia of all major enemy sanctuaries, including the headquarters of the communist military operation in South Vietnam. Accordingly, U.S. forces dropped an estimated 550,000 tons of bombs on Cambodia, about twenty-five times the explosive force of the atomic bomb that devastated Hiroshima and three and one-half times as many bombs as were dropped on Japan during World War II. Nearly half the population was uprooted, and Cambodians became refugees in their own country.[1] The communist headquarters was never found.

The fall of Sihanouk precipitated five years of total war on Cambodian soil. The U.S.-backed Lon Nol government proved incapable of coping with either international or domestic crises. The regime was corrupt; food shortages occurred for the first time in the country's modern history; inflation was out of control; and hundreds of thousands of Cambodians became refugees—Phnom Penh's population swelled from 600,000 to 2 million. One out of every ten Cambodians was killed in the war—most from U.S. bombing and suicide missions sent by Lon Nol to repel the Vietnamese. From his exile in Beijing, Prince Sihanouk announced his support for the radical rebels who opposed the Lon Nol regime. The country fell into a civil war that did not end until April 1975, when the Khmer Rouge rebel forces took control of the countryside and forced Phnom Penh into submission.

The massive bombings, the social dislocation, and the corruption of the Lon Nol government attracted support to the Khmer Rouge, which many believed was made up of nationalist "peasant reformers." That myth was quickly dispelled when the Khmer Rouge ordered the complete evacuation of Phnom Penh within hours of the takeover.

Pol Pot, the leader of one of several Khmer Rouge factions who eventually became the dominant individual in the new government, headed a tightly disciplined party vanguard called "the organization" *(angka)*, which ruthlessly ran the country. *Angka* represented itself as the leader of oppressed workers, farmers, and peasants against the "feudal, imperialistic, capitalist, reactionary, and oppressor classes" of the former regimes. The name Cambodia was changed to Democratic Kampuchea and Prince Sihanouk was brought back as the nominal head of state, but in reality he was under house arrest.

*Angka* used draconian measures to silence even potential voices of opposition and to reduce to impotency every person believed to be allied with the former ruling groups. The means to this end included strict discipline, total control, terror, and isolation from "impure" societies. The new regime's first undertaking, carried out immediately after the fall of Phnom Penh, was the evacuation of every person from Cambodia's major cities to the countryside. At first it was believed the evacuation was only to last for three days because the new government feared mass starvation in Phnom Penh and other cities, which had very limited supplies of rice. The evacuation, however, was meant to be permanent, to "purify" Cambodian society of decadent urban ways and to ensure internal security by ridding the country of "spies, imperialists, and enemies." The evacuations led to thousands of deaths and the separations of countless families.

*Angka* also purged persons who were in any way connected to the Lon Nol regime or were believed to harbor the slightest "bourgeois" values. Former residents of Phnom Penh were treated especially harshly by the regime. In places where displaced urban people settled, high death rates resulted from starvation, illness, and forced labor. An estimated one million persons were executed or worked to death between 1975 and 1979, an act of genocide that has few parallels in history. The country's entire intelligentsia was executed, often in hideous ways.

Further "enhancing" the Khmer Rouge's rule was the policy of forced labor, or collectivization, and the total restructuring of the economy. All Cambodian entrepreneurs lost their money when the regime halted the use of currency and nationalized private businesses. The family unit was replaced by collectives of up to a thousand households, which ate and worked together. Khmer Rouge troops enforced these harsh new policies and made sure that no one resorted to the "bourgeois" values of privatism, hierarchy, individualism, and the nuclear family.

Refugees reported that Cambodian society was rigidly organized into separate groups of men, women, the elderly, children six to fifteen years of age, and older teenagers. Only small quantities of food were available for communal workers. No schools were open, and no money was in circulation. Buddhist temples were converted into granaries for storing rice, and 80 percent of all books in Cambodia were thrown into rivers. Under Pol Pot, Cambodia became one of the most closed societies on Earth.

Following the communist victory in Vietnam in the spring of 1975, the Khmer Rouge began raiding Vietnam's border towns, thereby threatening Vietnam's important Mekong Delta region and causing thousands to lose their homes. An estimated 30,000 Vietnamese civilians were killed during these attacks. Pol Pot may have intended to reclaim the territory of the ancient Khmer Empire, which once included most of southern Vietnam. The fighting reflected the historically adversarial relationship between the two nations.

On Christmas Day 1978, a Vietnamese-led invasion overthrew Pol Pot's regime and installed Heng Samrin as president. Heng Samrin was an unknown former Khmer Rouge division commander who had sought refuge in Vietnam when his faction was overpowered by Pol Pot. Heng Samrin was soon replaced by Foreign Minister Hun Sen, who became the nation's most important leader for the next twenty years. Democratic Kampuchea became the People's Republic of Kampuchea (PRK). Vietnamese troops took Phnom Penh after less than two weeks of fighting and forced the Khmer Rouge to flee to the mountains in the western part of the country.

Vietnam announced that the purpose of its invasion was to end the constant border clashes, which jeopardized Vietnamese citizens, and to expel the hated Pol Pot regime. Certainly, Vietnam also desired a friendly government, not an ally of China, on its doorstep. The Khmer Rouge was viewed as Maoist and supportive of China, Vietnam's principal enemy.

The invasion has also been interpreted as a proxy war fought by surrogates of China and the Soviet Union. China provided aid to the Khmer Rouge, and the Soviet Union supported Vietnam; thus, some argue that these two world powers deliberately provoked the confrontation for the purpose of promoting their own self-interest and exercising control over client states in Southeast Asia. This interpretation sees Cambodia and Vietnam as pawns of major powers rather than as nations acting independently. However, historical precedents suggest that more was at issue in this conflict than competition between the major communist powers.

The new Vietnamese-installed government moved to undo the most onerous policies of the Khmer Rouge, and Phnom Penh was slowly repopulated. A market system was reestablished, and piped water and electricity were made available. Marriage and family restrictions were ended, forced collectives were abolished, and the practice of Buddhism was again allowed. Schools were reopened, and universal primary school education was instituted. After four years of the "killing fields," a semblance of normality appeared in Cambodian society.

Despite reforms, the new government faced severe problems. The Cambodians disliked and distrusted the Vietnamese officials and occupation soldiers (who numbered almost 200,000) but nevertheless realized that the Vietnamese were all that stood between themselves and the return of the Khmer Rouge. In addition, there was an administrative vacuum caused by Pol Pot's annihilation of virtually all skilled and educated Cambodians. For example, there were only forty-five doctors in the entire country. Few trained administrators had survived, and the country had no currency, no markets, no financial institutions, and no industry.[2]

The new government also faced a famine from 1978 to 1980 in which hundreds of thousands starved to death; to compound the problem, continued fighting between the Heng Samrin and Khmer Rouge forces disrupted the harvest of what little rice had been planted. Farmers were so physically weakened that they could not adequately care for their crops. International agencies were mobilized to provide food, and although thousands of people were saved from starvation, the rescue was only partially successful. As evidence of hoarding, favoritism, and corruption came to light, aid agencies were discouraged, but an even greater problem was the lack of qualified administrative personnel. In general, there was altogether too little food, and it arrived too late.

If Cambodia had not been drawn into the Vietnam War and had not suffered subsequently from its devastation; if Cambodia had not been depleted by genocide under a tyrannical regime, by famine, and by the flight of hundreds of thousands seeking food and freedom, the country's population in 1980 would have been 10 million. Instead, the total population in 1980 was about half that (though by 1997 it had again risen to 9 million). Few societies have sustained such tremendous losses.

Until 1991, when the United Nations assumed a direct role in supervising Cambodian affairs, Hun Sen's administration controlled the vast majority of the provinces. The Khmer Rouge, however, was still ensconced in the western mountains, controlling about 15 percent of the country's land area. The other two major resistance factions were the Sihanoukists, led by Sihanouk's son Prince Norodom Ranarridh, and the Khmer People's National Liberation Front (KPNLF), an anticommunist group led by Son Sann, a former prime minister.

These four groups agreed to participate in a newly created body, the Supreme National Council (SNC). Subsequently, the United Nations Transitional Authority in Cambodia (UNTAC) took over supervisory responsibilities in order to prepare the country for a cease-fire and elections in May 1993 for a 120-seat National Assembly. The assembly, in turn, was authorized to draft a new constitution and, as Cambodia's newly established legislature, to form the basis for the new government. However, even with 20,000 U.N. personnel in the country, the civil war continued, especially after the Khmer Rouge opted out of the peace process and renewed its terrorist activities. Thus, the world's foremost agency for peacekeeping was unable to bring harmony to this tortured country.

Despite the failed U.N. effort to bring Cambodia's factions together, popular support for the National Assembly elections was strong. Hun Sen organized the Cambodian People's Party (CPP), while Prince Ranarridh mobilized the United National Front for an Independent, Peaceful, and Cooperative Cambodia (FUNCINPEC). Both the CPP and FUNCIPEC campaigned on anti–Khmer Rouge platforms, and the dreaded Khmer Rouge did not participate in the campaign. The CPP argued that only the Hun Sen administration was strong enough to prevent a return of the Khmer Rouge. Prince Ranarridh's Sihanoukists, on the other hand, campaigned on the claim that the prince was the only Cambodian alive who had sufficient prestige to reconcile the murderous factions. FUNCINPEC candidates reminded voters that Hun Sen had once been a member of the Khmer Rouge and had been installed in power by the Vietnamese, who were detested by most Cambodians.

FUNCINPEC candidates also pointed out the CPP's blatant corruption, noting that Phnom Penh had become a boomtown catering to the whims of U.N. troops and foreign advisers who earned as much in a day as most Cambodians earned in a year. FUNCINPEC's campaign prevailed, winning with a plurality of 45 percent of the vote, which gave them fifty-seven seats in the National Assembly. Hun Sen's CPP followed with 38.2 percent and fifty-one seats. Various other parties split the remainder of the vote.

The UNTAC authorities declared the elections "free and fair," and the United Nations evacuated its peacekeepers in November 1993, leaving the government entirely in the hands of Cambodians for the first time since 1979. Prince Ranarridh and Hun Sen were designated co–prime ministers after Hun Sen threatened civil war if left out of the top position. (The prince was designated first prime minister and Hun Sen second prime minister.) The elderly Norodom Sihanouk was again named king, but he soon left the country for cancer treatment. The Khmer Rouge was kept out of the assembly and the executive branch.

By 1994, Cambodia had achieved a semifunctioning government, and life in the rural areas as well as in the cities had returned to some degree of normality. There was hope that the standard of living would improve with increasing foreign investment and political stability. However, underneath this appearance of normality were deep problems that included ubiquitous corruption, crime, and patronage. Factional struggles between the two prime ministers and their respective parties bogged down the government. The Khmer Rouge continued their terrorist attacks, which placed an immense financial burden on the national budget. The government could not maintain law and order; dissidents were regularly assassinated, and the government was widely blamed, or at least accused of being incapable of stopping the carnage.

The political rivalry between FUNCINPEC and the CPP was ongoing and involved the frequent ouster of prominent ministers, unsuccessful attempts at power sharing at the district levels, a bizarre situation in which all cabinet ministries were run by top officials from each of the rival parties, disagreements over policy issues such as how to deal with the Khmer Rouge, and anger on the part of Ranarridh's contingent over Hun Sen's forced entry into the government leadership. The rivalry culminated in Hun Sen's coup against First Prime Minister Ranarridh on July 6, 1997.

Both leaders had attempted to court dissident Khmer Rouge leaders, the most notorious being Ieng Sary, who announced that he was now opposed to his former comrade Pol Pot and desired to integrate his 3,000 troops (about one-third of the entire Khmer Rouge force) into the national army. Hun Sen feared a Khmer Rouge–FUNCINPEC alliance, which would isolate his CPP. Nevertheless, Hun Sen agreed to an amnesty for the former Khmer Rouge leader. This apparent concession did end the rivalry.

Prince Ranarridh was out of the country when Hun Sen's coup took place. To show that he was not simply seeking exclusive power, Hun Sen designated a new co–prime minister, Ung Huot, the foreign minister. Ung Huot was eventually approved by the National Assembly. Hun Sen charged Ranarridh with a variety of traitorous acts, including harboring Khmer Rouge hard-liners in Phnom Penh; for his part, he promised to respect the constitution, preserve the monarchy, and hold free and fair elections in 1998. King Sihanouk refused to endorse the new government, but he did nothing to stop the coup and its aftermath. Ranarridh remained in exile, unable to return to Cambodia, because Hun Sen promised to arrest him if he reentered the country.

The coup was reportedly financed by the alleged drug baron Theng Bunma, president of the Cambodian Chamber of Commerce, who publicly stated that he had given Hun Sen $1 million to stabilize the country's political situation. Following the coup, many FUNCINPEC supporters were assassinated; others were imprisoned while their homes were ransacked. Although Hun Sen apologized for the breakdown in law and order, the chaos continued for several months; the precarious balance that had emerged through the joint leadership of Cambodia had been destroyed.

Hun Sen's coup occurred at precisely the time that Pol Pot was found alive and brought before a "people's tribunal" in Anlong Veng Province in northern Cambodia. In a stunning turnaround, Pol Pot, the architect and perpetrator of the "killing fields," sat as an anguished old man, accused of a crime against a former Khmer Rouge comrade. He was denounced by the crowd, who screamed out "Crush! Crush! Crush!" when his prosecutor identified him. Pol Pot was found guilty and placed under house arrest for life. He was not turned over to the international courts for his crimes against humanity. The former tyrant's photograph (taken by the intrepid *Far Eastern Economic Review* correspondent Nate Thayer) was seen on the front page of newspapers around the world, and the American news show *Nightline* devoted an entire program to Pol Pot's "trial."

The discovery of Pol Pot's fallen status was a strong indication that the Khmer Rouge had dissipated and factionalized. Despite the group's impotence, it was Prince Ranarridh's ardent courting of Khmer Rouge factions that had caused Hun Sen to worry that the balance of power was tilting against him. Hun Sen was furious for being the odd man out and so launched his coup. The coup precluded any possibility of Pol Pot appearing before an international tribunal.

The world reacted strongly to the widely published photographs from Pol Pot's trial. Responsible for the torture and death of millions of people, he appeared like an elderly grandfather. His public statements to Nate Thayer were unrepentant; he asserted that he had a clear conscience. Pol Pot talked about his modesty, his lack of interest in leadership, his unobtrusive style of politics. He claimed that his opponents had been executed by the Vietnamese and that the skulls of those tortured and killed at Tuol Sleng prison could not have been Cambodian because they were too small. He seemed most eager to talk about his poor health (he was seventy-two in 1997) and his enjoyment of his new wife and twelve-year-old daughter, the apple of his eye. Pol Pot epitomized the fabled banality of the truly evil person. He died in April 1998 and was immediately cremated. He was one of history's mass murderers who escaped retribution.

## Institutions and Social Groups

### Prince Sihanouk

Since the 1940s, Prince Norodom Sihanouk has dominated all aspects of Cambodian society. Although placed on the throne by the French in 1941 (when he was nineteen) and thought by the French to be pliable, Sihanouk became the symbol of Cambodian independence. With his shrill voice, he rallied his people during an era when Cambodia was known as "an island of tranquillity in a sea of chaos." Conversant in ten languages, the author of five books, and a stage and movie actor and director, he has been the country's most cosmopolitan citizen.

Although Sihanouk ruled autocratically, allowing only his party to participate in elections, his government was supported by the overwhelming majority of the people. Sihanouk maintained the support of the rural population but eventually lost that of Cambodia's urban elites, who opposed his foreign and economic policies. After he was overthrown by his own premier in 1970, he allied himself with the Khmer Rouge rebels while in exile and, when the Khmer Rouge took power, returned to Phnom Penh as a "ceremonial" leader. Subsequently, he cooperated with the Khmer Rouge, even though it had murdered five of his sons and daughters, fourteen of his grandchildren, and more than a million of his former subjects. Sihanouk is an egotist who has been willing to prolong the civil war in order to maximize his own authority.

Sihanouk denounced the Vietnamese-backed Hun Sen administration; he lived in exile in Beijing and Pyongyang for much of this period, receiving medical treatment for his numerous maladies. His movement in and out of Cambodia solidified his reputation as a mercurial figure. Sihanouk lost much popular support by being out of power for over twenty years and allying himself with the Khmer Rouge. Nevertheless, he remained one of the country's major institutions, eventually returning to Cambodia to become king following the UNTAC-sponsored elections. However, Sihanouk has little formal power, and lives in China. He has said that if he were not a Buddhist he would kill himself, believing his life to be filled with shame, humiliation, and despair over Cambodia's past and future.

## Hun Sen

The opposite of Sihanouk in many ways, Prime Minister Hun Sen has been Cambodia's most important leader in the post–Khmer Rouge period. He was born in a peasant family and did not finish high school. Hun Sen was twenty-four when the Khmer Rouge came to power under Pol Pot. The Khmer Rouge evacuated his family from its rural home, killed his eldest son, and imprisoned his wife. Blinded in one eye by a U.S. cluster bomb, Hun Sen joined the Khmer Rouge as a senior commander before becoming aware of its genocidal fanaticism. He defected in 1977, as Pol Pot began his systematic executions of dissident Khmer Rouge members, and escaped to Vietnam.

In 1986, Cambodia was being administered by a Vietnamese-installed government. Hun Sen, the prime minister and foreign minister, had become the most influential figure in the People's Republic of Kampuchea although Heng Samrin, the head of state, held the highest position. Hun Sen's regime controlled the cities and most of the countryside with the aid of Vietnamese soldiers and advisers. However, few nations recognized this regime as Cambodia's legitimate government despite its control over virtually all aspects of the country's life.

As leader of the Vietnamese-backed PRK, Hun Sen traveled abroad to win foreign aid and support; he was known more as a pragmatist than as an ideologist. His attempts to make his government more independent of Vietnam greatly improved his popularity in Cambodia. This popularity, however, was not matched internationally, where he was still viewed as a leader who had come to power from aggression. These global assessments of Hun Sen's aggressive and self-serving nature were reinforced when he grabbed power in 1997.

## The State of Cambodia

For Cambodians, the central government, headquartered in Phnom Penh, was the only organization around which they could rebuild their lives after the disastrous Khmer Rouge years. The government remained weak partly because there was only a small number of experienced administrators and professionals. Its ruling body was the People's Revolutionary Party of Kampuchea (PRPK), a Marxist-Leninist party that monopolized power until 1989 when it lost that distinction to an elected National Assembly and executive state council. The National Assembly, not the PRPK, renamed the country the State of Cambodia, designated Buddhism the national religion, declared Cambodian foreign policy to be based on neutrality and nonalignment, abolished the death penalty, and altered the national flag to remove its communist imagery.

## Coalition Government and U.N. Authority

The Coalition Government of Democratic Kampuchea (CGDK) was a coalition of three disparate factions, formed in 1982, that was united solely in its opposition to the Vietnamese-sponsored regime in Phnom Penh. (The coalition was given Cambodia's seat in the United Nations in place of Phnom Penh government.) The largest of the factions, the Khmer Rouge, was nominally headed by Khieu Samphan, although it was generally believed that Pol Pot was actually in command. The military arm of the Khmer Rouge consisted of some 35,000 soldiers, also presumably led by Pol Pot. The Khmer Rouge was seated at the United Nations from 1979 to 1981 and again, as part of the coalition, from 1982 to the present.

Based in the western mountains of Cambodia near the Thai border, the Khmer Rouge was the best-equipped, most capable, and best-organized fighting force in the country. These rebels were supplied by China with infantry weapons, rocket-propelled grenades, and mortars. In 1990 Khieu Samphan continued to function as party head, partly because his reputation was less sullied than that of Pol Pot, Ieng Sary, and other Khmer Rouge notables. Earlier, Khieu Samphan had acted on behalf of the Khmer Rouge in negotiations toward a peace settlement.

Even though they had the strongest military force in the country, the Khmer Rouge controlled only a small amount of land. Periodically there were reports that the Khmer Rouge had taken new territory and was threatening to overrun Phnom Penh. These reports were usually exaggerated by the Khmer Rouge to remind its foes that it was still a force with which to be reckoned. The possibility of a Khmer Rouge return to power was one reason that the U.S. policy of indirect support changed in 1990 to total exclusion.

The second faction in the coalition was the KPNLF, an anticommunist right-wing group with about 5,000 troops. The group's leader, Son Sann, who had held numerous positions in former Cambodian administrations, was prime minister of the coalition. He was supported by the noncommunist ASEAN states and along with Prince Sihanouk's group enjoyed annual funding of about $7 million from the United States. The KPNLF was in turn factionalized between followers of Son Sann and followers of his armed forces commander, General Sak Sutsakhan. Corruption and power struggles weakened the KPNLF.

Prince Norodom Sihanouk, the president of the coalition, led the third faction, FUNCINPEC. Its military arm, the Armée Nationale Sihanoukiste, consisted of about 3,000 troops on the Thai-Cambodian border. Sihanouk was named coalition president largely because of his international fame, and his numerous "resignations" reflect his ambivalent feelings toward his coalition partners—especially the Khmer Rouge, which was responsible for the deaths of members of his family. Sihanouk's major goal was to oust the Vietnamese from Cambodia by whatever means necessary, including an alliance with those he loathed. He believed that the Vietnamese were systematically destroying Cambodian culture and therefore had to be removed before Cambodia ceased to exist as a separate entity.

Following the U.N.-sponsored Paris Peace Conference, held in October 1991 in an effort to resolve the Cambodian situation, the three coalition partners together with the Phnom Penh government agreed to a peace plan that featured a multinational force of U.N. peacekeepers and administrators, UNTAC, to be stationed in Cambodia. The force's success was dependent upon the remarkable notion that foreign troops, none able to speak the Cambodian language and all ignorant of Cambodian culture, could move into a chaotic situation and bring about a cease-fire, disarmament, free elections, and effective administration (including foreign affairs, national defense, and finance). At one point, when Cambodia had no indigenous government, the administration of the country was in the hands of the Japanese head of UNTAC, whereas the finance ministry was run by an American, the foreign ministry was led by a Pole, and the military was overseen by an Australian. The bizarre nature of the U.N. program was an indication of the desperate nature of the Cambodian imbroglio after years of civil war, genocidal rule, foreign aggression, and societal chaos.

The U.N. peace plan could not have been established without the concurrence of the major external players: the United States, Vietnam, China, and the Soviet Union. Vietnam's complete withdrawal from Cambodia and the collapse of communism in Eastern Europe had changed the views of these foreign powers, leading them to the agreement. Moreover, the agreement of the four factions, even though each had its own self-serving reasons, was necessary for the plan to be implemented. When the Khmer Rouge faction resisted, Chinese officials pressured the recalcitrants. Sihanouk's agreement to act as president of the SNC finally brought the accords to fruition.

All four factions were represented in the SNC, a frightening prospect for those critics who believed that the Khmer Rouge could not be trusted. The four factions continued to "administer" the areas they controlled, a situation that eventually undermined the accords when the Khmer Rouge reneged on its promises to carry out the terms of the accords. UNTAC was responsible for regrouping the factions into cantonment areas, disarming them, and demobilizing military forces. The Khmer Rouge, however, did not disarm or demobilize its area. Despite the Khmer Rouge boycott, elections took place May 23–27, 1993, to choose a representative legislature.

When Prince Sihanouk returned triumphantly to Phnom Penh in November 1991 to become the Cambodian head of state, Cambodians had hopes that the UNTAC experiment could succeed. Shortly thereafter, Khieu Samphan, the Khmer Rouge representative on the SNC, returned as well but was met by a mob that came close to tearing him apart limb from limb. Khieu Samphan was rescued and later returned to participate in the coalition, but the mob action clearly indicated the strong hatred Cambodians still felt toward the Khmer Rouge. UNTAC was not able to pacify the nation because of numerous violations of the cease-fire, mostly by the Khmer Rouge. The Hun Sen administration in Phnom Penh, which had turned over much of its power to UNTAC, engaged in its own violations and corruption, raising the question of whether any of the factions could run the government once elections had been held.

The tasks that UNTAC had set for itself were too great to be accomplished in only eighteen months. To run a government, oversee the repatriation of 350,000 refugees, supervise a cease-fire among factions that hated and distrusted one another, and conduct the first Cambodian election in decades were impossible goals even for an organization provided with $2.8 billion and more than 20,000 advisers, the most expensive and far-reaching plan of this type in world history. From November 1991 to May 1993, the period of UNTAC's involvement, the international media reported daily cease-fire violations by all factions, but especially by the Khmer Rouge, with the purpose of expanding their zones of influence and thereby controlling as many people as possible before the elections.

The Khmer Rouge refused to disarm and denied U.N. troops access to those areas under its control. The stated reasons for these violations were the Khmer Rouge's accusations that Vietnamese troops and citizens had remained in Cambodia and would take over the country once elections had been completed, and that UNTAC was biased in favor of the Hun Sen administration in Phnom Penh. No evidence was presented to substantiate these accusations. Throughout the transition period, Khmer Rouge forces routinely killed Vietnamese living in Cambodia, even those who had been there all their lives. Eventually, the Khmer Rouge leadership opted out of the U.N. plan, assassinated U.N. troops and advisers, and boycotted the election process. The Khmer Rouge's kidnappings and armed attacks against opposition candidates made campaigning impossible in many areas of the country under their control.

The chances for a free and fair election were bleak because of Khmer Rouge intransigence, the absence of Cambodian experience with open elections, reluctance on the part of the ruling Hun Sen administration to give up authority, and a general fear by the populace of the UNTAC foreigners who were essentially administering their country. Nevertheless, between May 23 and 27, 1993, 90 percent of the eligible voters cast ballots for members of a legislative assembly with powers to draft a new constitution. Although the Khmer Rouge did not participate in the elections, they did not sabotage them after it became clear that the overwhelming majority of Cambodians had rejected Khmer Rouge pressure. The largest plurality (45 percent) was won by Prince Ranarridh's FUNCINPEC; Hun Sen's CPP trailed with 38.6 percent of the vote. This result led to the ultimately unworkable system in which Ranarridh and Hun Sen shared the prime ministership.

The widespread support for elections was viewed as a great display of courage and hope by a people who had undergone indescribable horror during the previous two decades. Khmer Rouge terror continued after the elections to strengthen the guerrillas' claim that they should be incorporated into the government. After the elections were deemed free and fair by UNTAC authorities, the U.N. pulled out in November 1993, leaving Cambodia to cope with its newly elected government. The Coalition Government of Democratic Kampuchea came to an end and, for the first time since 1979, government administration was entirely in the hands of Cambodians, without significant influence from foreign powers.

## Refugees

On the Thai-Cambodian border, as many as 350,000 displaced Cambodians could be found in refugee camps at any time during the 1970s and 1980s; many individuals were held there for several years. There were different waves of refugees: after Lon Nol's rise to power, during the U.S. bombing, in the Khmer Rouge period, during the Vietnamese invasion when famine drove thousands from the country, and in 1990 when chances for a peace settlement were negligible. In 1990, some 1,800 Cambodians fled to Indonesia, where they were interred on Galang Island. Their fear of persecution by PRK authorities was judged to be poorly founded, so these Cambodians were not given refugee status and were referred to instead as displaced persons.[3] In total, almost one million persons fled Cambodia. The camps were controlled by U.N. agencies as well as by Khmer Rouge and noncommunist resistance forces. In effect, the displaced became a human buffer between Thailand and Cambodia. Periodic incursions and shelling brought further devastation to these already suffering people.

Refugees were still numerous in the region even fifteen years after the end of the Vietnam War, and they continued to be at the center of intractable warfare and conflict. The ASEAN members, while still the countries of first asylum for Cambodian and Vietnamese refugees, threatened to stop granting asylum unless the United States reversed its position against the forced repatriation to Vietnam and Cambodia of those judged to be "economic migrants." Malaysia turned back boat people for several years, in effect condemning them to roam the high seas. The U.S. position was that it was unthinkable to return refugees to nations ruled by reprehensible leaders.

The refugee camps ruled by the Khmer Rouge employed the same ruthless discipline, characterized by terror and slave labor, of the collective camps Pol Pot had established throughout Cambodia from 1975 to 1979. In 1988, for example, the Khmer Rouge forcibly removed an estimated 16,000 refugees from a border camp and marched them into the interior for resettlement as "the vanguard of the new revolution."[4] Refugee agencies were not allowed into these camps except under conditions dictated by the Khmer Rouge. By May 1993, all 350,000 refugees had been repatriated from Thai camps to various areas of Cambodia to participate in the UNTAC-supervised elections.

## Democratization

Cambodia has never experienced democratic rule. Since the days of ancient Angkor, Cambodian governments have been led by autocratic rulers with scarcely any accountability to the ruled. Even today, in the State of Cambodia, the characteristics of democracy are absent. One important reason for this is the omnipresent threat of foreign aggression, which has encouraged strong leadership at the expense of people's involvement in governmental affairs.

Cambodians have a long history of Hindu-Buddhist notions of hierarchy, status, and deference to those in authority. Indeed, the political order is still seen as a microcosm of the universe. The king was to his kingdom as God is to the cosmos. Great monuments were built to the glory of Cambodia's rulers, a practice that culminated in the great Khmer kingdoms. The principles of absolutism and hierarchy, introduced during the country's Hinduization centuries ago, remain essential aspects of Cambodian politics.

For over thirty years, Cambodia has been plagued by continuous civil war and terrorism. The devastating legacy of the Khmer Rouge social experiment has lingered. Although the new constitution called for adherence to human rights, factional power struggles bode poorly for a functioning civil society. Almost all of the nation's lawyers, legislators, and judges had been murdered by the Khmer Rouge. Memories of distrust and betrayal have hindered the evolution of democratic norms.

The devastation of Cambodia's economy also has boded poorly for democracy. The country's infrastructure is primitive, and most Cambodians have lived at a level of bare subsistence. The black market is larger than the legal market. Schools have only limited facilities, and there are not enough teachers.

The 1997 coup by Second Prime Minister Hun Sen against First Prime Minister Ranarridh fractured the already weak foundations of democracy. Newspapers were closed, and dozens of dissidents were assassinated, or at best jailed. Political killings once more became prominent. The most effective legislators, such as former Finance Minister Sam Rainsy, were separated from government positions, and the judicial system was incapable of implementing reforms or bringing to trial those accused of human rights abuses. It will take a Herculean effort to rebuild the trust and institutions necessary for Cambodia to move toward democratic rule.

## Economic Development

In addition to being one of the poorest countries in the world and having been ravaged by the Khmer Rouge and attacked by foreign forces, Cambodia is one of the only Third World nations that is denied governmental aid by most of the world's wealthy nations and the United Nations; thus, its prospects for economic development are dismal.

When the Vietnamese-sponsored regime took control in 1979, the government initially favored a command economy based on the Vietnamese model. Private enterprise and private property were not allowed. Beginning in the mid-1980s, however, the PRK regime instituted its own version of *perestroika* by liberalizing foreign investment laws, allowing private industries, increasing international trade, returning land to peasant ownership, permitting private transportation enterprises, guaranteeing the end of the nationalization of private enterprises, and legalizing the private sector.[5] This opening of the economy immediately improved the output of the industrial, agricultural, and private sectors, and Cambodia again became self-sufficient in rice production.

Twenty-seven nongovernmental organizations (NGOs) from Australia, Europe, and the United States provided approximately $10 million per year in relief and development assistance. These NGOs, which supported nutrition centers, hospitals, and artificial limb factories, also oversaw water supply, animal welfare, sanitation, irrigation, and educational projects.[6] Only certain U.N. agencies that provided emergency relief, such as UNICEF and the World Food Program, were allowed to operate inside Cambodia, whereas the U.N. Development Program, the World Health Organization, and other development-oriented U.N. agencies were not.[7] Even so, Cambodia's needs were far greater than what the NGOs provided.

The NGOs built good working relations with their bureaucratic and technical Cambodian counterparts. They were also the country's main contact with the outside world. However, even the small amount of NGO aid taxed the administrative capacity of the Cambodian government. Aid providers faced problems with accommodations, communications, travel, and visa relations. Even when a peace settlement was finally negotiated and the embargo lifted, planning, reconstruction and development would still be difficult because of severe constraints on the public sector's absorptive capacity. The country's technical and administrative cadres have been few in number, and they have been stretched to the limit.[8]

In 1997, there were only about sixty small industries operating in Cambodia, and they were operating at half capacity. The major prospects for foreign exchange were rubber, timber, and tourism. However, there were few tourists in Cambodia except for academic delegations and adventurous travelers. The magnificent ruins of Angkor were at one time a popular tourist attraction, but without political stability, roads, rail service, an administrative infrastructure, and airports, Cambodia has not attracted significant numbers of visitors.

For the great majority of Cambodians living in rural areas, the economy in 1997 was little improved over the disastrous 1980s. The nation's infrastructure continued to be inadequate. Bombed bridges and roads were still not repaired, the transportation system was abysmal, flooding had wiped out progress made in rice production, and undetonated land mines continued to kill or maim farmers.

In Phnom Penh, the economy changed dramatically in the 1990s with a boom in consumer goods, mostly from Thailand and China; increased car traffic; out-of-control land speculation; hyperinflation; and a huge supply of money, mostly from the high per diem payments made to the 20,000 UNTAC personnel. Their daily income was equivalent to Cambodians' average *yearly* income. Cambodia has had a limited capacity to manage foreign investment, because almost all economists and technocrats capable of administering the nation's economy were killed by the Khmer Rouge. Legal codes have been ad hoc, and there has been no mechanism for resolving contractual disputes. The black market, fueled by illegal trading by corrupt government officials, remained more important than the "authorized" economy.

By the beginning of 1997, fully 45 percent of Cambodia's budget came from international donors. However, the International Monetary Fund canceled major loans to Cambodia on the grounds that the government had no environmental program and that the country's forests were disappearing to loggers. They argued that deforestation changed weather patterns, leading to both droughts and floods and thereby destabilizing Cambodia's agricultural base. When Hun Sen launched his coup in 1997, the rest of the aid ceased and tourists disappeared, ending a brief period of growth and returning Cambodia's economy to catastrophe.

## The Cambodian State

In the twelfth century the Khmer Empire, under the great warrior Jayavarman VII, dominated much of mainland Southeast Asia. It was not until the fifteenth century that the empire was reduced in size to approximately the present boundaries of Cambodia. At its height, however, the Khmer Empire was among the strongest states in the world, able to mobilize the citizenry and protect its sovereignty. Modern Cambodia, in contrast, is one of the world's weakest states.

In the analysis of the other Southeast Asian states, massive social dislocation was seen as a necessary condition for a strong state. Cambodia qualifies in this respect but nevertheless has not become strong. Again, modern Cambodia history is the story of monumental dislocation as a result of the Khmer Rouge's systematic destruction of Cambodian social, cultural, economic, and political life. Although a strong state cannot emerge until its society has been weakened, and the latter did occur in Cambodia, a strong state has not evolved because the country has been largely bereft of capable administrative leadership. The PRK regime, installed by the Vietnamese, fulfilled state functions temporarily, but state officials did not have the wherewithal to mobilize or control public resources in the same manner as officials in Indonesia or Vietnam, both of which had also undergone major dislocations.

External support facilitates the rise of a strong state. For Cambodia, financial, administrative, and military support from Vietnam was minute compared to its needs, especially when virtually no other external support was provided by the nation's traditional sources of aid and trade. Military threats, including threat of internal rebellion, also facilitate the emergence of a strong state. Contemporary Cambodia has faced insurgency since the 1960s, and since the 1970s that insurgency has been supported financially and militarily by outside sources. From this perspective, too, Cambodia meets the criteria of a nation with the conditions for a strong state.

The explanation for Cambodia's weakness, then, must be the absence of a group that is both independent of existing bases of social control and skillful enough to execute the designs of state leaders. Cambodia has few experienced technocrats whose loyalty is primarily to the state; the army is weak and undependable; and politically skillful leaders are practically nonexistent. Indeed, there is no Cambodian leader who stands out even remotely as much as Ho Chi Minh in Vietnam, Lee Kuan Yew in Singapore, Ne Win in Burma, Suharto in Indonesia, or Ferdinand Marcos in the Philippines. The closest is Prince Sihanouk, but his prestige is tainted because of his alliance with the Khmer Rouge and the fact that he has not ruled since 1970. Hun Sen began his rule under global perception that he was a puppet of Cambodia's traditional adversary, Vietnam. Nevertheless, his capacity to bring some normality to Cambodia temporarily enhanced his image and moved the country toward more effective governance.

In 1997, the Cambodian state was weak, unable to control any aspect of the country's society. In transition to a system that it could not predict and that it had no capability to plan out, the state was in jeopardy of disintegration. In 1993, the United Nations had literally taken over all elements of the Cambodian state. UNTAC's departure left a situation similar to that of South Vietnam when the Americans extricated themselves in the early 1970s. In both cases, there was insufficient viability to sustain the goals of the state. The collapse of the South Vietnamese government in 1975 was a precursor to an inevitable collapse of Cambodia.

## Foreign Policy

Throughout its modern history, Cambodia has been the target of aggression by its larger neighbors and by Western and communist imperialists. The French, Americans, Soviets, Chinese, Vietnamese, and Thais have all attempted at various times to control Cambodian affairs. Since 1970, Cambodia has been the victim of direct U.S. and Vietnamese intervention as well as Chinese support for antigovernment rebels. The Vietnamese intervention of December 1978 could not have occurred without significant support by the Soviets, who funded the operation and provided much of the weaponry.

After the Vietnamese invasion, the United Nations continued to recognize the Pol Pot regime despite the fact that the Khmer Rouge controlled only about 2 percent of the population and that Pol Pot had been branded as one of history's worst violators of human rights. The vote of U.S. President Jimmy Carter's administration for Pol Pot was based on the view that his opponents, the Hun Sen government, had achieved power by aggression. The vote also reflected Carter's desire to strengthen ties with China and his displeasure with the growing Soviet role in Southeast Asia. The PRK was viewed as a puppet of Vietnam, which in turn was seen as a surrogate of the Soviet Union.

The late 1980s brought important international changes, which affected Cambodia by providing new opportunities for a comprehensive peace settlement after the country had floundered for a decade. Warmer relations between the United States and the Soviet Union were the primary influence on U.S. policy toward Cambodia. For many years, U.S. goals in Cambodia included the withdrawal of Vietnamese military forces; the repudiation of the Khmer Rouge; a political settlement that would permit Cambodians to choose their form of government; and an independent, neutral, and nonaligned Cambodia, protected from outside interference by international guarantees.[9]

These goals have been constant, but the means to achieve them have changed as the international situation has changed. President Mikhail Gorbachev elaborated a new Soviet policy toward Asia by emphasizing diplomacy, positive relations with ASEAN, and disengagement from Vietnam. In response to Soviet encouragement, the Vietnamese completed their withdrawal of troops from Cambodia in September 1989, and ASEAN—especially Thailand—agreed to meet with the State of Cambodia administration. Prior to 1989, the ASEAN nations and the United States had refused to talk with the Phnom Penh government and had vigorously supported the CGDK's credentials at the United Nations.

A series of conferences in Jakarta in 1988 and 1989 and an international peace conference in Paris in August 1989 failed to resolve the complex problems surrounding the principal actors such as Prince Sihanouk, the Khmer Rouge, and the State of Cambodia government. In order to break the stalemate, to react to U.S. congressional criticism of White House policy in Cambodia, and to indicate concern that the Khmer Rouge was gaining strength in Cambodia and threatening to win power once again, in July 1990 U.S. Secretary of State James Baker announced that the United States would withdraw diplomatic recognition of the CGDK in the United Nations and would henceforth deal directly with Vietnam in resolving the Cambodian crisis. Up to this time, the United States had supported the coalition rebels and had refused to negotiate with Vietnam.

The purpose of the new policy was to isolate the Khmer Rouge and to win concessions from Hanoi and Phnom Penh that would facilitate a peace settlement. In addition, the administration of President George Bush desired to end the contradiction in U.S. policy that both supported the Khmer Rouge as a component of the CGDK and at the same time opposed its return to power. The Khmer Rouge's noncommunist coalition partners had never had real autonomy, diplomatically or militarily; they were even coordinating military forays with the Khmer Rouge. Both lethal and nonlethal aid for the coalition had strengthened their forces, specifically the position of the Khmer Rouge against the Hun Sen government in Phnom Penh, which was the only obstacle to a return to power by the Khmer Rouge.

Before Vietnam withdrew its military from Cambodia, U.S. policymakers argued that the Hun Sen government was essentially a puppet of the Vietnamese, but that argument lost credibility once the withdrawal was completed. The decision to negotiate with Vietnam was a recognition of the Vietnamese withdrawal and an incentive to continue working toward a Cambodian peace settlement, necessary conditions before full normalization of relations between Vietnam and the United States could occur.

Moreover, the policy change recognized that U.S. relations with China did not dictate U.S. policies in Indochina. The United States had been reluctant to clash with China because China represented a bulwark against Soviet ambition in Southeast Asia. But Beijing's crackdown on the Tiananmen uprising in June 1989, Gorbachev's less threatening policies in Asia, and ASEAN's increased flexibility liberated U.S. policymakers from their dependence on China and permitted them to see Cambodia as autonomous rather than as a part of China's sphere of influence. The new policy also isolated China as the sole supporter of the Khmer Rouge. Signs of improved relations between China and Vietnam (such as increased border trade) mitigated Chinese opposition to the new U.S. policy and suggested that China might be seeking a face-saving solution to its unpopular ties with the Khmer Rouge.

The new U.S. policy also brought the United States back into Southeast Asia as a key force. During the fifteen years following the Vietnam War, U.S. foreign policy toward Indochina had been subordinated to that toward ASEAN and China. Nevertheless, U.S. policy had an important effect on Cambodia, isolating the country through the trade embargo and in effect strengthening rebel forces. Fear of a Khmer Rouge return to power mandated a new policy that could not be morally or strategically faulted for supporting such a frightening possibility.

ASEAN was not united on the best means by which to deal with Cambodia. Whereas Singapore took a hard-line stand against the Hun Sen government (while simultaneously developing trade and investment ties with that government), Thailand wished to convert Indochina from a battlefield into a marketplace, with the Thais themselves taking the leading economic role in mainland Southeast Asia. Prior to the change in U.S. policy, Prime Minister Chatichai met with Prime Minister Hun Sen on numerous occasions to negotiate trade programs and a settlement of the Cambodian imbroglio. Initially, ASEAN leaders protested the U.S. withdrawal of support for U.N. recognition of the CGDK, but the protests were short-lived as it became clear that the United States would continue to provide economic aid to the noncommunist resistance.

The future of Cambodia was seen in terms of alternative scenarios. The most unacceptable—but not impossible—outcome was the return of the Khmer Rouge to power. With the strongest military force in the country, the Khmer Rouge was quite capable of slowly taking power in the countryside through terrorist campaigns and eventually strangling Phnom Penh, just as it had done in April 1975. The unknown variable was the willingness of Vietnam and the international community to stop the Khmer Rouge and the support provided to it by China. In 1975, neither the Cambodians nor the rest of the world knew the kind of horror the Khmer Rouge was capable of perpetrating, something everyone knew by the 1990s.

The second alternative was a continuation of the stalemate and low-level civil war, perhaps for years. China would continue to support the Khmer Rouge, and the United States would support the noncommunist resistance led by Prince Sihanouk and Son Sann. The country would become increasingly partitioned between areas controlled by the Hun Sen government and areas controlled by factions of the CGDK. This state of permanent war would continue to destroy the fabric of Cambodian culture and would lead to the flight of even more of the country's most educated people.

Prince Sihanouk supported the third scenario, a quadripartite settlement with the Hun Sen administration and each of the three coalition members sharing equally in the running of the government until free, internationally supervised elections could be arranged. Sihanouk insisted on dismantling the Hun Sen administration before elections, leveling each faction's army to equal size, and establishing four-way leadership of key ministries.

The Hun Sen regime dismissed the quadripartite plan as unacceptable, tantamount, from its perspective, to bringing jackals into the tent in order to tame them. Also, the PRK leaders asserted that there was no evidence that the Khmer Rouge would not disrupt an interim or long-term coalition government. If Hun Sen were to allow a role for the Khmer Rouge in a future administration, such toleration would demolish the basis of his legitimacy as the liberator of Cambodia from the genocidal Khmer Rouge regime. Moreover, the other two factions of the CGDK were weak and could not compete with the highly organized and disciplined Khmer Rouge involvement. It was unlikely that the monarchical Sihanouk, the anticommunist Son Sann, and the fanatical Khmer Rouge would be willing to negotiate a plan for power sharing.

A tripartite settlement that excluded the Khmer Rouge was closer to the wishes of the United States. In this scenario, the Khmer Rouge would be isolated, assuming that Chinese support would end. Sihanouk, Hun Sen, and Son Sann would work together, with Sihanouk as head of state, Hun Sen as prime minister, and Son Sann in some other significant position of power. Hun Sen, moreover, agreed to free, multiparty elections and accepted Sihanouk's return as head of state. Elections would be supervised by an international commission, and restored diplomatic relations between Cambodia and the United States would lead to the end of the trade embargo and to larger aid programs.

The tripartite formula was criticized, however, for excluding one of the main forces in Cambodia. Prince Sihanouk in particular argued that integrating the Khmer Rouge into the government would co-opt it, whereas excluding it would perpetuate its insurgency. Also, the formula required a stable and capable administration, which none of the proposed tripartite groups were able to provide. Even the Hun Sen administration, which had been in power since 1979, had not been able to fashion a government that was effective throughout the countryside.

In October 1991, the United Nations announced an agreement aimed at ending the civil war by transferring temporary control of the country to the United Nations. The proposal involved employing some 20,000 U.N. peacekeeping troops who would virtually control all aspects of the Cambodian government, from foreign affairs to public security. The plan called for the Supreme National Council to represent Cambodia during the interim period before elections, with each faction having one-fourth of the representation. The SNC filled Cambodia's U.N. seat. The United Nations supervised elections; provided for internal security; administered foreign, economic, and defense affairs; and guaranteed human rights during the transition period.

After the October 1991 peace accords were signed, the SNC became the legitimate government of Cambodia, and the quadripartite group was given the U.N. seat to share. The Khmer Rouge lost Chinese aid when China and Vietnam moved to a rapprochement in 1992 and when China attempted to improve its international reputation following the Tiananmen Square tragedy. In addition, U.N.-imposed sanctions against the Khmer Rouge were directed primarily at Thailand, which had engaged in numerous trade and investment deals with the Khmer Rouge in logging and gems. To support the peace process, the United States ended its economic embargo against Cambodia, although the embargo against Vietnam continued.

Cambodia's international relations changed in 1995 when Vietnam became a member of ASEAN. Cambodia also applied for membership along with Burma and Laos but was rebuffed because of the 1997 Hun Sen coup; ASEAN required a higher degree of political and economic stability than Cambodia was able to demonstrate. Meanwhile, Cambodia improved its relations with China, agreeing to a Chinese military aid package and sponsoring state visits to and from Beijing. The United States had only peripheral relations with Cambodia in the mid-1990s.

## Conclusion

No country in Southeast Asia has undergone the same magnitude of horrific trauma suffered by Cambodia from the 1960s to the present. War, famine, and oppression have devastated the society once known as an oasis of tranquillity. With virtually its entire educated class decimated, Cambodia is attempting to rebuild. However, it is still buffeted by the world's great powers, by its neighbors, and by internal political rivalries. The phenomenal resilience of the Cambodians, who have endured a holocaust, is the most hopeful sign that the "killing fields" will never return and that Cambodia can develop and remain independent.

Nevertheless, for the foreseeable future Cambodia will continue under a weak state administration, threatened by internal political conflict. Without trained administrators, an effective infrastructure, or external aid, the immediate outlook is bleak. The problems of governing Cambodia and implementing lasting peace are among the most vexing issues facing contemporary Southeast Asia in the new international era. The demise of the cold war has thus far not made the crises in Cambodia less intractable.

## Notes

1. Eva Mysliwiec, *Punishing the Poor: The International Isolation of Kampuchea* (Oxford: Oxfam, 1988), p. 2.

2. Ibid., p. 11.

3. Robert J. Muscat, *Cambodia: Post-Settlement Reconstruction and Development* (New York: East Asian Institute, Columbia University, 1989), p. 98.

4. Frederick Z. Brown, *Second Chance: The United States and Indochina in the 1990s* (New York: Council on Foreign Relations, 1989), p. 71.

5. Muscat, *Cambodia*, pp. 88–89.

6. Mysliwiec, *Punishing the Poor*, p. 66.

7. Muscat, *Cambodia*, p. 2.

8. Ibid., p. 83.

9. Brown, *Second Chance*, p. 11.

# 12

## LAOS

Laos might best be described as a quasi-nation, having emerged from maps drawn by European colonialists rather than from a sense of territory and nationhood among a united people. The history of Laos is one of constant warfare among contending forces within the region as well as among external powers—mainly Thailand, Vietnam, China, France, and the United States. The present government faces the same problems as the governments of centuries ago: resettling the large refugee population stemming from past wars, uniting ethnic groups that have fought with each other for decades, closing the gap between urban and rural peoples, educating a citizenry in a nation without universities, and protecting the nation's sovereignty against encroachments by neighbors and by the major powers.

Contemporary Laos has changed little over the decades. It is still a rural, subsistence, agrarian society of some 4.5 million people divided among over forty ethnic groups, with the dominant lowland Lao consisting of just over 2 million people.[1] Most Lao are isolated from both their neighbors in Indochina and the world as well as from the hill peoples and other ethnic minorities within Laos. Almost all Lao are poor. The household economy is based on rice and relies on the water buffalo; modern farming techniques and equipment have not reached Lao farmers. The per capita GNP is only $370. About 90 percent of the population is Buddhist.

Contemporary problems in Laos originate from centuries-old conflicts, when ancient Lan Xang—"the Kingdom of a Million Elephants"—was a battleground for the expansionism of neighboring states. It was not until the fourteenth century that a semblance of national unity emerged. However, dynastic quarrels in the eighteenth century undermined this unity, and the area was divided into the kingdoms of Luang Prabang in the north, Champassak in the south, and Vientiane in the central region.

Vietnam and Thailand periodically plundered Laos until the French colonized the area beginning in the late 1880s. In 1899, the French claim of suzerainty consolidated Laos into a single political unit, but French rule did little to modernize or integrate the nation. On the contrary, a small group of elite Lao families was allowed to consolidate its power; thus, the Lao emerged from colonial rule (after World War II) more divided, isolated, and backward than ever.

From 1941 to 1945 the Japanese ruled Laos, although the collaborating Vichy French administered many governmental affairs. At the end of the war, the Gaullist French recaptured Vientiane, the administrative capital, and fought a group called the Lao-Issara (Free Laos), which established a government in Bangkok and became the forerunner and nucleus of the separate procommunist, anti-French, nationalist Neo Lao Hak Sat (NLHS)—the so-called patriotic front. Lao-Issara was led by Prince Souvanna Phouma and his half-brother, Prince Souphanouvong, who later broke off and joined the NLHS, which was operating in areas held by the Vietnamese Vietminh. By 1953 the NLHS's military force, known as the Pathet Lao, had seized control of the nation's northeastern provinces. In 1954 France accorded self-government to Laos at the Geneva Conference, which effectively gave Laos complete independence.

The aftermath of the Geneva Conference was a period of disarray for Laos, as the competing sides vied for control of the populace and the countryside. Also in 1954, when the Pathet Lao was making significant military gains in large areas of the countryside, the United States sponsored a coup by anticommunists against Premier Souvanna Phouma, who had become premier of the new nation but was considered too much a neutralist by the U.S. government. The coup failed, but Souvanna Phouma was given notice that left-wing or even neutralist policies were considered intolerable by the United States. When a right-wing government appeared in 1955, the United States immediately began a $45 million annual aid program.

In 1957 the neutralists, led by Souvanna Phouma—this time with backing from the United States—set up a government emphasizing national unity, with cabinet posts for leftists and rightists. In special elections as called for in the Geneva agreements, NLHS candidates won the majority of seats, an outcome deemed intolerable by Souvanna Phouma's government and by U.S. diplomats. To overturn the results of the election and reverse the apparent popular trend toward a communist government, the United States—principally through the Central Intelligence Agency—extended massive support to right-wing regimes that excluded NLHS representation. There were numerous coups d'état during this period as anticommunist leaders jockeyed for power. However, the major beneficiary of governmental chaos was the NLHS movement, which continued to expand its control as it received increasing amounts of military supplies and support from the Soviet Union.

At the second Geneva Conference in 1961, neutralist Souvanna Phouma, leftist Souphanouvong, and rightist Boun Oum agreed on coalition rule. The United States reversed its support of right-wing rule and supported Souvanna Phouma's appointment as prime minister (after he gave secret permission to the United States to bomb Pathet Lao areas). The coalition collapsed almost immediately, however, as factions maneuvered for power. The NLHS broke from the coalition, and Souvanna Phouma's Royal Lao government, a constitutional monarchy, became a virtual client of the United States.

Escalation of the Vietnam War changed the nature of the struggle between the NLHS and Royal Lao government forces. Hanoi's interest in Laos increased as its need for sanctuaries from U.S. bombing became paramount. Thus, Laos was swept up in the war as Hanoi, in violation of the Geneva agreements, escalated its presence in the northeastern provinces of Laos and as the United States, also in violation of the agreements, began its secret bombing missions in 1964. In the following years, the landlocked nation became one of the most heavily bombed countries in history; some 2.1 million tons of bombs were dropped between 1964 and 1972 (about two-thirds of a ton per Lao).[2] Despite this ferocity, the strategic effect of the bombing was minimal, prompting the Central Intelligence Agency to train and supply hill peoples, introduce military advisers, and use the U.S. Agency for International Development as a front for intelligence and training purposes. Laos became the battleground for a neighboring war fought by surrogate powers.

The Laos Peace Accords came in 1973 as the American withdrawal from Vietnam was completed. The accords called for stopping the bombing, disbanding foreign-supported forces, removing all foreign troops, and instituting the coalition Provisional Government of National Unity (PGNU). The new ministries were divided between the Royalists and the Pathet Lao. At the time of the signing of the accords, the NLHS controlled about three-fourths of all Lao territory and one-half of the population. Both sides were allowed to keep their zones of control until elections could be arranged.

The well-organized Pathet Lao (now called the Lao People's Liberation Army) prevailed over the Royal Lao faction in the coalition government, which lacked discipline, was enervated by family feuds, and was considered a puppet of the United States. The Pathet Lao spoke convincingly to the rural people of Laos, who had seen their agricultural base destroyed, their population dislocated, and their villages destroyed.[3] No family had been left unscathed by the civil war and the U.S. bombing.

In December 1975 the Pathet Lao dissolved the PGNU, abolished the 622-year-old monarchy, and established the Lao People's Democratic Republic. The change in government was preceded by communist victories in Vietnam and Cambodia and by procommunist demonstrations throughout Laos. The rightist ministers fled, and all power was eventually assumed by the communists. Souvanna Phouma resigned and Kaysone Phomvihan, general secretary of newly formed Lao People's Revolutionary Party (LPRP), became the new prime minister. A Supreme People's Council was set up with Prince Souphanouvong as president and chief of state, while Kaysone Phomvihan—virtually unknown to all but a handful of communist leaders before 1975—assumed political and administrative control of the country. In contrast to Vietnam and Cambodia, where communists came to power as a result of military victory, the change of government in Laos came about relatively peacefully.

The communist victory changed Lao politics fundamentally. For centuries the region had been dominated by a small group of wealthy families that wielded great political and economic influence. Most of those families fled to Thailand, Europe, or the United States, and those that remained underwent "reeducation" programs to cleanse them of their "bourgeois mentality." An estimated 400,000 persons, many of them the most educated in Laos, fled to Thailand following the change in government. The flight of educated Lao and the systematic expunging of civil servants of the former administration created a leadership vacuum that seriously impaired the government's ability to administer and implement new programs.

The new government moved quickly to eradicate the worst vestiges of what they considered bourgeois society by banning nightclubs, massage parlors, and dance halls. Private enterprise was stifled, and the government attempted to collectivize farms despite the peasants' resistance. Moreover, the government's reeducation program, affecting thousands of Lao, made the populace wary of the new regime. Refugees reported arrogant bureaucrats and repressive rules and regulations.

Another major change was the withdrawal of the United States as a principal player in Lao politics. Most Western aid, which had funded over 90 percent of the Royal Lao government budget, ended when the communists took power, although the countryside was still devastated from the war.

The virtual cessation of U.S. influence in Laos was a fundamental change. Although the United States did not break diplomatic relations with Laos after the communist takeover, U.S. involvement became peripheral, and the Soviet Union and Vietnam filled the vacuum. In 1979 the leaders of Laos and Vietnam signed a joint revolutionary declaration, a Treaty of Friendship and Cooperation, granting Vietnam the right to maintain some 40,000 troops in Laos. Vietnam's increased economic influence came about partially because Thailand initially cut off all trade with Laos. The fact that the port of Haiphong in Vietnam became the only outlet for Lao goods also gave Vietnam leverage over Lao policies. China's role in

Laos declined as Vietnam's grew. China soon accused Vietnam of working to create an Indo-Chinese federation dominated by the Vietnamese and withdrew its aid to Laos for numerous development projects. The Soviet Union, supplying some 2,000 advisers and $50 million in annual aid, was Laos's superpower patron until 1991, when the USSR collapsed.

The fact that Laos had been ruled since 1975 without a constitution disadvantaged the nation's leaders in their ability to govern and undermined foreign interest in providing assistance and investment. That problem was mitigated in August 1991 when the National Assembly adopted a constitution. The presidency (at that time held by Kaysone) was strengthened, although the LPRP retained its position as the primary institution. Civil liberties were allowed "as prescribed by law," but the major advantage of the document was to provide a semblance of stability and predictability with regard to governmental affairs.

President Kaysone's death in November 1992 provided an opportunity for Laos to usher in a new generation of leaders more in tune with the international movement away from communism and toward democracy. However, Prime Minister (and former Defense Minister) Khamtay Siphandone, sixty-six, was named leader of the LPRP, and National Assembly Chairman Noahak Phousavan, seventy-eight, was named president. Their hard-line conservatism and provincial outlook frustrated those who wanted Laos to look more toward the West for direction.

Laos, like China and Vietnam, attempted to open its economy along a market-based approach, while sustaining a one-party political dictatorship. Old-guard revolutionaries who had fought with the Pathet Lao were sidelined, and several persons were elected to the National Assembly who were not members of the LPRP. By 1995, the twentieth anniversary of LPRP rule in Laos, market economics was in command and the polity was far less authoritarian. For example, the funeral services for Prince Souphanouvong, the communist regime's first president, in 1995 was an entirely traditional Buddhist ceremony, with no ideological overtones. Clearly, the revolutionary leaders were no longer in the forefront and a new generation of leaders had moved into the important positions. The exception was the prime minister and party chief Khamtay Siphandone, who was a transitional figure between the old and new generations.

In 1996 the Sixth Congress of the LPRP further moved Laos toward comprehensive but slow economic reforms. Personalism, conservatism, and nationalism remained the dominant characteristics of the leading party. Military generals held six of the nine positions in the politburo; party leaders viewed the continuation of their unity (in a nation made up of numerous ethnic groups) as the primary national goal. This goal has been difficult to achieve because the economic reforms have made the urban areas wealthier whereas the rural areas, populated by minorities, have remained poor.

## Institutions and Social Groups

### The United States

Until 1975, the United States played the leading institutional role in Laos. By dominating the policies of the Vientiane administrations and financing the Lao military, the United States became the patron and the Lao government became a client of U.S. interests. The Lao government was so dependent on U.S. aid that American institutions in Vientiane had practically become the real government. To minimize opposition to U.S. involvement, the Central Intelligence Agency was given the principal responsibility of ensuring—by clandestine measures—the continuation of U.S. interests. One example of CIA involvement was its secret support of an army of Hmong hill people, who became the most important fighting force against communist Pathet Lao troops.

To secure the continuation in power of pro-U.S. forces, the United States engaged in a secret war in Laos in the 1960s, which cost $2 billion annually. The purpose of the bombing raids over Laos was to strengthen the anticommunist government in Vientiane, demolish the Pathet Lao infrastructure, and interdict soldiers from North Vietnam. In the long run, however, none of these goals was achieved.

After 1975, the United States no longer had influence over the Lao government. In 1987, however, the United States and Laos signed agreements for crop substitution programs. Laos had agreed to make a "maximum effort" to stop opium trafficking. In return, the United States removed Laos from its "decertification list" and reopened its aid program.

A major source of tension between the United States and Laos concerned some five hundred U.S. troops from the Vietnam War classified as missing in action (MIA) in Laos who had not been accounted for. The United States insisted on conducting excavations for their remains so that, if found, they could be transported back to the United States for burial. The Lao government was bitter about the U.S. demand because thousands of Lao were killed in the wartime bombings and hundreds continue to die every year from miniature "bombis" and land mines still scattered throughout the Lao countryside, with no offer of American compensation.

### Lao People's Revolutionary Party

Since 1975, the country's dominant institution has been the LPRP, the communist party that emerged from the Pathet Lao leadership. Led by elderly revolutionaries who fought against the French, Japanese, and Americans, the party has practiced democratic centralism requiring the unanimous support of all party leaders in all decisions. Policy was formu-

lated and implemented by the party politburo led by Kaysone Phomvihan. Kaysone had emerged in December 1975 from the caves of a northern province where he and his Pathet Lao colleagues had hidden to escape U.S. bombing. Outside of the inner circle of the Pathet Lao, few Lao
knew him or knew about him, and Kaysone eschewed a cult of personality, living quietly and making himself available to very few visitors except
communist allies. Little was known about his past except for his close association with Vietnam, where he had studied at the University of Hanoi.

Kaysone held the positions of prime minister and then president, as
well as general secretary of the LPRP. Surrounded by colleagues from his
revolutionary days in the 1950s, his rule changed little after 1975. Continuity and stability were the themes of governmental leadership until
1979, when reforms were instituted that significantly changed the hard-
line policies of the government.[4] After that time, and especially after 1986
when the "new thinking" reforms were instituted, Kaysone visited noncommunist countries, and his activities were even reported in the press.
Nevertheless, he remained one of the world's least-known leaders up to
his death in 1992.

The LPRP, with about 40,000 members—having failed to achieve popular support for its socialist policies—launched a series of reform policies
in 1986 to decentralize economic decisionmaking and to liberalize, both
economically and politically. In 1989—for the first time—the LPRP allowed elections for the National Assembly, Laos's nominal legislative
body. Some 121 government-approved candidates ran for 79 seats, and 65
of the victors were party members. The assembly then elected Noahak
Phousavan, second in command in the politburo, as chairman.[5]

There was no national constitution, so the LPRP was able to rule without guidelines or limits. Lacking a constitution until 1991, and further
lacking codified legislative, electoral, and criminal justice procedures,
Laos remained a government of men and not of law.[6] All the key men,
moreover, were LPRP members.

## Democratization

There is no semblance of democracy in Laos, nor has there ever been. The
country's communist leadership has not instituted reforms permitting a
representative system or civil liberties. Testimony to the Lao people's
view that their government is not legitimate is the fact that fully one-tenth
of the population has chosen to leave the country since 1975. Indeed, the
regime's insecurity regarding its legitimacy is shown by its refusal to allow any kind of opposition or free elections. Furthermore, the major hill
tribes, especially the Hmong, have not pledged allegiance to the communist regime and have even participated in national resistance movements.

Democracy is difficult to achieve even under the best of circumstances but is especially problematic in nations whose culture and traditions are antithetical to democratic practices. Laos was further disadvantaged by its severe war damage and by the fact that its economy had been heavily dependent on U.S. support. When that support suddenly ended in 1975, the country's economic collapse was not unexpected; the government's subsequent moves to collectivize farmers, nationalize the few industries, and rid the country of administrators who were part of the former regime exacerbated the siege mentality that made open politics impossible.

The fall of communist governments in Eastern Europe did not affect the Lao people because they did not have access to information about these changes. Following the democratization of Eastern Europe and the Philippines and the people's revolt in Burma, the LPRP made moves to liberalize the Lao economy. Oppression was lifted in the late 1980s so that the Lao people lived more normally.

## Economic Development

Laos, with Cambodia and Vietnam, is one of the world's poorest countries. With an estimated annual per capita income of $370, life expectancy of forty-five years, and infant mortality at 97 per 1,000 births, the standard of living is low. Less than 6 percent of the economy is industrial, and rice production, although largely subsistence, is poorly coordinated with any market or distribution system. Four out of ten children contract malaria, and diarrhea is a constant feature of life.

Although such extreme poverty is not new to Laos, the contrast with economic standards in the other ASEAN countries is more obvious than in the past, as most ASEAN countries have made great progress since the 1960s. The Lao watch Thai television programs in Vientiane and other border towns and see the great differences in economic conditions. Desperate conditions persist in Laos despite the fact that the country has been at peace for over twenty years.

After four years of rule, LPRP leaders realized that their agricultural and industrial policies had failed to revive the economy. In 1979, therefore, a process of decentralization was begun. In 1982, pragmatic policies were set forth at the Third Congress of the LPRP. The government's control over the economy was loosened; agriculture was decollectivized as the right to private property was established; and agricultural technology was introduced, resulting in larger crop output and self-sufficiency in rice for the first time since the revolution. These reforms were called *chin tanakan may* ("new thinking"), Laos's version of the Soviet Union's *perestroika* or Vietnam's *doi moi*.

The most fundamental changes, however, did not begin until 1986 at the Fourth Congress of the LPRP. These changes, called the New Economic Mechanism, allowed family farms to replace the unpopular agricultural cooperatives. Also, market mechanisms replaced centralized planning. In 1988, Kaysone admitted that the party's policy of putting private traders out of business, collectivizing farmers, and nationalizing industry had caused the production and circulation of goods to come to a halt, grievously affecting the people's livelihood.[7] The World Bank had been critical of the government's policy and cited Laos's agricultural inefficiency, declining industrial output, dependency on loans from socialist nations (on poor terms), stagnant exports, and huge balance of payment deficits, all of which acted to perpetuate underdevelopment.[8]

The reforms included a new foreign investment code designed to attract outside investment to finance the Lao infrastructure, but the results were disappointing. Most foreign investors were interested in small-scale manufacturing, particularly textiles. The fact that Laos did not have a constitution or a civil code frightened off many potential participants. Corruption also discouraged foreign investors, who were reluctant to pay "tea money" to officials whose salaries were insufficient for bare subsistence. An equally important problem was administrative capacity: Laos has no absorptive capability that allows follow-through on investment and aid projects.

In 1989 the United States granted its first assistance to Laos since 1975 by supporting a $1 million antinarcotics project. Australia, meanwhile, provided satellites for international telephone service and financed construction of the first bridge across the Mekong River between Thailand and Laos. Also in 1989, the World Bank and the Asian Development Bank pledged $238 million in no-interest loans. (Laos was not included in the trade embargo against Vietnam and Cambodia.)

The reforms emphasized grassroots economic units including factories, merchants' shops, and construction projects.[9] Rather than move directly from subsistence to large-scale collective farming, peasant families were encouraged to join the barter economy, trading their surplus production for commodities. In this way, the Lao were encouraged to become small-scale capitalists and consumers. State land was distributed to individual families on a long-term basis, and consideration was given to making such land inheritable.[10]

Following the reforms, there was a noticeable improvement in the standard of living of many Lao; house construction was up and more consumer goods were available in the major towns, and more Lao owned bicycles. However, the reforms did little to benefit rural people, who have very few roads on which to transport their farm products.

The early 1990s were not kind to the Lao economy, despite the regime's commitment to liberalization. The loss of Soviet aid, high levels of inflation, poor infrastructure, bureaucratic meddling, and crop failures resulting from droughts and floods seriously undermined the economy. Increased aid from the capitalist world helped offset these problems, but the country's standard of living barely improved. Ecologically, Laos is suffering from deforestation because of timber exported to Thailand. Laos's forests fell from 70 percent of the country's area one hundred years ago to 30 percent in 1990, reflecting the nation's only major natural resources: forests and water for hydroelectricity.

In the midst of this dismal picture is a national economy that experienced relatively high growth rates of 8 percent in 1994 and 7 percent in 1995. Thailand and South Korea have extensive investments in Laos, mostly garment factories. Laos has plans to sell its hydroelectricity to Thailand in exchange for much-needed capital. The concern is that the dams needed for this hydroelectricity project will negatively affect the nation's environment. Even without the dams, Laos's forests are rapidly falling to the logging industry, mostly to make up for the shortfall of timber in Thailand as a result of the ban on logging in that country.

## The Lao State

Laos, like Cambodia, is an example of a state with little capacity to meet the needs of its citizenry or to mobilize its collective strength. Like most Southeast Asian states, it has dual elements of strength and weakness. Certainly, it meets one criterion for all strong states: massive social dislocation. Laos was exploited by a self-serving colonial regime, was occupied by the Japanese and later became a client state of the United States, was bombed during the Vietnam War to an even greater extent than Japan was bombed in World War II, and was finally taken over by a hardline communist government; thus, Laos qualifies as a nation whose society has been weakened by massive social dislocation.

Although the United States provided financial and military support to its client regimes, administrations in Laos never achieved stability. However, massive Soviet aid to the LPRP regime helped strengthen the state's stability by undermining potential societal threats to the regime. The LPRP dominated every aspect of Lao political life, having co-opted virtually the entire administrative class.

Laos does not have a societal group that is independent of social controls and capable of executing the designs of state leaders. Its bureaucrats and technocrats are not independent of LPRP authorities. Those who were autonomous left the country for Thailand. There is no intellectual class in the country capable of competing with the state leaders. The Lao government has purposely precluded the rise of autonomous groups; thus, the Lao state can be considered strong. This lack of autonomy, however, has reduced the regime's legitimacy and its ability to meet the needs of the people, thereby undermining state strength. Whereas Thailand enjoys the symbolic importance of the king to provide legitimacy, since 1975 Laos has had no parallel institution.

Weakening the Lao state is the absence of a charismatic and skillful leader such as Suharto, Ho Chi Minh, or Ne Win. Kaysone Phomvihan's leadership resulted more from his control of the LPRP and from repression than from his capacity to gain the approbation of the Lao people.

## Foreign Policy

As a landlocked nation, Laos has always had to rely on its neighbors for security. Traditionally, Thailand, China, and Vietnam have had the greatest impact on Lao political affairs because these nations share long borders with Laos and control its access to the oceans. After World War II, however, the United States became the paramount power, with almost total control over every aspect of Lao political and economic life.

The United States supported the series of right-wing regimes that ruled Laos after the war, but following the communist takeover in 1975, the United States no longer played an important role in Lao affairs. Vietnam, which had approximately 50,000 troops in Laos after 1975, became the major influence on foreign and domestic policies. Although there was fear in the 1980s that Laos and Cambodia would be assimilated into a greater Indochina federation under Vietnamese dominance, such a confederation never occurred. For some time Laos was dependent upon Vietnam and echoed Vietnam's line on most international questions. By 1990, however, all Vietnamese troops had been withdrawn, and Laos was asserting a more independent policy as well as strengthening its relations with Western powers, China, and Thailand.

Relations with the United States have been low-key since 1975. The United States has maintained diplomatic relations with Vientiane, since 1995 at the ambassadorial level. The two nations have negotiated such issues as MIAs, drug trafficking, and human rights. Laos has worked with the United States on MIAs and has agreed to cooperate in narcotics control; however, the United States decertified Laos because of alleged government involvement in the illicit drug trade. Because of decertification, Laos was no longer eligible for U.S. aid, and U.S. officials were required to vote against loans to Laos from international institutions such as the World Bank. Laos was recertified in 1990.

In 1989 Laos moved to end its near-total dependence on the Soviet Union and Vietnam. Prime Minister Kaysone traveled to Japan, China, and France to request aid and investment. Australia agreed to build a bridge over the Mekong River, creating the first road link ever between Laos and Thailand.

Laos's relations with Thailand have been tense since the Pathet Lao took power because the Thais view Laos as a base for support of insurgency and because the hundreds of thousands of Lao (and Cambodian) refugees who have crossed into Thailand are viewed as an economic burden. In 1988, Laos and Thailand fought a bloody three-month war over a disputed border area. Later, as relations warmed, Thai businesspeople took advantage of the economic reforms in Laos to set up businesses, and border towns became market centers for Thailand. Indeed, in 1990 Prime Minister Chatichai visited Vientiane, the first trip to Laos by a Thai prime minister in a decade.

Improved relations did not resolve the centuries-old problem of a strong Thailand versus a weak Laos. Semiofficial commentaries noted that having failed to destroy Laos with its military power, Thailand had employed a new strategy: attacking Laos with economic power. Although the Lao government later distanced itself from this view, many Lao feared that Thailand—with more than ten times the population of Laos and a history of aggression against its smaller neighbor—might once again intervene. The Lao government was particularly concerned about Thai support for right-wing insurgent forces, which were formed to oust the Kaysone administration.

The demise of the Soviet Union caused the communist Lao leadership to hunker down even more, determined not to be overwhelmed by the forces of democratization. No longer able to rely on Soviet aid, Laos moved to improve relations with China, especially to balance the increasing influence of Thailand and Vietnam. Notwithstanding fears of Thai intentions, Thailand became Laos's most important trade and investment partner. The shops in Vientiane were stocked primarily with Thai products. Thai television was beamed throughout the country with images of more developed societies. Burma and Laos also improved ties, and the leaders of the two nations exchanged visits, reflecting the fact that Laos was following the Burmese model of a strongly authoritarian and nationalist centralized administration, with a central role for the military. In addition, both nations have a distrust and fear of Thailand and have accused the Thai government of harboring insurgents plotting against their respective governments.

In a move reflecting the tremendous changes that were occurring in Southeast Asia, Laos became a member of ASEAN in 1997. The move was made to improve Lao relations with the flourishing economies of the region. Relations with the United States also improved when the latter announced that Laos was making progress in ending opium production. As a result of this progress and Lao willingness to investigate the MIA issue, the United States agreed to upgrade diplomatic relations by naming an ambassador.

By 1993, hopes had arisen that the nation's isolation would end. The new constitution made foreign investment more attractive, the Australian-built bridge over the Mekong River had the potential to open up Laos to increased trade with Thailand and the West, and tourists were returning to Vientiane as well as to the beautiful provincial and former royal capital of Luang Prabang, declared a UNESCO World Heritage site in 1995. China remained an important trade ally and a major supplier of weaponry.

## Conclusion

Laos is the "forgotten country" of Southeast Asia because it is small and is no longer strategically important to the world's major powers. Its total population is far smaller than that of the city of Bangkok. Laos's leadership is unknown to the world, and its military capacity is practically nonexistent. In contrast to Thailand, Laos has changed little over the past several decades. The appearance of the country's towns, its available resources, and its level of development have remained largely static, although some changes have been evident in more recent years since the country abandoned its rigid socialism. (These changes have had the negative effect of jeopardizing Laos's environment.) Thus, the prospects for Laos in terms of improving the standard of living of its people remain uncertain.

## Notes

1. W. Randall Ireson and Carol J. Ireson, "Laos," in *Coming to Terms: Indochina, the United States, and the War,* ed. Douglas Allen and Ngo Vinh Long (Boulder: Westview Press, 1991).

2. Ibid., p. 66.

3. Ibid.

4. Macalister Brown and Joseph J. Zasloff, *Apprentice Revolutionaries: The Communist Movement in Laos, 1930–1985* (Stanford: Hoover Institution, Stanford University, 1986), p. 165.

5. Geoffrey C. Gunn, "Laos in 1989: Quiet Revolution in the Marketplace," *Asian Survey,* vol. 30, no. 1 (January 1990), p. 84.

6. Charles A. Joiner, "Laos in 1987," *Asian Survey,* vol. 28, no. 1 (January 1988), p. 104.

7. Far Eastern Economic Review, *Asia Yearbook, 1990* (Hong Kong: Far Eastern Economic Review, 1990), p. 161.

8. Joiner, "Laos in 1987," p. 19.

9. Ibid., p. 96.

10. Martin Stuart-Fox, "Laos in 1988," *Asian Survey,* vol. 29, no. 1 (January 1989), pp. 81–82.

# 13

# CONCLUSION

Since World War II, nearly all the conflicts in Southeast Asia have been related to cold war politics: communist versus anticommunists in the Vietnam War; support for the right-wing Suharto regime after 1965; and support for the Marcos regime in the Philippines. Today, those issues are a part of the past and the cold war is no longer the driving force. No communist power threatens the sovereignty of any Southeast Asian nation today.

Russia is no longer a major player in Southeast Asia and has disengaged even from Vietnam. China is more concerned with trade ties with its Southeast Asian neighbors than with support for insurgent forces. Vietnam, vitally concerned with internal economic issues, is no longer a threat, and has even joined the ASEAN alliance, once established in part to stop Vietnamese aggression. The Clinton administration's decision to lift the trade embargo and establish diplomatic relations helped provide economic security to Vietnam and end any thought of Vietnamese aggression in the region.

In short, Southeast Asia is a region of non-crisis, with the former historical flash points no longer volatile. The struggles for independence from colonialism are over, charismatic leaders have disappeared, and large-scale war no longer plagues the region. Instead, economic development is the new emphasis, with virtually all of Southeast Asia (Burma being the obvious exception) eager to join the international capitalist world. Security matters have taken a secondary position.

The new economic crises in 1997 confirm the importance of understanding economics and underscore the close ties between economics and politics. A new breed of foreign policy specialists has emerged who know the language of economics: trade, aid, the World Trade Organization (WTO), intellectual property rights, and economic growth triangles. The fall of Prime Minister Chavalit in Thailand in November 1997 because of Thailand's currency crisis is an indication of the close relationship between economics and politics.

In the new international era, ASEAN has grown to include nearly all of Southeast Asia. It is not clear whether ASEAN can be sustained without an "outside enemy," because the alliance has primarily developed into an economic one, with each nation in competition with the others for similar exports.

The economic crisis stemmed from imprudent supervision of the nations' economies. The high economic growth rates caused governments to be lax as they basked in the "Asian miracle," not sensing that the economic foundations of their societies were weak. Moreover, pervasive corruption that blocked infrastructure projects and held up educational reform further undermined the economies. As foreign capital flowed in, too many investments went to unnecessary projects designed solely for fast profit. The currencies became overvalued, so that speculators were able to support currency devaluation. Many of the region's economies then collapsed, causing political as well as economic instability. The high capacity of the Southeast Asian nations to resolve complicated problems, the generally well-educated populations, the global nature of the economies, and astute leadership all will work toward a rapid resolution of the crisis.

American involvement in Southeast Asia during the region's postindependence period was traumatic. The United States, which carried on a long, costly, and controversial war in Indochina and developed patron-client relationships (and all the attending obligations) with the region's noncommunist nations, was integrally involved in Southeast Asian affairs.

Thus, the subordination of Southeast Asia in U.S. foreign policy during the 1980s and 1990s was a striking change in the new international era. Analysts did not predict the breadth or direction of this change. During the Vietnam War, every ASEAN nation was deemed susceptible to communist-inspired insurgencies; the region's economies were among the poorest in the world; authoritarian governments ruled in virtually every country; and Vietnam, Cambodia, and Laos were overwhelmed by war. The United States was the only superpower with significant influence in Southeast Asia at that time, and its failure to achieve its short-term aim to stop communist aggression in Vietnam led to a pessimistic evaluation of the region's overall future.

In many respects, the present era in Southeast Asia suggests that the pessimistic view was unwarranted and that U.S. aims have been achieved. The area is dominated by economically vital, democratically aligned nations, and it shelters no adversarial superpower that threatens U.S. interests. With varying degrees of success, the ASEAN nations have moved toward semidemocratic rule. In the new international era, Vietnam and Laos are no longer at war, and both countries have launched economic reforms aimed to integrate their economies more intimately with the world capitalist system. Except for the Philippines, the ASEAN nations have terminated their insurgent threats and are now an anticommunist bastion in the Third World. Rather than falling like dominoes, the noncommunist Southeast Asian countries became dynamic models for successful development, at least until the 1997 economic crisis. U.S. interests in the region have correspondingly changed, becoming primarily economic rather than military.

Still, the United States has interests in Southeast Asia, even if no "Clinton Doctrine" has been elaborated. First, America seeks continued political stability, which has essentially been achieved (except in Burma). Second, America supports economic development through capitalism. This interest includes the lowering of trade barriers to American products. Two-way trade across the Pacific between the United States and all of Asia is three times greater than trade between the United States and Europe. Each 1 percent increase in Asian economic growth can create as many as 300,000 American jobs.

Third, the United States seeks to preserve access to Asia as a "balance" to China and Japan. The access problem has been achieved through the establishment of a floating depot for America's Seventh Fleet and of facilities throughout Southeast Asia for training, repair, refueling, and shore leave for crew members. Lacking a comprehensive Southeast Asian policy, Americans are relying on an ad hoc flexibility should any crises arise. The disadvantage to this situation is that American policy objectives remain unclear, so that Southeast Asian leaders are unable to take them into account.

Rather than relying exclusively on the United States for support as in preceding decades, the Southeast Asian countries widened their relations with the old Soviet bloc, western Europe, China, and Japan. At the same time, there was movement toward normalizing relations between Vietnam and the United States as the former Soviet Union reduced its involvement in Indochina. Vietnam, Laos, and Burma joined ASEAN, and Cambodia is expected to join soon, as the cold war mentality continues to dissipate.

The most salient unresolved issue is the instability in Cambodia, which has thus far resisted resolution despite the movement toward reform and the end of the genocidal Khmer Rouge regime.

Another difficult issue concerns the refusal of the Burmese military to respect the desire of the populace for democratization by turning the government over to the winners of the 1990 election. The possibility of a civil war makes this an issue of great importance both for the Burmese people and for the stability of Southeast Asia.

A third issue, closer to resolution under the Ramos administration, is the instability of the Philippines, which is caused by a democratic but weak government, an insurgency that continues to feed upon widespread poverty (and the large gap between the few rich and the many poor), the feudal nature of society, and the gross corruption of officials. These problems were initially exacerbated by negotiations with the United States over U.S. military bases in the Philippines. However, the ousting of the American military caused Filipinos to view their problems more realistically, as they were no longer able to blame "American neo-imperialism" for their country's many ills.

The future role of Vietnam in Southeast Asia and in the international system is another problem. Viewed as a pariah by the United States and the ASEAN nations at the end of the Vietnam War, Vietnam has since made clear its desire to participate in the new international arena. This aim was partially achieved when the United States and Vietnam agreed to normalize relations.

The success of the ASEAN nations in improving their citizens' standard of living and in opening their political systems is an important change for Southeast Asia in the new international era. Virtually every social-political indicator (such as life expectancy, infant mortality, number of doctors, and literacy) shows improvement compared with ten years ago. Nevertheless, economic inequality in Southeast Asia has become greater even as per capita income has increased. The elites live in urban areas and tend to neglect the rural peasantry. Economic development is concentrated in urban industrial centers in the expectation that resources will eventually "trickle down" to the masses. These changes stem in part from the nations' integration into the world economic system and the international division of labor in which ASEAN provides cheap labor for export products to the West. Moreover, the rapid growth of ASEAN's primary cities has led to overcrowding and insufficient services, resulting in vast slums and urban alienation.

Vietnam, Cambodia, and Laos have made slow but significant strides toward economic development. Since around 1986, the Indo-Chinese countries have initiated reforms that are beginning to show results. Despite these reforms, the Indo-Chinese people are still impoverished, the nations' infrastructures are dilapidated, and the bureaucracy is oppressive. In Vietnam, the government was led in the postwar decades by an elderly generation of communists who were out of touch with the needs of the citizenry. The outcome of factional disputes between reformers and hard-line conservatives will determine Vietnam's capacity to participate in the new international era.

The analysis of the role of the state in explaining high economic growth rates does not indicate a clear pattern. Where the states have acted autonomously, independent of societal groups, economic development has both flourished and deteriorated. For example, Singapore is a strong state with a flourishing economy, whereas Vietnam is also a strong state but, until the 1990s, with a stagnant economy. In Thailand, the state has been strong enough to allow the private sector to propel economic growth, but in Burma the authorities increased the state's role in economic policymaking with disastrous results. Weak and inefficient governments hinder economic growth; however, strong states do not necessarily realize rapid development and often cause as many problems as they solve.

The clearest explanation for economic growth is the pattern of openness in a state's polity. Democratization correlates positively with high growth rates. The semidemocracies of Thailand and Malaysia have the highest rates of growth, in contrast to Vietnam, Laos, Cambodia, and Burma, all of which have relatively closed polities and the region's lowest growth rates. Indonesia's controlled democracy is in the middle in terms of economic growth. Singapore, because of its city-state character, and Brunei, because of its oil revenues and small population, cannot be compared with other Southeast Asian countries. It seems, therefore, that no country in the region is likely to develop economically if it is ruled by a closed political system, whereas an open system committed to a market economy has a good chance of leading to development. The longevity and strength of the 1997 economic and currency crisis could undermine this generalization.

The future of Southeast Asia is inextricably tied to the policies of the great powers. Southeast Asia is of secondary importance to the United States, compared to primary U.S. interests in the Middle East, Russia, Europe, China, and Japan. The obvious potential power in Southeast Asia is Japan, which is already significantly involved in the economic affairs of the region. Although the United States will continue to pressure Japan to do more in terms of burden sharing, the memories of the Japanese occupation during World War II are strong enough to raise fears about the renewal of Japanese militarism.

At the same time, the nations of Southeast Asia are moving in the direction of greater national resilience and self-reliance. Their prospects rest on each nation's internal capacity to meet the needs of its people and to assure them of a higher standard of living. Each nation must strike its own bargain between its requirements for growth and stability, authority and freedom, regional interdependence and nationalism, and modernization and cultural integrity.

*Southeast Asia in the New International Era* suggests that the region is diverse, with political systems as varied as in any region of the world. The new international era is influencing each nation in different ways, with some nations—such as Singapore and Thailand—moving rapidly toward westernization and others—such as Burma—moving toward further isolation. Each nation, however, is coping with change in ways that create difficult problems and choices. The choices should not be evaluated against Western standards but against each nation's own history. In short, Southeast Asia is worthy of consideration on its own terms.

# BIBLIOGRAPHY

For up-to-date analyses of politics in Southeast Asia, consult the following journals: *Asian Survey, Pacific Affairs, Far Eastern Economic Review, Asian Thought and Society, The Journal of Asian Studies, Asiaweek,* and *Indochina Chronology.* Each year the January and February issues of *Asian Survey* feature articles that summarize the previous year's events in each Southeast Asian nation.

Following is a selected bibliography of books written since 1980, organized according to country.

## General Southeast Asia

Clad, James. *Behind the Myth: Business, Money and Power in Southeast Asia.* London: Unwin and Hyman, 1989.

Diamond, Larry, Juan J. Linz, and Seymour Martin Lipset, eds. *Democracy in Developing Countries: Asia.* Boulder: Lynne Rienner Publishers, 1989.

Djiwandono, J. Soedjati, and Yong Mun Cheong, eds. *Soldiers and Stability in Southeast Asia.* Singapore: Institute of Southeast Asian Studies, 1988.

Ghee, Lim Teck. *Reflections on Development in Southeast Asia.* Singapore: Institute of Southeast Asian Studies, 1988.

Jackson, Karl D., Sukhumbhand Paribatra, and J. Soedjati Djiwandono, eds. *ASEAN in Regional and Global Context.* Berkeley: Institute of East Asian Studies, University of California, 1986.

Kallgren, Joyce K., Noordin Sopiee, and J. Soedjati Djiwandono, eds. *ASEAN and China: An Evolving Relationship.* Berkeley: Institute of East Asian Studies, University of California, 1988.

Mauzy, Diane K., ed. *Politics in the ASEAN States.* Kuala Lumpur: Maricans, 1986.

McVey, Ruth T., ed. *Southeast Asian Capitalists.* Ithaca: Southeast Asia Program, Cornell University, 1992.

Neher, Clark D., and Ross Marlay. *Democracy and Development in Southeast Asia: The Winds of Change.* Boulder: Westview Press, 1995.

Rigg, Jonathan. *Southeast Asia: A Region in Transition.* London: Unwin and Hyman, 1991.

Robison, Richard, Kevin Hewison, and Richard Higgott, eds. *Southeast Asia in the 1980s: The Politics of Economic Crisis.* Sydney: Allen and Unwin, 1987.

Scalapino, Robert A., Seizaburo Sato, and Jusuf Wanandi, eds. *Asian Economic De-velopment: Present and Future.* Berkeley: Institute of East Asian Studies, Univer-sity of California, 1985.

_____. *Asian Political Institutionalization.* Berkeley: Institute of East Asian Studies, University of California, 1986.

_____. *Internal and External Security Issues in Asia.* Berkeley: Institute of East Asian Studies, University of California, 1986.

Scalapino, Robert A., Seizaburo Sato, Jusuf Wanandi, and Sung-joo Han, eds. *Asia and the Major Powers: Domestic Politics and Foreign Powers.* Berkeley: Institute of East Asian Studies, University of California, 1988.

Snitwongse, Kusuma, and Sukhumbhand Paribatra, eds. *Durable Stability in Southeast Asia.* Singapore: Institute of Southeast Asian Studies, 1987.

Steinberg, David Joel, ed. *In Search of Southeast Asia.* Honolulu: University of Hawaii Press, 1985.

Wurfel, David, and Bruce Burton, eds. *The Political Economy of Foreign Policy in Southeast Asia.* London: Macmillan, 1990.

Yoshihara, Kunio. *The Rise of Ersatz Capitalism in South-East Asia.* New York: Ox-ford University Press, 1988.

## Thailand

Dhiravegin, Likhit. *Demi Democracy.* Singapore: Times Academic Press, 1992.

Girling, John L. S. *Thailand: Society and Politics.* Ithaca: Cornell University Press, 1981.

Jackson, Karl D., and Wiwat Mungkandi, eds. *United States–Thailand Relations.* Berkeley: Institute of East Asian Studies, University of California, 1986.

Keyes, Charles. *Thailand: Buddhist Kingdom as Modern Nation-State.* Bangkok: Duang Kamol, 1989.

Kulick, Elliott, and Dick Wilson. *Thailand's Turn: Profile of a New Dragon.* New York: St. Martin's Press, 1992.

Laothamatas, Anek. *From Bureaucratic Polity to Liberal Corporatism: Business Associ-ations and the New Political Economy of Thailand.* Boulder: Westview Press, 1991.

Morell, David, and Chai-Anan Samudavanija. *Political Conflict in Thailand: Reform, Reaction, Revolution.* Cambridge, England: Oelgesclager, Gunn and Hain, 1981.

Muscat, Robert. *Thailand and the United States.* New York: Columbia University Press, 1990.

Neher, Clark D., and Wiwat Mungkandi, eds. *U.S.-Thailand Relations in a New In-ternational Era.* Berkeley: Institute of East Asian Studies, University of Califor-nia, 1990.

Ramsay, Ansil, and Wiwat Mungkandi, eds. *Thailand-U.S. Relations: Changing So-cial, Political and Economic Factors.* Berkeley: Institute of East Asian Studies, Uni-versity of California, 1988.

Randolph, Sean. *The United States and Thailand: Alliance Dynamics, 1950–1985.* Berkeley: Institute of East Asian Studies, University of California, 1986.

Wright, Joseph. *The Balancing Act: A History of Modern Thailand.* Bangkok: Asia Books, 1991.

Xuto, Somsakdi, ed. *Government and Politics of Thailand.* Oxford: Oxford University Press, 1987.

## The Philippines

Bonner, Raymond. *Waltzing with a Dictator.* New York: Times Books, 1987.

Brillantes, Alex. *Dictatorship and Martial Law: Philippine Authoritarianism in 1972.* Manila: Great Books, 1987.

Broad, Robin. *Unequal Alliance: The World Bank, the International Monetary Fund, and the Philippines.* Berkeley: University of California Press, 1978.

De Guzman, Raul P., and Mila A. Reforma, eds. *Government and Politics of the Philippines.* Singapore: Oxford University Press, 1988.

Greene, Fred, ed. *The Philippine Bases: Negotiating for the Future.* New York: Council on Foreign Relations, 1988.

Hawes, Gary. *The Philippine State and the Marcos Regime: The Politics of Export.* Ithaca: Cornell University Press, 1987.

Johnson, Bryan. *The Four Days of Courage.* New York: The Free Press, 1987.

Kerkvliet, Benedict. *Everyday Politics in the Philippines.* Berkeley: University of California Press, 1990.

Kessler, Richard J. *Rebellion and Repression in the Philippines.* New Haven: Yale University Press, 1989.

Lande, Carl H. *Rebuilding a Nation: Philippine Challenges and American Policy.* Washington, D.C.: The Washington Institute, 1987.

Steinberg, David Joel. *The Philippines: A Singular and Plural Place.* 2d ed. Boulder: Westview Press, 1990.

Timberman, David. *A Changeless Land: Continuity and Change in Philippine Politics.* New York: M. E. Sharpe, 1991.

Wurfel, David. *Filipino Politics: Development and Decay.* Ithaca: Cornell University Press, 1988.

## Indonesia

Crouch, Harold A. *The Army and Politics in Indonesia.* Ithaca: Cornell University Press, 1988.

Jackson, Karl D., and Lucian Pye, eds. *Political Power and Communications in Indonesia.* Berkeley: University of California Press, 1978.

MacAndrews, Colin, ed. *Central Government and Local Development in Indonesia.* Oxford: Oxford University Press, 1986.

Robison, Richard. *Indonesia: The Rise of Capital.* Sydney: Allen and Unwin, 1986.

Vatikiotis, Michael. *Indonesian Politics Under Suharto.* London: Routledge, 1993.

## Malaysia

Bowie, Alasdair. *Crossing the Industrial Divide: State, Society, and the Politics of Economic Transformation in Malaysia.* New York: Columbia University Press, 1991.

Jomo, Kwame Sundaram. *A Question of Class: Capital, the State, and Uneven Development in Malaya*. New York: Oxford University Press, 1986.

Mauzy, Diane K. *Barisan Nasional: Coalition Government in Malaysia*. Kuala Lumpur: Marican and Sons, 1983.

Milne, R. S., and Diane K. Mauzy. *Malaysia: Tradition, Modernity and Islam*. Boulder, Westview Press, 1985.

Scott, James C. *Weapons of the Weak: Everyday Forms of Peasant Resistance*. New Haven: Yale University Press, 1983.

## Singapore

Josey, Alex. *Lee Kuan Yew: The Struggle for Singapore*. Sydney: Angus and Robertson, 1980.

Minchin, James. *No Man Is an Island: A Portrait of Singapore's Lee Kuan Yew*. Sydney: Allen and Unwin, 1990.

Quah, Jon S. T., Chan Heng Chee, and Seah Chee Meow, eds. *Government and Politics of Singapore*. Singapore: Oxford University Press, 1987.

Rodan, Garry. *The Political Economy of Singapore's Industrialization: National, State, and International Capital*. New York: St. Martin's Press, 1989.

## Negara Brunei Darussalam

Hamzah, B. A. *The Oil Sultanate: Political History of Oil in Brunei Darussalam*. Seremban, Malaysia: Mawaddaw Enterprise, 1991.

Leake, David, Jr. *Brunei: The Modern Southeast Asian Islamic Sultanate*. Jefferson, N.C.: McFarland and Co., 1989.

Singh, D. S. Ranjit. *Brunei 1839–1983: The Problems of Political Survival*. New York: Oxford University Press, 1984.

## Burma

Lintner, Bertil. *Outrage*. Hong Kong: Review Publishing Co., 1989.

Silverstein, Josef. *Independent Burma at Forty Years: Six Assessments*. Ithaca: Cornell University Press, 1989.

Steinberg, David I. *Burma: A Socialist Nation of Southeast Asia*. Boulder: Westview Press, 1982.

_____. *The Future of Burma: Crisis and Choice in Myanmar*. Lanham, Md.: University Press of America, 1990.

Taylor, Robert H. *The State in Burma*. Honolulu: University of Hawaii Press, 1987.

## Vietnam

Brown, Frederick Z. *Second Chance: The United States and Indochina in the 1990s*. New York: Council on Foreign Relations, 1989.

Cima, Ronald, ed. *Vietnam: A Country Study*. Washington, D.C.: Library of Congress, 1989.

Duiker, William J. *China and Vietnam: The Roots of Conflict.* Berkeley: Institute of East Asian Studies, University of California, 1986.

Goodman, Allan E. *The Search for a Negotiated Settlement of the Vietnam War.* Berkeley: Institute of East Asian Studies, University of California, 1986.

Kahin, George McT. *Intervention: How America Became Involved in Vietnam.* New York: Alfred A. Knopf, 1986.

Karnow, Stanley. *Vietnam: A History.* New York: Viking Press, 1983.

Marr, David G., and Christine P. White, eds. *Postwar Vietnam: Dilemmas in Socialist Development.* Ithaca: Southeast Asia Program, Cornell University, 1988.

Tai, Ta Van. *The Vietnamese Tradition of Human Rights.* Berkeley: Institute of East Asian Studies, University of California, 1988.

Turley, William S. *The Second Indochina War.* Boulder: Westview Press, 1986.

Vu, Tran Tri. *Lost Years: My 1,632 Days in Vietnamese Reeducation Camps.* Berkeley: Institute of East Asian Studies, University of California, 1986.

## Cambodia

Bit, Seanglim. *The Warrior Heritage.* El Cerrito, Calif.: Seanglim Bit, 1991.

Chanda, Nayan. *Brother Enemy: The War After the War.* New York: Macmillan, 1986.

Chandler, David P. *Brother Number One: A Political Biography of Pol Pot.* Boulder: Westview Press, 1992.

Chandler, David P., and Ben Kiernan. *Revolution and Its Aftermath in Kampuchea: Eight Essays.* New Haven: Southeast Asia Studies, Yale University, 1983.

Kiernan, Ben, and Chanthou Boua, eds. *Peasants and Politics in Kampuchea: 1942–1981.* New York: M. E. Sharpe, 1982.

Muscat, Robert J. *Cambodia: Post-Settlement Reconstruction and Development.* New York: East Asian Institute, Columbia University, 1989.

Mysliwiec, Eva. *Punishing the Poor: The International Isolation of Kampuchea.* Oxford: Oxfam, 1988.

## Laos

Brown, Macalister, and Joseph J. Zasloff. *Apprentice Revolutionaries: The Communist Movement in Laos, 1930–1985.* Stanford: Hoover Institution, Stanford University, 1986.

Dommen, Arthur J. *Laos: Keystone of Indochina.* Boulder: Westview Press, 1985.

Gunn, Geoffrey. *Rebellion in Laos: Peasant and Politics in a Colonial Backwater.* Boulder: Westview Press, 1990.

Merritt, Jane Hamilton. *Tragic Mountains: The Hmong, the Americans, and the Secret Wars for Laos, 1942–1992.* Bloomington: Indiana University Press, 1993.

Stuart-Fox, Martin. *Contemporary Laos: Studies in the Politics and Society of the Lao People's Democratic Republic.* New York: St. Martin's Press, 1982.

_____. *Laos: Politics, Economics, and Society.* Boulder: Lynne Rienner Publishers, 1986.

# INDEX